Blackstone's

Police Q&A

Evidence and Pr 2011

Blackstone's
Police Q&A

Evidence and Procedure 2011

Ninth edition

Huw Smart and John Watson

OXFORD
UNIVERSITY PRESS
Great Clarendon Street, Oxford OX2 6DP

Oxford University Press is a department of the University of Oxford.
It furthers the University's objective of excellence in research, scholarship,
and education by publishing worldwide in

Oxford New York

Auckland Cape Town Dar es Salaam Hong Kong Karachi
Kuala Lumpur Madrid Melbourne Mexico City Nairobi
New Delhi Shanghai Taipei Toronto

With offices in

Argentina Austria Brazil Chile Czech Republic France Greece
Guatemala Hungary Italy Japan Poland Portugal Singapore
South Korea Switzerland Thailand Turkey Ukraine Vietnam

Published in the United States
by Oxford University Press Inc., New York

First published 2010

British Library Cataloguing in Publication Data
Data available

Library of Congress Cataloging in Publication Data
Data available

Typeset by MPS Limited, A Macmillan Company
Printed in Great Britain
on acid-free paper by CPI William Clowes, Beccles

ISBN 978-0-19-959240-1

10 9 8 7 6 5 4 3 2 1

Contents

Introduction

Before you get into the detail of this book, there are two myths about multiple-choice questions (MCQs) that we need to get out of the way right at the start:

1. that they are easy to answer;
2. that they are easy to write.

Take one look at a professionally designed and properly developed exam paper such as those used by the Police Promotion Examinations Board or the National Board of Medical Examiners in the US and the first myth collapses straight away. Contrary to what some people believe, MCQs are not an easy solution for examiners and not a 'multiple-guess' soft option for examinees.

That is not to say that all MCQs are taxing, or even testing—in the psychometric sense. If MCQs are to have any real value at all, they need to be carefully designed and follow some agreed basic rules.

And this leads us to myth number 2.

It is widely assumed by many people and educational organisations that anyone with the knowledge of a subject can write MCQs. You need only look at how few MCQ writing courses are offered by training providers in the UK to see just how far this myth is believed. Similarly, you need only to have a go at a few badly designed MCQs to realise that it is a myth nonetheless. Writing bad MCQs is easy; writing good ones is no easier than answering them!

As with many things, the design of MCQs benefits considerably from time, training and experience. Many MCQ writers fall easily and often unwittingly into the trap of making their questions too hard, too easy or too obscure, or completely different from the type of question that you will eventually encounter in your own particular exam. Others seem to use the MCQ as a way to catch people out or to show how smart they, the authors, are (or think they are).

There are several purposes for which MCQs are very useful. The first is in producing a reliable, valid and fair test of knowledge and understanding across a wide range of subject matter. Another is an aid to study, preparation and revision for such examinations and tests. The differences in objective mean that there are slight differences in the rules that the MCQ writers follow. Whereas the design of fully validated MCQs to be used in high stakes examinations which will effectively determine who passes and who fails have very strict guidelines as to construction, content and style, less stringent rules apply to MCQs that are being used for teaching and revision. For that reason, there may be types of MCQ that are appropriate in the latter setting which would not be used in the former. However, in developing the MCQs for this book, the authors have tried to follow the fundamental rules of MCQ design but they would not claim to have replicated the level of psychometric rigour that is—and has to be—adopted by the type of examining bodies referred to above.

These MCQs are designed to reinforce your knowledge and understanding, to highlight any gaps or weaknesses in that knowledge and understanding and to help focus your revision of the relevant topics.

I hope that we have achieved that aim.

Good luck!

Blackstone's Police Q&As—Special Features

References to Blackstone's Police Manuals

Every answer is followed by a paragraph reference to Blackstone's Police Manuals. This means that once you have attempted a question and looked at an answer, the Manual can immediately be referred to for help and clarification.

Unique numbers for each question

Each question and answer has the same unique number. This should ensure that there is no confusion as to which question is linked to which answer. For example, Question 2.1 is linked to Answer 2.1.

Checklists

The checklists are designed to help you keep track of your progress when answering the multiple-choice questions. If you fill in the checklist after attempting a question, you will be able to check how many you got right on the first attempt and will know immediately which questions need to be revisited a second time. Please visit www.blackstonespolicemanuals.com and click through to the Blackstone's Police Q&As 2011 page. You will then find electronic versions of the checklists to download and print out. Email any queries or comments on the book to: police.uk@oup.com.

Acknowledgements

This book has been written as an accompaniment to Blackstone's Police Manuals, and will test the knowledge you have accrued through reading that series. It is of the essence that full study of the relevant chapters in each Police Manual is completed prior to attempting the Questions and Answers. As qualified police trainers we recognise that students tend to answer questions incorrectly either because they don't read the question properly, or because one of the 'distracters' has done its work. The distracter is one of the three incorrect answers in an MCQ, and is designed to distract you from the correct answer, and in this way discriminate between candidates: the better-prepared candidate not being 'distracted'.

So particular attention should be paid to the ***Answers*** sections and students should ask themselves, 'Why did I get that question wrong?' and, just as importantly, 'Why did I get that question right?' Combining the information gained in the ***Answers*** section together with re-reading the chapter in the Police Manuals should lead to a greater understanding of the subject matter.

The authors wish to thank all the staff at Oxford University Press who have helped put this publication together. We would particularly like to dedicate these books to Alistair McQueen who sadly passed away in 2008. It was his vision and support that got this project off the ground. Without his help neither Huw nor John would have been able to make these Q&As the success they are. We would also like to show appreciation to Fraser Sampson, consultant editor of Blackstone's Police Manuals, whose influence on these Q&As is appreciated.

Huw would like to thank Caroline for her constant love, support and understanding over the past year—and her ability to withstand the pressures of being the partner to a workaholic! Special thanks to Lawrence and Maddie—two perfect young adults. Last but not least, love and special affection to Haf and Nia, two beautiful young girls.

John would like to thank Sue, David, Catherine and Andrew for their continued support, and understanding that 'deadline' means 'deadline'.

1 Sources of Law

STUDY PREPARATION

This chapter examines what could be best described as the building blocks of criminal law, the body of laws; common, statutory and delegated legislation. This chapter also examines what are known as 'precedents' or the details of cases that have been 'decided' in the higher courts and the impact these have on current and future cases. Students should recognise that what they have erroneously called 'stated cases' for years are probably not 'stated'. But more importantly, they should recognise the importance of these authorities, not just in their working lives as police officers, but as students of the law in any capacity; particularly candidates for promotion.

QUESTIONS

Question 1.1

Common law is still very much part of modern law, and it is still commanding legislation.

As a whole, where do its sources lie?

A Principles of the law declared by the judges in the course of deciding particular cases.

B Principles of the law declared by High Court judges in the course of deciding particular cases.

C Principles of the law declared by the most senior law courts in the course of deciding particular cases.

D Principles of the law that have evolved over time.

Question 1.2

STRUTHERS is appearing at Crown Court charged with robbery, and has been convicted at Crown Court. His barrister was successful in gaining an acquittal on a point of law following appeal to the Court of Appeal. The High Court judge also commented that the police action in obtaining witness evidence had been on the point of being unlawful.

Which of the following is true in relation to precedent?

A In future cases lower courts will have to follow the point of law made by the High Court judge.

B In future cases lower courts will have to follow the point of law, and the comments made by the High Court judge about the police action.

C In future cases lower courts will have to follow the point of law, and the comments made by the High Court judge about the police action, but only if it is the same police officers.

D The decision is not binding on lower courts as it was not a judgment laid down by the Law Lords in the Supreme Court.

Question 1.3

On 1 October 2009 the Supreme Court replaced the House of Lords as the highest court in the United Kingdom.

To what, if any, extent is the new Supreme Court of the UK bound by decisions made in the European Court of Justice?

A The Supreme Court is not bound at all by decisions made in the European Court of Justice.

B The Supreme Court is bound to consider, but not necessarily act on decisions made in the European Court of Justice.

C The Supreme Court is bound to an extent by the decisions made in the European Court of Justice.

D The Supreme Court is fully bound by the decisions made in the European Court of Justice.

Question 1.4

In considering points of law the courts must consider judicial precedents and consider whether they are bound by those judicial precedents.

Which of the following is correct in relation to being bound by other courts' decisions?

A A judge in the Divisional Court is not bound by decisions made in the Court of Appeal.
B A magistrates' court is never bound by the decisions of a Crown Court.
C An opinion about a point of law expressed by a High Court judge is always binding on inferior courts.
D The Supreme Court is never bound to follow decisions made in the European Court of Justice.

Question 1.5

Parliament has enacted a new statute and it has received Royal assent.

Who, if anyone, is responsible for interpreting the new Act?

A The Supreme Court only.
B The Supreme Court or the High Court.
C It is the duty of any court to interpret the new Act to fall in line with existing legislation.
D It is the duty of any court to interpret the new Act to give effect to the intention of Parliament.

Question 1.6

The system of courts in England and Wales is a hierarchy, the various courts being related to one another as superior and inferior. An inferior court is generally bound by the decision and directions of a superior court.

In relation to this which of the following is correct?

A The Supreme Court is always bound by decisions made by the European Court of Justice.
B The Divisional Court is bound by decisions made by the Court of Appeal.
C The Crown Court is sometimes bound by decisions made by other Crown Courts.
D The Magistrates' court is sometimes bound by decisions made by the Crown Court.

ANSWERS

Answer 1.1

Answer **A** — There is no authoritative text of the common law and, as a whole, its sources lie in the principles of the law declared by the judges in the course of deciding particular cases; answers B, C and D are therefore incorrect. It should be noted that the common law can only be declared authoritatively by the judge(s) of the superior courts (i.e. from the High Court) and then only to the extent that it is necessary to do so for the purpose of deciding a particular case. For this reason, the development of the common law has always been dependent upon the incidence of cases arising for decision, and the particular facts of those cases.

Evidence and Procedure, para. 2.1.2

Answer 1.2

Answer **A** — The system of courts in England and Wales is a hierarchy, the various courts being related to one another as superior and inferior. An inferior court is generally bound by the decision and directions of a superior court. For example, judges of the Divisional Court and Crown Courts are bound by the decisions of the Court of Appeal; answer D is therefore incorrect. The Appeal Court is in turn bound by the decisions of the Supreme Court, which is also bound—to an extent—by decisions of the European Court of Justice. It should be noted that, although the Crown Court is superior to a magistrates' court and enjoys wider powers, it is still a 'lower' court and its decisions are not generally binding on other courts.

When it is said that a decision is binding, or more fully, a binding and authoritative precedent, what is meant is that the principle of law on which the decision was based, or the reason for the decision, is binding. This principle of the law is known as the *ratio decidendi* of the case. An example of this would be the decision that, once the prosecution have proved that a defendant was carrying a weapon that is 'offensive' *per se*, there is no need to prove any intention to use that weapon offensively.

The *ratio decidendi* consists only of the principle(s) of law essential to a decision. A judge, or court as a whole, may sometimes go beyond the facts of a particular case and give an opinion on some connected matter, which is intended to be of guidance in future cases. Such an opinion is known as an *obiter dictum*, and may be persuasive, but not binding, on other courts in a future case, even if the same parties are involved; answers B and C are therefore incorrect.

Evidence and Procedure, para. 2.1.4.1

Answer 1.3

Answer **C** — The system of courts in England and Wales is a hierarchy, the various courts being related to one another as superior and inferior. An inferior court is generally bound by the decision and directions of a superior court. For example, judges of the Divisional Court and Crown Courts are bound by the decisions of the Court of Appeal. The Court of Appeal is in turn bound by the decisions of the Supreme Court, which is also bound—to an extent—by decisions of the European Court of Justice; answers A, B and D are therefore incorrect.

Evidence and Procedure, para. 2.1.4.1

Answer 1.4

Answer **B** — The system of courts in England and Wales is a hierarchy, the various courts being related to one another as superior and inferior. The directions of a superior court generally bind an inferior court. For example, judges of the Divisional Court and Crown Courts are bound by the decisions of the Court of Appeal. The Appeal Court is in turn bound by the decisions of the Supreme Court, which is also bound—to an extent—by decisions of the European Court of Justice; answer A is therefore incorrect. Although the Crown Court is superior to a magistrates' court and enjoys wider powers it is still a 'lower' court and its decisions are not generally binding on other courts.

A judge, or court as a whole, may sometimes go beyond the facts of a particular case and give an opinion on some connected matter, which is intended to be of guidance in future cases. Such an opinion is known as an *obiter dictum*, and may be persuasive, but not binding, on other courts in a future case. Such *obiter dicta* are often made where an important point has arisen from the arguments in an appeal case but that point has not been directly raised by either party to the case, and even when made by a High Court judge they remain only persuasive; answer C is therefore incorrect.

The Supreme Court is bound, to a certain extent, to follow decisions made in the European Court of Justice; answer D is therefore incorrect.

Evidence and Procedure, para. 2.1.4.1

Answer 1.5

Answer **D** — Statutes, in the form of Acts of Parliament, have always been regarded as supplementary to the common law. It is true that the major part of criminal law and procedure is now in statutory form, but it is equally true that the principles of common law, notably in relation to criminal liability generally, homicide and the rules of evidence and procedure at a criminal trial, have not lessened in importance.

Statutes are enacted by Parliament and it is the duty of the court, as and when the occasion arises, to interpret and give effect to the intention of Parliament as expressed in the words of the statute. This is any court which is asked, where appropriate, to interpret the intention of the statute maker, it is not restricted to the higher courts, and answers A and B are therefore incorrect.

The court however will not interpret the Act to make it fall in line with existing legislation; it is interpreted so as to ensure that Parliament's wishes (the wording of the actual statute) are given effect; answer C is therefore incorrect.

Evidence and Procedure, para. 2.1.3

Answer 1.6

Answer **B** — The system of courts in England and Wales is a hierarchy, the various courts being related to one another as superior and inferior. An inferior court is generally bound by the decision and directions of a superior court. For example, judges of the Divisional Court (High Court) and Crown Courts are bound by the decisions of the Court of Appeal. The Appeal Court is in turn bound by the decisions of the Supreme Court, which is also bound—to an extent, but not always—by decisions of the European Court of Justice; answer A is therefore incorrect. It should be noted that, although the Crown Court is superior to a magistrates' court and enjoys wider powers, it is still a 'lower' court and its decisions are not generally binding on other courts; answers C and D are therefore incorrect.

Evidence and Procedure, para. 2.1.4.1

2 The Courts

STUDY PREPARATION

Building on how laws are made, this chapter looks at how the law is decided and interpreted in the courts.

The nature of an offence will determine in which court a case is heard. In England and Wales offences can be tried in either the magistrates' court or the Crown Court. Offences committed by a child or young person are generally heard in the youth court.

This chapter tests your knowledge of the categories of offences and the criminal courts where these are dealt with.

QUESTIONS

Question 2.1

MULCAHY is appearing before the magistrates' court for an either-way offence. He wishes the matter to be dealt with by the magistrates, as he fears a substantial prison sentence at Crown Court. The magistrates, however, feel the matter should be committed due to the serious nature of the offence.

Which of the following is correct?

A The matter must be committed to Crown Court in these circumstances.

B The matter must be dealt with fully in the magistrates' court as the defendant wishes summary trial.

C The matter can be committed to Crown Court, but only if the defendant agrees.

D The matter can only be committed to Crown Court for sentencing as the defendant wishes summary trial.

Question 2.2

HELPS is appearing before the magistrates' court for the offence of carrying an insecure load, contrary to reg. 100(2) of the Road Vehicles (Construction and Use) Regulations 1986 and s. 42 of the Road Traffic Act 1988. He has received a computer-generated requisition as a result of a written charge.

The date of the alleged offence was 16 June. The information date printed at the head of the requisition was 10 December; that is six days before the effluxion of the six months' limitation period. The summons, which was dated 9 January, included a statement of facts. It also bore the date when the information was printed, 20 December; that is four days outside the limit.

Bearing in mind this discrepancy in 'information' dates in the requisition, which of the following is correct as to whether the information was laid in time?

A The date at the top should be accepted as correct, as it was computer-generated information.

B It is for the defence to prove, on the balance of probabilities, that it was *not* laid in time.

C It is for the magistrates to decide if it was laid in time, applying the criminal standard of proof.

D It is for the Clerk of the Court to decide if it was laid in time, on the balance of probabilities.

Question 2.3

PETTIGREW is 17 years of age and appearing in youth court charged with an offence.

Under what circumstances will PETTIGREW be sent to Crown Court for trial and not tried in the youth court?

A Only where the offence is one with a fixed sentencing tariff, i.e. murder.

B Only if the youth is jointly charged with an adult, and the adult opts for trial by jury.

C PETTIGREW will make the choice. He can elect trial by jury provided he is charged with an indictable offence.

D If the offence is one carrying a sentence of 14 years or more imprisonment in the case of an adult.

Question 2.4

DICKENS is appearing at magistrates' court on two counts of theft. He has been found guilty and the bench is considering sentence. Theft is an offence that is triable either way.

What is the maximum sentence that can be imposed by the magistrates?

A 6 months for each which must run concurrently.

B 6 months for each which must run consecutively.

C 12 months for each which must run concurrently.

D 12 months for each which must run consecutively.

Question 2.5

DAY is appearing at magistrates' court at a mode of trial hearing. She wishes to know what sentence she might receive if she pleads guilty, and how much higher the sentence would be should she plead not guilty and be convicted.

Which of the following is correct?

A The court can give an indication as to the likely sentence in both cases, but the magistrates have a broad discretion as to whether or not to provide such an indication.

B The court can give an indication as to the likely sentence but only where the accused indicates that they will plead guilty at the first opportunity to claim credit for a guilty plea.

C The court can give an indication and they are bound by this indication when sentencing is considered either after a guilty plea or on conviction.

D The court can give an indication for a guilty plea and are then only bound by this indication where the accused enters a guilty plea.

Question 2.6

Section 2 of the Criminal Appeal Act 1968 provides that the Court of Appeal shall allow an appeal against conviction in certain circumstances.

What are those circumstances?

A The Court of Appeal should allow an appeal if it was of the view that the conviction was unsafe.

B The Court of Appeal should allow an appeal if it was of the view that the conviction was unsafe or unsatisfactory.

C The Court of Appeal should allow an appeal if it was of the view that the judgment of the court of trial should be set aside because of an error of law.

D The Court of Appeal should allow an appeal if it was of the view that there had been a material irregularity in the course of the trial.

Question 2.7

DE KLERK was convicted at Crown Court of an offence of burglary. At the *voir dire* during this trial, the defence sought to have a vital piece of evidence excluded, as they believed it had been obtained unlawfully. The trial judge refused their application, the evidence was adduced and the jury convicted DE KLERK. He appealed, and the Court of Appeal decided that the judge's adverse ruling amounted to a wrong decision on a question of law and the evidence should have been excluded. The prosecution now wish to challenge the ruling made by the Court of Appeal.

Which of the following is true?

A The prosecution cannot appeal any decision made in the Court of Appeal.

B The prosecution can only appeal on a general point of law that is of legal importance.

C The prosecution can only appeal on a point that is of general public importance.

D The prosecution can only appeal on a point of law of general public importance.

Question 2.8

Sections 35 and 36 of the Criminal Justice Act 1988 provide that where the Attorney General considers an offender was sentenced unduly leniently by the Crown Court he may refer the case to the Court of Appeal for a review of the sentence.

Which of the following is true in relation to what action the Attorney General can take?

A The Attorney General can refer any case provided the sentence passed appears unduly lenient.

B The Attorney General can refer certain cases where the sentence passed appears unduly lenient, however leave of the Court of Appeal is required.

C The Attorney General can refer certain cases where the sentence passed appears unduly lenient and leave of the Court of Appeal is not required.

D The Attorney General can only refer cases where the sentence tariff is fixed, i.e. murder.

Question 2.9

A serving police officer has been called to jury service and is awaiting selection. One of the trials about to go ahead contains contentious police evidence and the court is considering whether the police officer should sit on this jury.

In relation to this which of the following is correct?

A The officer should not sit on this jury unless absolutely necessary.

B The officer should not sit on this jury in any circumstances.

C The officer should only sit on this jury with the express approval of the trial judge.

D The officer can sit on the jury; there is no reason why they cannot.

Question 2.10

The Court of Appeal may make an order to quash the person's acquittal on a charge and order a retrial in line with the Criminal Justice Act 2003.

In which of the following cases would this be likely?

A Where certain evidence was not allowed in the original trial and that evidence would be compelling if allowed.

B Where new evidence becomes available, and it is in the interests of justice that this evidence be adduced.

C Where evidence not used at the previous trial becomes available and it is compelling evidence.

D Where the person has been convicted of a similar charge since the acquittal and it is in the interests of justice for a retrial to be held.

ANSWERS

Answer 2.1

Answer **A** — This is known as a mode of trial hearing, the power to conduct a mode of trial hearing arises whenever an adult appears or is brought before a magistrates' court charged with an offence triable either way. The object of this hearing is to determine whether the case should be dealt with by a magistrates' court or by the Crown Court. The magistrates decide initially whether or not to deal with the case, basing their decision mainly on the seriousness of the offence and whether their powers of punishment are adequate; their decision is not affected by the conformity of the defendant, therefore, answer C is incorrect.

They will hear representations from both the prosecution and the defence. If they decide not to deal with the case it will be committed to the Crown Court. Where the magistrates accept jurisdiction, the defendant has the right to choose or elect between being dealt with in the magistrates' court or the Crown Court. Note, this choice only arises when the justices agree to hear the case. Answers B and D are therefore incorrect.

A magistrates' court dealing with the trial of an either-way offence may, on conviction of the defendant, commit them to the Crown Court for sentencing in certain circumstances. These circumstances are usually linked to the seriousness of the offence and/or the seriousness of the defendant's previous convictions, which the magistrates will not usually be aware of until the end of the trial.

Evidence and Procedure, para. 2.2.2.4

Answer 2.2

Answer **C** — A magistrates' court may not try a defendant for a summary offence unless the information was laid within six months of the time when the offence was allegedly committed (Magistrates' Courts Act 1980, s. 127(1), as qualified by s. 127 (2)(a)); this is subject to any enactment which expressly permits a longer period.

In *Atkinson* v *DPP* [2004] EWHC 1475 it was held that, where there is uncertainty as to whether an information has been laid in time, the question should be determined according to the criminal standard of proof and the magistrates should decline to hear the matter unless they are sure that the information was laid in time.

The ratio of the decision is that if, on evidence of whatever nature before the court, magistrates doubt the date of the information, such that it could have been laid outside the time limit, they are entitled to, and should, decline jurisdiction. It is a matter of fact for their determination in accordance with the ordinary criminal burden and standard of proof; therefore answers A, B and D are incorrect.

Evidence and Procedure, para. 2.2.4.1

Answer 2.3

Answer **D** — The general principle is that persons under the age of 18 years should be tried and sentenced in the youth court for both summary and indictable offences. They have no ability to elect jury trial; answer C is therefore incorrect.

However, s. 51A of the Crime and Disorder Act 1998 provides those occasions where a juvenile will be sent directly to the Crown Court for trial. Those occasions are when the juvenile is charged with:

- homicide (murder, manslaughter, or causing or allowing the death of a child or vulnerable adult) (Domestic Violence, Crime and Victims Act 2004, s. 5);
- an offence involving firearms under the Firearms Act 1968, s. 51A, or where s. 29 (3) of the Violent Crime Reduction Act 2006 applies (minimum sentences in certain cases of using someone to mind a weapon);
- an offence mentioned within the terms of s. 91 of the Powers of Criminal Courts (Sentencing) Act 2000 (offenders under 18 convicted of certain serious offences: powers to detain for specified periods); namely offences carrying a sentence of 14 years or more imprisonment in the case of an adult;
- a 'specified' offence as provided by s. 224 of the Criminal Justice Act 2003 (specified violent offence or specified sexual offence (dangerous offenders)); or where the juvenile is:
- (jointly charged) with an adult who has been sent for trial for the same or related indictable offence (s. 51(5) of the Crime and Disorder Act 1998).

Although answers A and B are covered by the above they both state that they are the 'only' offences that apply. This is not the case, they are not exclusive and therefore they are both incorrect.

Evidence and Procedure, para. 2.2.3

Answer 2.4

Answer **B** — The maximum aggregate term of imprisonment which magistrates' can impose is six months unless two of the terms are imposed for offences triable either way in which case the maximum aggregate term is 12 months (Courts Act 1980, s.133).

Evidence and Procedure, para. 2.2.2.1

Answer 2.5

Answer **D** — The accused may require the magistrates to indicate the type of sentence they would consider appropriate if they pleaded guilty to the offence(s) charged, not a 'not guilty' plea; answer A is therefore incorrect. The magistrates have a broad discretion as to whether or not to provide such an indication. The court is only bound by this indication where the accused has entered a guilty plea (s. 20(3)–(9)); answer C is therefore incorrect. It is a matter for the court's discretion and not based on a promise to plead guilty; answer B is therefore incorrect.

Evidence and Procedure, para. 2.2.2.4

Answer 2.6

Answer **A** — By virtue of s. 2 of the Criminal Appeal Act 1968, the principal question for the Court of Appeal in the determination of an appeal against conviction is whether or not the conviction is unsafe.

Prior to the amendment of s. 2 by the Criminal Appeal Act 1995, it provided that the Court of Appeal should allow an appeal if it was of the view that the conviction was unsafe or unsatisfactory, or that the judgment of the court of trial should be set aside because of an error of law, or that there had been a material irregularity in the course of the trial. Even if the point in issue concerning a point of law or material irregularity was decided in favour of the appellant, the Court of Appeal could exercise the proviso and dismiss the appeal if they were satisfied that no miscarriage of justice had occurred. Despite the change in wording, the authorities which developed in relation to the application of the earlier version of s. 2 are relevant to the operation of the provision as now amended and the consideration of the ultimate question of the safety of the conviction; answers B, C and D are therefore incorrect.

Evidence and Procedure, para. 2.2.5

Answer 2.7

Answer **D** — Appeals can be made to the Supreme Court by both the prosecution and defence from a decision of the Criminal Division of the Court of Appeal; answer A is therefore incorrect. This decision must involve a point of law of general public importance. Note that it must be a point of law, and that that point of law must be of general public interest, not legal interest. Answers B and C are therefore incorrect (the Court of Appeal must certify this for the appeal to be heard).

Evidence and Procedure, para. 2.2.5

Answer 2.8

Answer **B** — Sections 35 and 36 of the Criminal Justice Act 1988 provide that where the Attorney General considers an offender was sentenced unduly leniently by the Crown Court he may refer the case to the Court of Appeal for a review of the sentence (the procedure to be followed is set out in Sch. 3 to the 1988 Act and the Criminal Procedure Rules 2005, Part 70). The cases that can be referred are contained in Sch. 1 to the 1988 Criminal Justice Act 1988 (Reviews of Sentencing) Order 2006 (SI 2006/1116) and include:

- offences which are triable only on indictment (para. 1);
- listed miscellaneous offences (para. 2);
- listed offences under the Sexual Offences Act 2003 (para. 3);
- attempting to commit or inciting the commission of most offences listed in paras 2 and 3 (para. 4).

So it is only these cases that can be referred, not all cases; answer A is therefore incorrect. As the list is not limited to fixed sentencing tariff offences answer D is also incorrect.

In each case, however, leave of the Court of Appeal is required before a referral can be made; answer C is therefore incorrect.

Evidence and Procedure, para. 2.2.5.2

Answer 2.9

Answer **D** — Serving police officers, and staff of the CPS, can serve on juries as this does not offend against principles of fairness where there are no circumstances which would give rise to concerns of bias (*R* v *Abdroikov, Green and Williamson* [2007] UKHL 37). In *R* v *Yemoh* [2009] EWCA Crim 930, the court held that even where a case contained contentious police evidence there was no reason why a police officer should not be a juror; answers A, B and C are therefore incorrect.

Evidence and Procedure, para. 2.2.8.4

Answer 2.10

Answer **B** — Two statutes provide for those occasions where a person may be tried again even though they have been acquitted.

The Criminal Procedure and Investigations Act 1996 deals with what is referred to as 'tainted acquittals'. This is where an accused has been wrongly acquitted of an offence due to the interference with, or intimidation of, a juror or witness (ss. 54 to 57). In such cases the High Court may grant an order quashing the acquittal.

The Criminal Justice Act 2003, ss. 75 to 97, provides that a prosecutor, with the written consent of the Director of Public Prosecutions, can apply to the Court of Appeal to quash a person's acquittal for a qualifying or lesser qualifying offence (an offence listed in part 1 of Sch. 5 (s. 75(8)). A retrial must be ordered if there is new and compelling evidence that was not adduced in previous proceedings and that evidence is considered reliable, substantial and appears highly probative of the case against the acquitted person and it is in the interest of justice to make the order (ss. 78 and 79 of the 2003 Act).

This refers only to 'new' evidence. Evidence that existed at the original trial but which was not used for whatever reason will not be applicable in the decision; answers A and C are therefore incorrect.

Any subsequent finding of guilt on a similar charge is of no relevance; answer D is therefore incorrect.

Evidence and Procedure, para. 2.2.5.1

3 Instituting Criminal Proceedings

STUDY PREPARATION

This chapter looks at the way in which prosecutions are started. Laying informations and securing the attendance of witnesses, defendants and evidence are basic mechanics of the criminal justice procedure. As with other areas of practical relevance, this means that they will be of interest to trainers and examiners.

QUESTIONS

Question 3.1

The Criminal Justice Act 2003 provides a new method of instituting criminal proceedings where a public prosecutor may issue a document (a 'written charge'), which charges the person with an offence (s. 29(1)). At the same time as issuing a written charge the public prosecutor must also serve on the person concerned a document (a requisition) that requires the person to appear before a magistrates' court to answer the written charge (s. 29(2)).

In relation to this which of the following is correct?

A The written charge must give exact technical information about the nature of the charge.

B The written charge need not specify the relevant statutory provision.

C The written charge should ordinarily be for one offence only.

D The written charge should be written in ordinary language.

Question 3.2

FLAHERTY wishes to take action to have a dangerous dog destroyed by attending the local magistrates' court and obtaining a destruction order under s. 2 of the Dogs Act 1871.

In relation to this which of the following is correct?

A The information must be laid in writing by FLAHERTY.

B The information must be laid in writing by FLAHERTY or personally by him at the court.

C Following the laying of the information by FLAHERTY the justice can issue a warrant to arrest the dog owner.

D Following the laying of the information by FLAHERTY the justice can only issue a summons to the dog owner.

Question 3.3

One of the processes to put a matter before a court is known as 'laying an information'.

For which of the following can a 'public prosecutor' lay an information?

A For the purpose of obtaining the issue of a summons under s. 1 of the Magistrates' Courts Act 1980 for an offence.

B For the purpose of obtaining the issue of a summons under s. 1 of the Magistrates' Courts Act 1980 for an either way offence.

C For the purpose of obtaining the issue of a summons under s. 1 of the Magistrates' Courts Act 1980 for a breach of the peace.

D For the purposes of securing the grant of an arrest warrant.

Question 3.4

Under the Criminal Procedure Rules 2010 a summons or requisition may be served on a person by, amongst other methods, delivering it to an address.

Which of the following properly represents the wording of the Rules in relation to serving a summons?

A By leaving it at, or sending it to, an address where it is reasonably believed that he or she will receive it.

B By leaving it at, or sending it to, an address where it is known that he or she will receive it.

C By leaving it at, or sending it to, the registered address of the person to receive it.

D By leaving it at, or sending it to, the registered, or last known, address of the person to receive it.

Question 3.5

KEENE had been summonsed to attend court following the laying of a written charge in relation to an indictable offence. KEENE has, however, failed to appear in court and the public prosecutor wishes to apply for an arrest warrant.

In relation to this, which of the following is correct?

A The public prosecutor must lay an information personally.

B The public prosecutor can lay an information in writing.

C The public prosecutor must lay an information personally, but must also lay the original written charge.

D The public prosecutor can lay an information in writing, but must also lay the original written charge.

Question 3.6

Under certain circumstances a warrant can be issued to arrest a witness and compel them to attend court. The power for this comes from the Magistrates' Courts Act 1980.

In which of the following circumstances can a warrant be issued?

A Where a witness is appearing at magistrates' court only, and only where they have failed to comply with a witness summons.

B Where a witness is appearing at Crown Court only, and only where they have failed to comply with a witness summons.

C Where a witness is appearing at Crown Court only and only where the judge is certain that it is in the interests of justice to compel the witness to attend.

D In any court where it is in the interests of justice to secure the attendance of a witness and where there is evidence that a summons would not ensure attendance.

Question 3.7

WATKINS is a civilian enforcement officer who is executing a warrant of arrest. The male who is the subject of the warrant demands that WATKINS gives him his name.

Which of the following is correct in relation to the information WATKINS is required to show in relation to executing the warrant?

A WATKINS must provide documentary evidence of his name.

B WATKINS must provide his name, but this can be done verbally.

C WATKINS need only give documentary evidence showing the authority by which he is employed.

D WATKINS need only give documentary evidence showing that he is authorised to execute warrants.

Question 3.8

Constable HUSSEIN is a serving officer in a Welsh police force, but he is Scottish in origin. Before going on leave he reads a Police National Computer (PNC) broadcast about an arrest warrant for an offence issued in Glasgow, which concerns a student he was at university with whom he knows well. Whilst on holiday on the south coast of England, he sees his friend against whom the warrant was issued.

Can he arrest his friend by executing the warrant?

A Yes, a warrant issued in Scotland can be executed in England or Wales by any constable.

B Yes, but only if the Scottish offence corresponds with an English law offence.

C No, the warrant would have to be in his possession to arrest in England.

D No, because he is not acting within his own force area.

Question 3.9

McGWYER is a civilian enforcement officer employed by the local court and authorised in the prescribed manner. McGWYER is executing a distress warrant at an address when he notices RYAN, for whom he knows an arrest warrant has been issued. McGWYER does not have this warrant in his possession.

Can McGWYER execute the warrant for arrest?

A Yes, a civilian enforcement officer can execute any warrant.

B Yes, an arrest warrant is one that can be executed by a civilian enforcement officer.

C No, a civilian enforcement officer must have possession of an arrest warrant.

D No, a civilian enforcement officer cannot execute an arrest warrant.

Question 3.10

Constable NICHOLS, from the Metropolitan Police, carried out a check on the police national computer (PNC) on an Irish male. The check showed that a warrant was outstanding against the male, and that it had been issued in the Republic of Ireland.

Which of the following is correct in relation to the officer executing the warrant?

A The warrant can be executed provided the offence to which it relates corresponds to an offence in England and Wales.

B The warrant can be executed provided the offence to which it relates corresponds to an offence in England and Wales and has been issued for the purposes of arrest and prosecution.

C The warrant can be executed provided the person is accused of the commission of a specified offence and that the warrant has been issued for the purposes of arrest and prosecution.

D The warrant cannot be executed under any circumstances in England and Wales.

Question 3.11

Constable PONTING is an officer in an English police force. She has been given a summons, which was issued in Scotland (called a 'citation'). She has been asked to serve the summons on behalf of the police in Glasgow.

In relation to the serving of this summons, which of the following is correct?

A The summons must be served in person by the officer.

B The officer can post the summons, provided it is recorded delivery.

C The officer can post the summons, provided it is sent first class.

D The officer can post the summons to the person's last known or usual place of abode.

Question 3.12

Proceedings may be instigated against a person suspected of a criminal offence.

In relation to these proceedings, which of the following options is available for a public prosecutor under the Criminal Justice Act 2003?

A A public prosecutor must lay information before a justice for a summons to be issued.

B A public prosecutor can issue a 'written charge' charging the person to appear before the magistrates' court.

C The public prosecutor must lay written signed information before a justice for a summons to be issued.

D The public prosecutor must substantiate the information on oath before a justice for a summons to be issued.

Question 3.13

A judge at Crown Court sentences an offender in their absence. The judge issues a warrant to commit the person to prison for a period of 18 months and specifies the place to which they should go. Constable DEAKINS executes the warrant at the offender's home address.

Where should the officer take the offender?

A To the nearest police station, which need not be specified; from there the offender should be taken to Crown Court.

B To the nearest designated police station; from there the offender should be taken to Crown Court.

C To the place specified on the warrant.

D To the nearest prison, even if it is not the one specified on the warrant.

Question 3.14

Detective Constable MATHERS is dealing with a case at magistrates' court where a material witness has refused to attend. The officer also believes that they will not respond to a summons and is considering applying for the district judge to issue a warrant to arrest the witness.

In relation to this which of the following is correct?

A The officer must satisfy the district judge that it is in the interests of justice to secure the attendance of a person who could give material evidence.

B The officer must satisfy the district judge that it is in the interests of justice to secure the attendance of a person who could give material evidence, and that a summons would not procure the attendance of the person.

C The officer must satisfy the district judge by giving evidence on oath that it is in the interests of justice to secure the attendance of a person who could give material evidence.

D The officer must satisfy the district judge by giving evidence on oath that it is in the interests of justice to secure the attendance of a person who could give material evidence, and that a summons would not procure the attendance of the person.

ANSWERS

Answer 3.1

Answer **D** — Part 7 of the Criminal Procedure Rules 2010 outlines that the written charge, as with an information, must contain a statement describing the offence in ordinary language and identify any relevant statutory provision; answers A and B are therefore incorrect. Such particulars must be included of the conduct constituting the commission of the offence as to make clear what the prosecutor alleges against the defendant. The written charge must be for one offence only. However, more than one incident of the commission of the offence may be included in the written charge if those incidents taken together amount to a course of conduct having regard to the time, place or purpose of commission; answer C is therefore incorrect.

Evidence and Procedure, para. 2.3.2

Answer 3.2

Answer **C** — In the case of private prosecutions a person may lay an information, orally or in writing (answer A is therefore incorrect), alleging that a person has committed an offence, or make a verbal complaint that a person has committed a breach of the law not being a criminal offence; for example, breach of the peace (Criminal Procedure Rules 2010, r. 7.1).

On an information being laid, or a complaint made, a justice or justice's clerk may issue either a summons requiring the person named in the information to appear before a magistrates' court, or a justice may issue a warrant to arrest that person and bring them before a magistrates' court (s. 1(1) of the Magistrates' Courts Act 1980); answer D is therefore incorrect.

Although a private individual can lay an information this can also be done on his behalf. In the case of a private prosecution, an information can be laid by the prosecutor before a magistrate resulting in the issue of a summons requiring the accused to attend at court on a specified day to answer the allegation in the information; answer B is therefore incorrect.

Evidence and Procedure, para. 2.3.1

Answer 3.3

Answer **D** — The Criminal Justice Act 2003 provides the method of instituting criminal proceedings where a public prosecutor may issue a document (a 'written charge'), which charges the person with an offence (s. 29(1)). At the same time as issuing a written charge the public prosecutor must also serve on the person concerned a document (a requisition) that requires the person to appear before a magistrates' court to answer the written charge (s. 29(2)).

The written charge and requisition must be served on the person concerned and a copy of both must be served on the court named in the requisition (s. 29(3)).

The written charge, as with an information, must contain a statement describing the offence in ordinary language and identify any relevant statutory provision. Such particulars must be included of the conduct constituting the commission of the offence as to make clear what the prosecutor alleges against the defendant. The written charge must be for one offence only. However, more than one incident of the commission of the offence may be included in the written charge if those incidents taken together amount to a course of conduct having regard to the time, place or purpose of commission (Criminal Procedure Rules 2010, r. 7.3).

The requisition, as with a summons, must state the name of the justice or public prosecutor 'responsible for' issuing it, specify each offence in respect of which it is issued, and state the time and place at which the defendant is required to appear at the magistrates' court (Criminal Procedure Rules 2010, r. 7.4).

Public prosecutors no longer have the power to commence proceedings by means of laying an information for the purpose of obtaining the issue of a summons under s. 1 of the Magistrates' Courts Act 1980 (s. 29(4)). However, a public prosecutor may still lay an information in order to secure the grant of an arrest warrant; answers A, B and C are therefore incorrect.

Evidence and Procedure, para. 2.3.2

Answer 3.4

Answer **A** — A summons may be served on a person under the Criminal Procedure Rules 2010 by:

(a) handing it to him or her; or

(b) leaving it at an address where it is reasonably believed that they will receive it, or by sending it to that address by first class post or by the equivalent of first class post (r. 4.4(1) and (2)(a)).

(c) by sending it to that address by first class post or by the equivalent of first class post.

Answers B, C and D are therefore incorrect.

Evidence and Procedure, para. 2.3.4

Answer 3.5

Answer **D** — Section 1(1)(b) of the Magistrates' Courts Act 1980 provides that, whenever a justice before whom an information is laid has power to issue a summons, they may alternatively issue a warrant for the arrest of the person named in the information, save that:

- the information must be in writing (s. 1(3)); and
- where the person in respect of whom the warrant is to be issued has attained the age of 18, the offence is an indictable offence or is punishable with imprisonment or else the person's address is not sufficiently established for a summons, or a written charge and requisition, to be served on them (s. 1(4)).

Where the offence charged is an indictable offence and a written charge and requisition have previously been issued, a warrant may be issued by a justice upon a copy of the written charge being laid by a public prosecutor.

It is therefore a written submission together with the original written charge which is answer D; answers A, B and C are therefore incorrect.

Evidence and Procedure, para. 2.3.6.1

Answer 3.6

Answer **D** — The Magistrates' Courts Act 1980 provides that a justice of the peace may issue a warrant where they are satisfied that it is in the interests of justice to secure the attendance of a person who could give material evidence. However, a warrant may only be issued where the justice of the peace is satisfied, by evidence on oath, that a summons would not procure the attendance of the person (s. 97(2)). In addition, a warrant may also be issued where a person fails to attend the court in answer to a summons where there is proof of its service if it appears to the court that there is no just excuse for the failure (s. 97(3)).

Similar powers exist for witness warrants (and summonses) for the High Court and the Crown Court. Answers A, B and C are therefore incorrect.

Evidence and Procedure, para. 2.3.6.2

Answer 3.7

Answer **A** — Rule 18.11(1) of the Criminal Procedure Rules 2010 provides that where a constable executes a warrant of arrest, commitment or detention they must, when arresting the relevant person:

- show the warrant (if they have it with them) to the relevant person; or
- tell the relevant person where the warrant is and what arrangements can be made to let that person inspect it;
- explain, in ordinary language, the charge and the reason for the arrest; and
- (unless a constable in uniform) show documentary proof of their identity.

If the person executing the warrant is one of the persons referred to in r. 18.10(b)(ii) (civilian enforcement officers or approved enforcement agencies), they must also show the relevant person a written statement under s. 125A(4) or s. 125B(4) of the Magistrates' Courts Act 1980, as appropriate. The written statement must include: the officer's name; the authority by which they are employed; and the fact they are authorised to execute warrants.

All of this must be shown by WATKINS, not just the authority by which he is employed and the fact he is authorised to execute warrants; answers C and D are therefore incorrect. The proof must be documentary and not just provided orally; answer B is therefore incorrect.

Evidence and Procedure, para. 2.3.7.1

Answer 3.8

Answer **D** — Section 136(2) of the Criminal Justice and Public Order Act 1994 states:

> A warrant issued in—
> (a) Scotland; or
> (b) Northern Ireland,
> for the arrest of a person charged with an offence may (without any endorsement) be executed in England and Wales by any constable of any police force of the country of issue or of the country of execution, or by a constable appointed under s. 53 of the British Transport Commission Act 1949, as well as by any other persons within the directions of the warrant.

There is no requirement that the offence the warrant relates to has a corresponding offence; answer B is therefore incorrect. The officer making the arrest also need not be in possession of the warrant at the time of the arrest; answer C is therefore incorrect.

However r. 18.10 of the Criminal Procedure Rules 2010 states:

> A warrant of arrest, commitment or detention may be executed by—
> (a) the persons to whom it is directed; or
> (b) by any of the following persons, whether or not it was directed to them—
> (i) a constable for any police area in England and Wales, acting in his own police area . . .

In this scenario the officer is not within their own force area; answer A is therefore incorrect.

Evidence and Procedure, paras 2.3.7, 2.3.7.3

Answer 3.9

Answer **B** — Section 125A of the Magistrates' Courts Act 1980 enables certain warrants to be executed in England and Wales by a civilian enforcement officer, provided he or she has been authorised in the prescribed manner, and answer D is therefore incorrect. However, this does not extend to all warrants, and answer A is therefore incorrect. An arrest warrant is one of those that can be executed by a civilian enforcement officer, but it does not stipulate that the warrant has to be in the officer's possession, and answer C is therefore incorrect.

Evidence and Procedure, para. 2.3.7.2

Answer 3.10

Answer **C** — The execution of warrants from other countries is dealt with by the Extradition Act 2003. This provides a fast-track extradition arrangement with Member States of the European Union and Gibraltar. Such warrants must state that the person in question is accused in the territory issuing the warrant of the commission of a specified offence and that the warrant has been issued for the purposes of arrest and prosecution.

There are therefore two factors, both of which must be present, prior to the warrant being lawfully executed:

- The person in question is accused in the territory issuing the warrant of the commission of a specified offence.
- The warrant has been issued for the purposes of arrest and prosecution.

This is answer C; answers A, B and D are therefore incorrect.

Evidence and Procedure, para. 2.3.7.3

Answer 3.11

Answer **C** — The Criminal Law Act 1977, s. 39 deals with the service of summons etc. in Scotland and Northern Ireland. The Scottish term for 'summons' is 'citation'. A 'summons, written charge and requisition' is said to be 'served' in England and Wales, and a 'citation' is said to be 'effected' in Scotland. Postal service of a summons, written charge and requisition issued in England and Wales is permitted throughout Great Britain, and a Scottish citation may be serviced by post in England and Wales; answer A is therefore incorrect.

This means that it must comply with posting rules in England and Wales. The Criminal Procedure Rules 2010 provide that a summons or requisition may be served on a person by:

(a) handing it to him or her (r. 4.3(1)(a)); or

(b) leaving it at an address where it is reasonably believed that he/she will receive it (r. 4.4 (2)(a)); or

(c) sending it to that address by first class post or by the equivalent of first class post (r. 4.4(1)).

So this means first class post to an address where it is reasonably believed the person will receive it; answers B and D are therefore incorrect.

Evidence and Procedure, para. 2.3.5

Answer 3.12

Answer **B** — Section 29 of the Criminal Justice Act 2003 changes the way proceedings can be instituted in the magistrates' court. The section removes the power to lay an information for the purpose of obtaining the issue of a summons under s. 1 of the Magistrates' Courts Act 1980 (note, this does not apply to warrants), therefore answers A, C and D are incorrect. The purpose of this is to reduce the work of the magistrates' court, and it allows the 'public prosecutor' (which includes a police force in its definition) a new method of instituting proceedings.

Section 29 states:

(1) A public prosecutor may institute criminal proceedings against a person by issuing a document (a 'written charge') which charges the person with an offence.

(2) Where a public prosecutor issues a written charge, it must at the same time issue a document (a 'requisition') which requires the person to appear before a magistrates' court to answer the written charge.

Evidence and Procedure, para. 2.3.2

Answer 3.13

Answer **C** — A warrant to commit to prison is a warrant of arrest directing that the person be taken to a specified place.

On arrest the constable should take the person to the place specified and obtain a receipt. This is one of the very rare occasions where a person need not be taken to a police station after arrest; answers A, B and D are therefore incorrect.

Evidence and Procedure, para. 2.3.6.4

Answer 3.14

Answer **D** — The Magistrates' Courts Act 1980 provides that a justice of the peace may issue a warrant where they are satisfied that it is in the interests of justice to secure the attendance of a person who could give material evidence. However, a warrant may only be issued where the justice of the peace is satisfied, by evidence on oath, that a summons would not procure the attendance of the person (s. 97(2)). In addition, a warrant may also be issued where a person fails to attend the court in answer to a summons where there is proof of its service, if it appears to the court that there is no just excuse for the failure (s. 97(3)).

Similar powers exist for witness warrants (and summonses) for the High Court and the Crown Court.

The person issuing the warrant must be satisfied of both parts, and the evidence must be on oath; answers A, B and C are therefore incorrect.

Evidence and Procedure, para. 2.3.6.2

4 Bail

STUDY PREPARATION

In terms of constitutional powers, the granting—and more importantly the denial—of bail is an area of fundamental importance. While there are lots of areas where tenuous human rights arguments have been raised since the 1998 Act was introduced, this one is for real. This area raises lots of questions about an individual's human rights—and therefore potentially lots of questions in exam papers.

For sergeants and inspectors, it is vital to know the extent of powers that exist to restrict or deny a person's bail. Practically this area is sometimes misunderstood, with many police officers (and lawyers) confusing the areas which will permit the police and courts to restrict a person's bail or to deny it altogether.

QUESTIONS

Question 4.1

Officers have arrested ELLIOT for an offence of theft and place him before the custody officer. The custody officer decides that, although further inquiries are necessary, there is currently insufficient evidence to charge and that there are no grounds to detain ELLIOT.

In relation to releasing ELLIOT, what can the custody officer do?

A She can release ELLIOT on bail, which must be unconditional.

B She can release ELLIOT on bail, which can have conditions.

C She can release ELLIOT on bail, which can have conditions and these cannot be varied later.

D She cannot release ELLIOT on bail where there are no grounds for detention.

Question 4.2

When a person is charged at a police station, the custody officer must make a decision about bail.

In relation to this decision and any representations made, which of the following is true?

A Only the person charged is allowed to make representations prior to the decision being made.

B If the person is legally represented, only the solicitor is allowed to make representations prior to the decision being made.

C Either the person charged or a solicitor is allowed to make representations prior to the decision being made.

D The custody officer does not need to listen to representations from anyone prior to the decision being made.

Question 4.3

HEAD was tried and convicted for an offence of manslaughter nine years ago, for which he was *not* given a prison sentence due to the circumstances of the case. HEAD has recently been arrested for murder. However, HEAD has been charged with manslaughter again. The custody officer is considering bail.

Which of the following is true?

A HEAD cannot be given bail in any circumstances, as he has within the last ten years been convicted of a manslaughter offence.

B HEAD cannot be given bail in any circumstances, as he has previously been convicted of a manslaughter offence.

C HEAD should be bailed, unless one of the grounds under s. 38(1) of the Police and Criminal Evidence Act 1984 applies.

D HEAD should be granted bail only if there are exceptional circumstances justifying it.

Question 4.4

The custody officer is considering whether DENNY, having been charged with an offence of burglary, should be granted bail. The investigating officer believes that bail should be refused, as she suspects that DENNY will commit further offences. The investigating officer believes this because DENNY has previously offended whilst on bail.

Is the previous offending on bail relevant to the custody officer's decision?

A No, any reasonable grounds for refusing bail cannot be gained from previous incidents.

B No, 'commission of further offences' relates to non-imprisonable offences only.

C Yes, provided those offences committed on bail were burglary offences.

D Yes, provided it is considered with other factors, e.g. the strength of the evidence.

Question 4.5

ABID was on street bail for a fraud offence and as part of the conditions attached to that bail he had to surrender his passport. ABID has made an application to the magistrates' court to have his passport back. Police officers have attended court hoping to give reasons why the application should be refused. They have evidence that ABID is liquidating his assets with a view to fleeing the country.

In relation to this what evidence should the police give to the court to allow it to consider the application?

A The police must give the court their evidence relating to the asset liquidation.

B The police must give the court the evidence relating to the asset liquidation provided it did not interfere with their on-going inquiries.

C The police need only give evidence of their suspicions that ABID may flee, no actual evidence is required.

D The police cannot give evidence in relation to the application, it is a decision of the court based only on the applicant's submission as it relates only to bail conditions variation.

Question 4.6

MARCATO was charged with rape and remanded in custody as the custody officer believed he would commit further offences. On his first court appearance his legal team argued that there was no case to answer due to the lack of evidence and the court agreed; MARCATO was released from custody. MARCATO wishes to seek redress through damages for the decision to refuse bail whilst charged.

Which of the following is correct?

A He could well win his case as there was clearly no evidence to support the charge.

B He could well win his case, particularly if the police could not produce reasonable grounds to believe he would commit further offences.

C He cannot win his case as he was not given bail by court.
D He cannot win his case as the police were in the process of investigating a crime with a view to prosecution.

Question 4.7

GREENING is being bailed by the custody officer and indicates he has had enough of the local police and may well be moving away from the area to live with his brother, who is well known to police in that area. The custody officer asks for that address and if the move is imminent. GREENING replies that it's none of her business.

What is the most appropriate action that the custody officer can now take?

A The custody officer should now refuse bail as she does not know the address of GREENING.
B The custody officer can impose a condition of bail that any change of address must be notified.
C The custody officer can take no action as GREENING has not indicated he is definitely moving address.
D The custody officer can take no action as the brother's address can be easily ascertained.

Question 4.8

FINCH is on police bail for a robbery offence and is due to return next week. Despite a very thorough investigation no eyewitness has been obtained. The investigating officer asks the custody officer to supply to the defendant a notice under s. 47(4) of the Police and Criminal Evidence Act 1984 that their attendance is no longer required. This is done; however two days later an eyewitness comes forward identifying FINCH as the robber.

Which of the following is correct in relation to action the police may now take?

A The police must serve a notice on FINCH that the bail date has been re-instated.
B The police must attend at his home address and give him a street bail notification.
C The police can re-arrest FINCH and can do so without warrant.
D The police can re-arrest FINCH, but this must be done with a warrant issued by the court.

Question 4.9

MICHAEL is an 11-year-old boy charged with burglary. There are clear grounds for the custody officer to refuse bail to prevent further offending. There is no secure local authority accommodation available, and the local authority can only provide accommodation from which it would be easy to escape.

In relation to detaining MICHAEL at the police station, which of the following is true?

A MICHAEL can be detained as no secure accommodation is available.

B MICHAEL can be detained provided there would be a risk to the public by placing him in the insecure accommodation.

C MICHAEL can be detained provided the custody officer certifies that it would have been impractical to find local authority accommodation.

D MICHAEL can be detained provided the custody officer certifies that it would have been impractical for him to be taken into local authority care.

Question 4.10

GRIEVE was dealt with by police officers in a shop for an offence of theft by shop-lifting. She was granted 'street bail' to attend at the police station in three days time. She asked her twin sister to attend in her place, as she had a hospital appointment that day.

In relation to this which of the following is correct in relation to s. 34 of the Forgery Act 1861?

A This is an offence unless GRIEVE can prove she had an excuse.

B This is an offence unless GRIEVE's sister can prove she had an excuse.

C This is not an offence as it relates only to appearing at court on bail.

D This is not an offence as it is not bail granted by a custody officer.

Question 4.11

ROWLANDS was on unconditional bail on a charge of assault. The magistrates' court granted bail for a period of four weeks. ROWLANDS failed to appear and a warrant was issued. He was arrested three weeks later and taken before the court. When he gave evidence relating to a charge of absconding, ROWLANDS stated he had been in hospital at the time of the court date and left hospital a week later. He also stated he had not been given a copy of the court record of the date of his next appearance.

In relation to ROWLANDS's potential offence of absconding, which of the following is true?

A ROWLANDS did not commit the offence as he had reasonable cause not to surrender.

B ROWLANDS did not commit the offence because he did not receive a copy of the court record.

C ROWLANDS still committed the offence even though he had reasonable cause.

D ROWLANDS committed the offence simply by failing to appear in the first place.

Question 4.12

HENRY, aged 19 years, has been charged with an offence of theft and is appearing before magistrates' court where bail is being considered. The prosecution apply for bail to be denied asserting that HENRY is a habitual drug user and likely to commit further offences whilst on bail. The prosecutor also maintains that bail should be refused as HENRY was shown to have a Class A drug present in his body and has refused to undergo an assessment as to his dependence or propensity to misuse any specified Class A drug.

In these circumstances will bail be granted by the magistrates' court?

A As HENRY has refused to undergo an assessment as to his dependence or propensity to misuse any specified Class A drug, bail must be denied.

B Bail can be granted but only where HENRY agrees to an assessment (or follow-up assessment) and it will be a condition of bail that it is undertaken.

C HENRY can be granted bail in these circumstances but only where the court is satisfied that there is no significant risk of his committing an offence while on bail.

D HENRY must be granted bail, as the prosecutor has not shown the use of a Class A drug contributed to the offence.

Question 4.13

WEBSTER was on bail to attend at magistrates' court at a date in the future. Constable NEWELL received firm evidence that WEBSTER was not going to surrender but was certain to abscond. Constable NEWELL arrested WEBSTER at 11.20 am on Monday, under s. 7(3) of the Bail Act 1976, and detention was authorised at 11.50 am. WEBSTER was taken to court at 10 am on Tuesday and appeared before a justice of the peace at 12 noon. The justice is of the opinion that WEBSTER will fail to surrender in the future.

In relation to what the justice may do next, which of the following is true?

A He may remand WEBSTER in custody as he was brought to court within 24 hours of detention being authorised.

B He may remand WEBSTER in custody as he was brought to court within 24 hours of the time he was arrested.

C He may *not* remand WEBSTER in custody as he was not put before a justice within 24 hours of detention being authorised.

D He may *not* remand WEBSTER in custody as he was not put before a justice within 24 hours of the time he was arrested.

Question 4.14

SIMPSON was required to surrender her passport and not to leave the country as part of her bail conditions set by the Crown Court. She was to attend at the court that afternoon and surrender her passport; however, she failed to do so and travelled that evening to Spain. On the day of her trial SIMPSON returned and appeared in court on time.

In relation to SIMPSON's actions which of the following is correct?

A SIMPSON has committed an offence of breaching her bail conditions and can be arrested for so doing.

B SIMPSON has committed an offence of breaching her bail conditions and can be dealt with by the Crown Court there and then.

C SIMPSON has committed no offences.

D SIMPSON has committed an offence of contempt of court by not complying with her bail conditions.

Question 4.15

WEST has been charged with several serious offences. The custody officer is deciding whether to grant bail or not, and needs to be aware of and give consideration to the rights and freedoms guaranteed under the European Convention on Human Rights when reaching that decision. There is no evidence that WEST has previously interfered with the course of justice while on bail.

In relation to the grounds on which to refuse bail, which of the following is true?

A The fact that the person had *not* previously 'interfered with the course of justice' whilst on bail would make refusing bail difficult to justify.

B The serious nature of the offences charged alone will be sufficient reason when considering 'fear of absconding' to justify remanding him in custody.

C Any previous offences need not be comparable with the offence charged when considering the prevention of crime to justify remanding him in custody.

D The fact there may be a public reaction that threatens 'the preservation of public order' to a release on bail would not help to justify remanding him in custody.

Question 4.16

BALLINGER wishes to stand surety for his friend by providing a security and is making inquiries as to what this would mean for him should certain events happen after he stood surety and provided a security.

In relation to acting as a surety, which of the following is correct?

A If the accused fails to appear any valuable item left as security would not be forfeited, a sum of money would have to be used.

B If an asset was given to the accused as a security and then forfeited due to non-appearance BALLINGER would have to be informed by the courts.

C In circumstances where the accused absconds a security need not be forfeited.

D BALLINGER can give any item as a security, but the accused must hand the item over as such security.

Question 4.17

Constable WASSELL attends a local major retail shop to deal with GREAVES, aged 17, for shoplifting. The officer listens to the store detective's evidence in the presence and hearing of GREAVES. Constable WASSELL detains the suspect and cautions her. Constable WASSELL then satisfies herself regarding the identity of GREAVES (who is a first-time offender) and considers how best to deal with this offence.

Which of the following is true?

A The officer cannot 'street bail' GREAVES as she is a youth offender.

B The officer can 'street bail' GREAVES, but this must be to the local police station.

C The officer can 'street bail' GREAVES to a police station, but this can only be to a designated police station.

D The officer can 'street bail' GREAVES to the local youth offending team office, which is in a non-designated police station.

Question 4.18

Constable GREIG granted street bail to HENTY and set conditions of bail. HENTY believes that these conditions are unreasonable and wishes to have them varied. He is due at Central Police Station (a designated station) on bail next week.

In relation to varying bail conditions in these circumstances which of the following is correct?

A HENTY has to attend court to have 'street' bail conditions overturned, they cannot be varied.

B HENTY should attend at Central Police Station and request the custody officer to vary the conditions.

C HENTY should attend at Central Police Station and ask the officer in the case to vary the conditions.

D HENTY should attend at any police station and ask any officer, other than the officer in the case, to vary the conditions.

Question 4.19

MALLARD has stood surety for her son who was charged with a serious fraud offence. MALLARD put up her matrimonial home, valued at £200,000, which was owned jointly with her husband as surety. Her son did not appear and the judge is considering forfeiture, however since the surety was taken MALLARD and her husband have divorced and the house has been sold.

In relation to this which of the following is correct?

A The judge may only order forfeiture of the entire sum, not part of it.

B The judge may order forfeiture of the whole of, or part of, £200,000 as that was the means of MALLARD at the time the surety was taken.

C In deciding whether part or the whole of the surety will be forfeited the judge should take into the account the means of MALLARD as it stands now.

D The judge cannot order any forfeiture as the surety was based on the house, which MALLARD no longer owns.

Question 4.20

Short-term prisoners on home curfew are subject to a specific period of curfew.

In relation to that period, which of the following is true?

A The minimum period is nine hours and there is no maximum.

B The minimum period is nine hours and the maximum is 12 hours.
C The minimum period is 12 hours and there is no maximum.
D The minimum period is 10 hours and the maximum is 12 hours.

Question 4.21

HENDRICKS has been released from prison and is subject to a home-detention curfew. He is arrested for an offence of theft and is taken before the local custody officer.

What action should the custody officer now take?

A Inform HM Prison Service Parole Unit and ask them to attend and collect the prisoner.
B Inform HM Prison Service Parole Unit and seek their directions on HENDRICKS' disposal.
C Inform HM Prison Service Parole Unit and deal with the prisoner as normal, but he is not entitled to bail.
D Inform HM Prison Service Parole Unit and deal with the prisoner as normal.

Question 4.22

DEWBURY is on a home-detention curfew, and is seen by Constable WYATT in the early hours in breach of his curfew.

What action should Constable WYATT take?

A Arrest DEWBURY and take him to the nearest HM Prison.
B Arrest DEWBURY and take him to the custody officer.
C Follow local policy as there is no power to arrest DEWBURY.
D Request HM Prison Service Parole Unit to revoke DEWBURY's licence. There is no power of arrest.

ANSWERS

Answer 4.1

Answer **B** — The meaning of 'bail in criminal proceedings' is contained in s. 1 of the Bail Act 1976 which states:

> (1) In this Act 'bail in criminal proceedings' means—
> (a) bail grantable in or in connection with proceedings for an offence to a person who is accused or convicted of the offence, or
> (b) bail grantable in connection with an offence to a person who is under arrest for the offence or for whose arrest for the offence a warrant (endorsed for bail) is being issued, or
> (c) bail grantable in connection with extradition proceedings in respect of an offence.

This is further endorsed by s. 1(6) which states:

> Bail in criminal proceedings shall be granted (and in particular shall be granted unconditionally or conditionally) in accordance with this Act.

As the person, although not charged, has clearly been released 'in criminal proceedings', bail can be granted and answer D is therefore incorrect. Bail can be granted conditionally, because s. 47(1A) of the Police and Criminal Evidence Act 1984 has been amended by the Police and Justice Act 2006 to include conditional bail prior to charge, and these conditions may be varied at a later time; answers A and C are therefore incorrect.

Evidence and Procedure, para. 2.4.1

Answer 4.2

Answer **C** — This is a review of the person's detention. Therefore, to comply with the Police and Criminal Evidence Act 1984, the person, or his or her legal representative, should be given an opportunity to make representations to the custody officer prior to that officer's decision whether or not to grant bail. The review should be conducted with regard to PACE Code C, paras 15.1 to 15.7. Note that if the detained person was a juvenile, the opportunity to make representations should be extended to the 'appropriate adult'. This can also be extended, by the new Code of Practice, para. 15.3A, at the discretion of the person carrying out the review. This allows for representations from other people who have an interest in the detainee's welfare.

As it is either the person or his or her solicitor who can make representations, answers A and B are therefore incorrect. Also, the custody officer has to allow opportunities for representations to be made and answer D is therefore incorrect.

Evidence and Procedure, para. 2.4.4

Answer 4.3

Answer **C** — Section 25 of the Criminal Justice and Public Order Act 1994 deals with the issue of bail for those charged with certain offences such as manslaughter. In *R (on the application of O)* v *Crown Court at Harrow* [2006] UKHL 42, it was held that this section is compatible with Art. 5 of the European Convention. Generally speaking, a person charged with manslaughter should not be given bail if he or she has a previous conviction for that offence, unless there are exceptional circumstances for granting bail, and answer B is therefore incorrect. Note that there is, however, a caveat where the previous conviction is manslaughter, as it says in s. 25 (3), 'in the case of a previous conviction for manslaughter or of culpable homicide, if he was then sentenced to imprisonment'. As this was not the case (and there is no time limit on that conviction), the 'exceptional circumstances' do not apply, and HEAD must be granted bail unless one of the grounds under s. 38(1) of the Police and Criminal Evidence Act 1984 apply; and answers A and D are therefore incorrect.

Evidence and Procedure, para. 2.4.5

Answer 4.4

Answer **D** — Section 38(1) of the Police and Criminal Evidence Act 1984 provides that a custody officer need not grant bail if there are reasonable grounds for believing that bail should be refused to prevent the accused, among other things, committing other offence(s). The custody officer should give due weight to whether the accused had committed offences when previously on bail (therefore answer A is incorrect) and also other factors. These factors are:

- the nature and seriousness of the offence and the probable method of dealing with the offender for it;
- the character, antecedents, associations and community ties of the accused;
- the accused's 'record' for having answered bail in the past;
- the strength of the evidence against the accused.

Although there are grounds for refusing bail that relate to non-imprisonable offences only, the one relating to 'commission of further offences' relates to imprisonable offences only (i.e. burglary), and therefore answer B is incorrect. The previous offending is not specific to the offence currently charged, and would therefore relate to any offence, and therefore answer C is incorrect—it is information which should be taken as a factor by the custody officer.

Evidence and Procedure, para. 2.4.6

Answer 4.5

Answer **B** — Section 30CB(1) of the Police and Criminal Evidence Act 1984 states:

> Where a person released on bail under s. 30A(1) is on bail subject to conditions, a magistrates' court may, on an application by or on behalf of the person, vary the conditions if—
>
> (a) the conditions have been varied under s. 30CA(1) since being imposed under s. 30A(3B),
>
> (b) a request for variation under s. 30CA(1) of the conditions has been made and refused, or
>
> (c) a request for variation under s. 30CA(1) of the conditions has been made and the period of 48 hours beginning with the day when the request was made has expired without the request having been withdrawn or the conditions having been varied in response to the request.

Where the court vary the conditions they must be seen as necessary for any of the purposes mentioned in s. 30A(3B)(a) to (d), and bail continues subject to the varied conditions (s. 30CB(3)(b) and (c)). It was held in *R (on the application of Ajaib)* v *Birmingham Magistrates' Court* [2009] EWHC 2127 (Admin), that in deciding to vary bail conditions, the court was entitled to rely on a police officer's evidence whilst allowing him to withhold specific information; answer D is therefore incorrect. That particular case related to police assertions that they held material that would prejudice their inquiries to disclose, namely suggesting that the suspect was liquidating his assets to travel abroad; answers A and C are therefore incorrect.

Evidence and Procedure, para. 2.4.2.6

Answer 4.6

Answer **D** — A detained person should be informed of the bail decision as soon as it is made. This can be delayed if the conditions set out in Code C, para. 1.8 apply, in which case the detainee should be informed as soon as practicable. The conditions are that the detained person:

- is incapable of understanding what is said;
- is violent, or likely to become violent; or
- is in urgent need of medical attention.

In reaching a decision as to whether a person should be refused bail the custody officer should consider whether the same objective can be achieved by imposing conditions to the bail, that is, for the person to appear at an appointed place at an appointed time. If conditions attached to a person's bail are likely to achieve the same objective as keeping the person in detention, bail must be given.

In *Gizzonio* v *Chief Constable of Derbyshire* [1998] EWCA Civ 543, Gizzonio had been remanded in custody in respect of certain charges which had not ultimately been pursued. Damages (for the wrongful exercise of lawful authority) were sought on the basis that the police had wrongly opposed the grant of bail. The court held that the decision by a police station custody sergeant whether or not to grant bail to a suspect after charge, and on what terms, has immunity from action so long as it forms part of the process of prosecution. No abuse of process or malicious prosecution action or misfeasance in public office could be maintained against him for such a decision; answers A, B and C are therefore incorrect.

Evidence and Procedure, para. 2.4.5.1

Answer 4.7

Answer **B** — Under s. 3A of the Bail Act 1976, conditions can be imposed where it is necessary to do so for the purpose of preventing a person from:

- failing to surrender to custody; or
- committing an offence while on bail; or
- interfering with witnesses or otherwise obstructing the course of justice, whether in relation to himself or any other person.

One or more of the following conditions can be imposed:

- the accused is to live and sleep at a specified address;
- the accused is to notify any changes of address;
- the accused is to report periodically (daily, weekly or at other intervals) to their local police station;
- the accused is restricted from entering a certain area or building or to go within a specified distance of a specified address;

- the accused is not to contact (whether directly or indirectly) the victim of the alleged offence and/or any other probable prosecution witness;
- the accused is to surrender their passport and/or identity card;
- the accused's movements are restricted by an imposed curfew between set times (i.e. when it is thought the accused might commit offences or come into contact with witnesses);
- the accused is required to provide a surety or security.

It is incorrect to state that there is no action the custody officer can take. Where they feel that it is necessary to ensure surrender to custody they may impose a condition of bail that any change of address must be notified; answers C and D are therefore incorrect. The grounds for refusing bail are that the person's name and address cannot be ascertained or that which is given is doubted. This is not the case here as they know who GREENING is and have an address, they even have an indication where GREENING intends to go (although no actual definitive intent was given). The brother is known so his address can be ascertained; it would not be the most appropriate action to deny bail in these circumstances; answer A is therefore incorrect.

Evidence and Procedure, paras 2.4.6.1, 2.4.7.2

Answer 4.8

Answer **C** — The Police and Criminal Evidence Act 1984 provides that a person may be released on bail with a duty to surrender at a given time and date whilst inquiries are on-going.

A custody officer, having granted bail to a person subject to a duty to appear at a police station, may give notice in writing to that person that their attendance at the police station is not required (s. 47(4)).

However nothing in the Bail Act prevents the re-arrest without warrant (answer D is therefore incorrect) of a person released on bail subject to a duty to attend at a police station if new evidence justifying a further arrest has come to light since their release (s. 47(2)).

Answers A and B both have 'must do' but as stated there is nothing preventing re-arrest; they are both incorrect.

Evidence and Procedure, para. 2.4.3

Answer 4.9

Answer **D** — A custody officer who authorises an arrested juvenile to be kept in police custody must ensure that the arrested juvenile is moved to local authority accommodation unless he or she certifies that, by reason of such circumstances as are specified in the certificate, it is impracticable to do so, or that, in the case of a juvenile who has attained the age of 12, no secure accommodation is available *and* that keeping him in other local authority accommodation would not be adequate to protect the public from serious harm from him (s. 38(6) of the Police and Criminal Evidence Act 1984). PACE Code C, Note 16D clearly states:

> The availability of secure accommodation is only a factor in relation to a juvenile aged 12 or over when the local authority accommodation would not be adequate to protect the public from serious harm from the juvenile.

As MICHAEL is only 11 years of age, answers A and B are incorrect. Note 16D also states, 'the lack of secure local authority accommodation shall not make it impracticable for the custody officer to transfer him'. This means that, unless the exception applies, the custody officer must physically hand him over to the care of the local authority. However, this does not apply to MICHAEL who is only 11 years old, and therefore answer C is incorrect.

Evidence and Procedure, para. 2.4.9

Answer 4.10

Answer **A** — Section 34 of the Forgery Act 1861 states:

> Whosoever, without lawful authority or excuse (the proof whereof shall lie on the party accused), shall in the name of any other person acknowledge any recognisance or bail, . . . or judgment or any deed or other instrument, before any court, judge, or other person lawfully authorised in that behalf, shall be guilty of felony . . .

Provided the bail or recognisance is valid, this offence would appear to apply equally to bail granted by a court or the police, and not necessarily a custody officer; answers C and D are therefore incorrect.

If there is an 'excuse' the proof lies with GRIEVE, not her sister; answer B is therefore incorrect.

Evidence and Procedure, para. 2.4.11.3

Answer 4.11

Answer **C** — Section 6 of the Bail Act 1976 creates the offence of absconding. By s. 6(1), if a person released on bail fails without reasonable cause to surrender to custody, he is guilty of an offence. The burden of showing reasonable cause is on the accused (s. 6(3)). Moreover, a person who had reasonable cause for failing to surrender on the appointed day nevertheless commits an offence if he fails to surrender *as soon after the appointed time as is reasonably practicable* (s. 6(2)). The fact that ROWLANDS did not surrender to the court until being arrested means that, although he had reasonable cause, he failed to surrender and therefore still commits the offence (answer A is incorrect). The offence is not absolute and is not committed simply by failing to surrender to custody, and therefore answer D is incorrect. Section 6(4) of the 1976 Act states:

> A failure to give a person granted bail in criminal proceedings a copy of the record of the decision shall not constitute a reasonable cause for that person's failure to surrender to custody.

Therefore answer B is incorrect.

Evidence and Procedure, para. 2.4.11

Answer 4.12

Answer **C** — Section 19(4) of the Criminal Justice Act 2003 adds paras 6A to 6C to the Bail Act 1976, Sch. 1, part I. These provide that an accused aged 18 or over who has been charged with an imprisonable offence will not be granted bail where the three conditions set out in para. 6B apply, namely:

(1) there is drug test evidence that the person has a specified Class A drug in his body (by way of a lawful test obtained under the PACE 1984, s. 63B or the Criminal Justice Act 2003, s. 161);

(2) either he is charged with an offence under the Misuse of Drugs Act 1971, s. 5(2) or (3), and the offence relates to a specified Class A drug, or the court is satisfied that there are substantial grounds for believing that the misuse of a specified Class A drug caused or contributed to the offence with which he is charged, or that offence was motivated wholly or partly by his intended misuse of a specified Class A drug; and

(3) the person does not agree to undergo an assessment (carried out by a suitably qualified person) of whether he is dependent upon or has a propensity to misuse any specified Class A drugs, or he has undergone such an assessment but does not agree to participate in any relevant follow-up which has been offered.

All three conditions must apply, and as the scenario gives no evidence that the use of a Class A drug contributed to the offence answer A is therefore incorrect. In this scenario this particular ground for denying bail is not met, however the court is under no obligation to grant bail where it believes the person may commit offences whilst on bail; answer D is therefore incorrect.

However, even where all three elements are present, the court may still grant bail if it is satisfied that there is no significant risk of his/her committing an offence whilst on bail; answer A is therefore incorrect.

Although bail can be granted if an assessment or follow-up is proposed and agreed to this is not conditional on bail being granted, the court can grant bail if it is satisfied that there is no significant risk of his/her committing an offence whilst on bail; answer B is therefore incorrect. Where a defendant agrees to an assessment (or follow-up assessment) it will be a condition of bail that it is undertaken (Bail Act 1976, s. 3(6D)).

Evidence and Procedure, para. 2.4.13.1

Answer 4.13

Answer **D** — Section 7(3) of the Bail Act 1976 states:

> A person who has been released on bail in criminal proceedings and is under a duty to surrender into the custody of a court may be arrested without warrant by a constable—
> (a) if the constable has reasonable grounds for believing that that person is not likely to surrender to custody ...

Following arrest under s. 7(3), the person arrested must be brought before a magistrate as soon as practicable, and in any event within 24 hours (s. 7(4)). Note that the section clearly states that the person must be brought before a magistrate (justice) and not brought merely to the court precincts, and therefore answers A and B are incorrect. This requirement is absolute and requires that a detainee be brought not merely to the court precincts or cells but actually be dealt with by a justice within 24 hours of being arrested (*R (on the application of Culley)* v *Crown Court sitting at Dorchester* [2007] EWHC 109 (Admin)). The 24 hours is calculated from the time of arrest and not the time detention was authorised and therefore answer C is incorrect.

Evidence and Procedure, para. 2.4.11.2

Answer 4.14

Answer **C** — The Divisional Court has held that the purpose of placing restrictions on an individual's movement under the Bail Act 1976 is to ensure that they attend the trial. If the conduct breaching bail is known about at the time, that bail could be revoked, and s. 7 of the Bail Act 1976 provides a power of arrest without warrant if the constable:

- has reasonable grounds for believing that the person is not likely to surrender to custody;
- has reasonable grounds for believing that the person is likely to break, or reasonable grounds for suspecting that the person has broken, any conditions of bail.

However, s. 7 does not itself create any offence. Answers A and B are therefore incorrect.

In *R* v *Ashley* [2004] 1 WLR 2057, the accused was accused of contempt of court, arising out of breaches of bail conditions. He had been released on bail subject to conditions that required him to surrender his passport and not to leave the country. He broke both conditions but returned to face trial on the appointed day. Although the defendant had breached bail conditions by leaving the country, he did return for his trial. It followed that the judge did not have power to deal with him by way of contempt of court. Answer D is therefore incorrect.

Evidence and Procedure, para. 2.4.11

Answer 4.15

Answer **A** — The European Court and Commission have identified four grounds where the refusal of bail may be justified under the European Convention on Human Rights:

- fear of absconding;
- interference with the course of justice;
- the prevention of crime;
- the preservation of public order.

In relation to fear of absconding, the seriousness of the offence alone has been deemed not to be a sufficient reason to suppose a person will necessarily abscond (*Yagci and Sargin* v *Turkey* (1995) 20 EHRR 505), and answer B is therefore incorrect. In considering the prevention of crime, the European Court has held that, where the offender's previous convictions were not comparable either in nature or seriousness with the offence(s) charged, their use as grounds for refusing bail would not be acceptable for the purposes of Art. 5 of the Convention (*Clooth* v *Belgium* (1991) 14 EHRR 717), and answer C is therefore incorrect. The temporary detention of a person where the particular gravity of the offence(s) and the likely public reaction mean that the release may give rise to public disorder was considered in *Letellier* v *France* (1991) 14 EHRR 83 in relation to the preservation of public order. This was held to be a sound reason for remanding in custody, and answer D is therefore incorrect. In *Ringeisen* v *Austria* (1971) 1 EHRR 455, interference with the course of justice was considered. If the detained person has previously been bailed and there was no evidence of interference with the course of justice, remanding in custody to prevent interference with the course of justice would be very difficult to justify.

Evidence and Procedure, para. 2.4.16

Answer 4.16

Answer **C** — Section 3(4) of the Bail Act 1976 provides that before a person is granted bail he or she may be required to provide one or more sureties to secure his or her surrender to custody. A custody officer is entitled (as a court) to require such sureties. Section 3(5) of the Bail Act 1976 provides that, before a person is granted bail, he or she may be required to give security for his or her surrender to custody. As with sureties, a custody officer is entitled (as a court) to require such security, as far as s. 3(6)(a) to (c) (surrender to custody, not commit an offence on bail, interfere with witnesses, etc.) applies. The security required may be a sum of money or other valuable item and may be given either by the accused or someone on his/her behalf; answer D is therefore incorrect. A third party may make an asset available to an accused for the purpose of providing a security and where the security is forfeited there is no requirement for the third party to be informed (*R (Stevens)* v *Truro Magistrates' Court* [2002] 1 WLR 144); answer B is therefore incorrect.

As with sureties, where an accused absconds this would result in forfeiture of the security, whether this be cash or a valuable item; answer A is therefore incorrect. This would not be the case if there appears reasonable cause for the (accused's) failure to surrender to custody (s. 5(7) to (9) of the 1976 Act).

Evidence and Procedure, paras 2.4.7.4, 2.4.7.5

Answer 4.17

Answer **D** — The Criminal Justice Act 2003 allows an officer to 'street bail' an offender as an alternative to arresting him or her and taking him or her straight to the police station, as was required by s. 30 of PACE prior to being amended by the 2003 Act. Section 30A of PACE now states:

(1) A constable may release on bail a person who is arrested or taken into custody in the circumstances mentioned in s. 30(1).

(2) A person may be released on bail under subs. (1) at any time before they arrive at a police station.

(3) A person released on bail under subs. (1) must be required to attend a police station.

(3A) Where a constable releases a person on bail under subs. (1)—
- (a) no recognisance for the person's surrender to custody shall be taken from the person,
- (b) no security for the person's surrender to custody shall be taken from the person or from anyone else on the person's behalf,
- (c) the person shall not be required to provide a surety or sureties for their surrender to custody, and
- (d) no requirement to reside in a bail hostel may be imposed as a condition of bail.

(3B) Subject to subs. (3A), where a constable releases a person on bail under subs. (1) the constable may impose, as conditions of the bail, such requirements as appear to the constable to be necessary—
- (a) to secure that the person surrenders to custody,
- (b) to secure that the person does not commit an offence while on bail,
- (c) to secure that the person does not interfere with witnesses or otherwise obstruct the course of justice, whether in relation to themselves or any other person, or
- (d) for the person's own protection or, if the person is under the age of 17, for the person's own welfare or in the person's own interests.

(4) Where a person is released on bail under subs. (1), a requirement may be imposed on the person as a condition of bail only under the preceding provisions of this section.

(5) The police station which the person is required to attend may be any police station.

As can be seen in s. 30A(5) above, the person can be bailed to any police station, including non-designated ones; answers B and C are incorrect. There is nothing in the 2003 Act that restricts street bail to adult offenders, and therefore answer A is incorrect. It is perfectly acceptable, and some might add inherently sensible, to 'street bail' a youth offender straight to the youth offending team office. The only consideration outlined in the 2003 Act in relation to bail to non-designated stations is contained in s. 30C(2) of the 1984 Act:

(2) If a person is required to attend a police station which is not a designated police station he must be—
(a) released, or
(b) taken to a designated police station,
not more than six hours after his arrival.

Evidence and Procedure, paras 2.4.2.2, 2.4.2.4

Answer 4.18

Answer **B** — Where a person released under the Police and Criminal Evidence Act, s. 30A(1) is on bail subject to conditions—

(a) a relevant officer at the police station at which the person is required to attend, or

(b) where no notice under s. 30B specifying that police station has been given to the person, a relevant officer at the police station specified under s. 30B(4A)(c),

may, at the request of the person but subject to subs. (2), vary the conditions; answer A is therefore incorrect.

The 'relevant officer' (s. 30CA(3)(c)) means a custody officer in relation to a designated police station, or a constable or person designated as a staff custody officer in any other police station. A constable involved in the investigation should not deal with the request unless no other constable or officer is available (s. 30CA (5)); answer C is therefore incorrect. HENTY was given notice of which police station to attend, so cannot attend any police station; answer D is therefore incorrect.

Evidence and Procedure, para. 2.4.2.26

Answer 4.19

Answer **C** — If an accused bailed with sureties fails to surrender at the appointed time, the court must forfeit their recognisances (i.e. order them to pay the amounts in which they respectively stood surety). This is the normal consequence of the accused's absconding, although the court has a discretion in exceptional circumstances to order that the surety pay less than the full sum or even to order that none of the sum it previously declared forfeited should in fact be forfeited; answer A is therefore incorrect.

However, in *R* v *Stipendiary Magistrate for Leicester, ex parte Kaur* (2000) 164 JP 127, it was held that the means of the surety at the time of enforcement must be taken into account when the court decides whether or not to remit the whole or part of the forfeited recognisance. This takes into account that people's means change; answer B is therefore incorrect.

The house was not the surety, it merely represented a financial sum; the money would still be owed even though the actual property entered as surety was no longer in the possession of the suretor.

Evidence and Procedure, para. 2.4.7.4

Answer 4.20

Answer **A** — Release of short-term prisoners subject to home curfew is provided by s. 253 of the Criminal Justice Act 2003.

The home-detention curfew is set up for a prisoner to complete their sentence and runs for a minimum period of 14 days and a maximum period of 60 days. The prisoner is required to agree to the curfew conditions. The governor at the relevant prison determines the details of the curfew. This will normally be from 7 pm to 7 am and may be varied. The minimum period of curfew is nine hours but there is no maximum. This leaves option A as the correct answer; answers B, C and D are therefore incorrect.

Evidence and Procedure, para. 2.4.18.2

Answer 4.21

Answer **D** — The guidance provided to police forces in relation to persons who are subject to a home-detention curfew, and subsequently arrested for other offences is as follows.

Where arrested, the custody officer is to notify the monitoring contractor immediately of:

- details of the prisoner,
- details of the offence,
- whether the prisoner is to be bailed or retained in custody,
- whether the prisoner continues to wear the electronic tag,
- custody officer to notify the monitoring contractor when the prisoner is released.

Where charged the custody officer is to:

- immediately inform HM Prison Service Parole Unit,
- inform the contractor if the prisoner is to be returned to prison,
- remove and collect the monitoring unit.

Where a person is charged with an offence whilst subject to a home-detention curfew, PACE Code C in relation to detention following charge continues to apply. The question of bail is not affected by their curfew breach, and answer C is therefore incorrect. The custody officer is responsible for their treatment and disposal, not the prison service, therefore answers A and B are incorrect. Note, this is an arrest for an offence, and is a separate issue from that of the enforcing of his home-detention curfew.

Evidence and Procedure, para. 2.4.18.4

Answer 4.22

Answer **C** — Any reports of a breach of curfew are to be made to HM Prison Service Parole Unit. This unit may make a decision to revoke or vary the curfew order. The relevant prison governor may also make variations to the order. There is no power to arrest any person solely found breaching his or her curfew, as no actual offence has been committed and local policy should be followed, therefore answers A and B are incorrect. Where the police consider that a prisoner subject to a home-detention curfew represents a serious risk to the public, they may make a request for the curfew order to be revoked. Any such request should be authorised by an officer of the rank of superintendent or above and made to HM Prison Service Parole Unit at the Home Office. So the constable cannot seek revocation of the licence directly herself, and answer D is therefore incorrect.

Evidence and Procedure, paras 2.4.18.4, 2.4.18.5

5 Court Procedure and Witnesses

STUDY PREPARATION

This is what the whole process is all about. Although, logically, this chapter should appear at the end of the book, it makes practical sense to consider its contents here. The mechanics of getting evidence before a court largely come from statute and, as you would expect, contain a fair amount of detail.

It is important to understand who can give what evidence and under what circumstances; it is also important to know some of the more general restrictions that are placed on witnesses' evidence-in-chief and cross-examination.

QUESTIONS

Question 5.1

GUNTER is a 14-year-old boy who was summonsed to court for riding a moped other than in accordance with a licence. He wishes to plead guilty by post to that offence.

In relation to this which of the following is correct?

A He can plead guilty by post, and if he does the matter will be held in the magistrates' court.

B He can plead guilty by post and the matter will be held in the youth court.

C He cannot plead not guilty by post as he is not an adult, and must appear in the youth court.

D He cannot plead guilty by post as he is not aged 16 or 17, he must appear in the youth court.

Question 5.2

MUDGE was charged with dangerous driving and elected summary trial. He made his first appearance 21 days ago and was initially remanded in custody by the magistrates. He served a total of 14 days in custody prior to being bailed by a judge in chambers at Crown Court.

Within which time limit must MUDGE's trial commence?

A 35 days.
B 41 days.
C 56 days.
D No specific time limit.

Question 5.3

SUTHERLAND has been convicted of an offence of assault at magistrates' court. The district judge is going to pass a community sentence on SUTHERLAND and is considering whether he needs to give reasons for, and explain the effects of, the sentence passed under s. 174 of the Criminal Justice Act 2003.

Does the district judge have to give reasons as to why a community sentence has been passed?

A No, s. 174 of the Criminal Justice Act 2003 only applies to a judge handing down a sentence at Crown Court.
B No, s. 174 of the Criminal Justice Act 2003 only applies where a custodial sentence is imposed.
C Yes, and the district judge must mention any important aggravating factors.
D Yes, and the district judge must mention any important aggravating or mitigating factors.

Question 5.4

KHAN, who is 21 years of age, was due to appear in magistrates' court for an offence of theft. Whilst waiting in the foyer outside the court room someone accused him of being there as a suicide bomber and a fight ensued. The court security ejected KHAN from the building and refused to let him re-enter even for his trial. When his case was called he did not appear and the magistrates decided to hear the case in his absence as KHAN had, by virtue of his conduct, voluntarily absented himself from the hearing of his case.

Should the trial take place in KHAN's absence?

A Yes, as through his actions he has voluntarily absented himself from the hearing.

B Yes, as his behaviour is likely to disrupt the trial they may proceed in his absence.

C No, KHAN is willing and wanting to attend court, but is being prevented from doing so.

D No, only where it would be in the interest of justice can any trial be held without the accused being present.

Question 5.5

FOOT and her partner have been jointly charged with an offence of theft. They have cohabited together for the last 10 years. They have separate defence teams who are each trying to blame the other co-accused. Their defence teams are considering whether they can call the other co-accused to give evidence.

In relation to competence and compellability which of the following is correct?

A Both are competent witnesses, and can be compelled to give evidence as they are not married.

B Both are competent witnesses and can be compelled as they are neither civil partners nor married.

C Both are competent witnesses and cannot be compelled as they are civil partners.

D Both are competent witnesses, but cannot be compelled to give evidence as they are co-accused.

Question 5.6

BURGESS and PURDY are security staff working at a secure unit holding asylum seekers. A riot takes place and the two security officers will be witnesses at the forthcoming trial of some of the detainees. Prior to the court hearing, a legal training consultancy was used by the security company to provide training for all staff, and BURGESS and PURDY took part in the training. A case study prepared by the training consultancy, for training purposes, contained similarities with the events of the real riot. The training process included a mock cross-examination.

In respect of this training session which of the following is correct in relation to the forthcoming trial of some of the detainees?

A This is coaching of witnesses; it is prohibited by law.

B This is coaching of witnesses; it is prohibited by the courts.

C This is not coaching of witnesses, as it is part of an on-going training programme.

D This is not coaching of witnesses, as it was not training on the exact evidence that the witnesses would give.

Question 5.7

JOHNSTONE is 17 years old and a witness to an offence of kidnapping. She is to be called to the Crown Court to give evidence for the prosecution, but JOHNSTONE has been receiving threats from the accused's family who have yet to be dealt with for this intimidation. To avoid the accused's family attending and intimidating the witness, the prosecution seek a special measures direction to have JOHNSTONE's evidence given in private.

Who, if anyone, can the court exclude under this special measures direction?

A Any person, including the accused, but not his or her legal representatives.

B Any person except the accused and his or her legal representatives.

C The public only; the press would be allowed to stay, as would the accused and his or her legal representatives.

D In this case the special measures direction may not be given as it is not a sexual offence.

Question 5.8

Constable GUNTER and Constable HUNT are witnesses in a case of theft. Both officers made pocket notebook entries regarding the incident, and have refreshed their memory from those notebooks prior to giving evidence. Constable GUNTER is now giving her evidence-in-chief and wishes to consult her pocket notebook.

In relation to refreshing memory, which of the following is true?

A She cannot refer to her pocket notebook as she made the notes in consultation.

B She cannot refer to her pocket notebook as she refreshed her memory prior to giving evidence.

C She can refer to her pocket notebook, but only for exact details, i.e. index numbers.

D She can refer to her pocket notebook, provided she states that it records her recollection of the case.

Question 5.9

KHAN and BRADFIELD are jointly charged with robbery. KHAN goes into the witness box and gives an account of events, but BRADFIELD does not give sworn testimony. Counsel for BRADFIELD asks no questions of KHAN in cross-examination. Counsel for BRADFIELD suggests to the jury in her closing speech that the co-accused and a prosecution witness had committed the offence charged, and not her client.

Which of the following is correct?

A Counsel for BRADFIELD can make this suggestion as it relates to the co-accused.

B Counsel for BRADFIELD can make this suggestion as she is not prosecuting counsel.

C Counsel for BRADFIELD cannot make this suggestion as it was not put to him in cross-examination.

D Counsel for BRADFIELD cannot make this suggestion as her client did not give evidence.

Question 5.10

PERKINS has received a summons for a motoring offence and intends pleading guilty by post. PERKINS has previous motoring convictions within the last three years.

In relation to these previous convictions and pleading guilty by post which of the following is correct?

A If the court wishes to use the previous convictions they must give the accused notice of that intention, but allow the guilty plea by post.

B If the court wishes to use the previous convictions they must give the accused notice of that intention, and direct the accused attend in person.

C The court can use the previous convictions, without giving the accused notice of that intention, but can only use a certified court record of those convictions.

D The court can use the previous convictions, without giving the accused notice of that intention, and can use a DVLA print out to do so.

Question 5.11

ALBERTS is standing trial at Crown Court for an offence of rape. His defence is based on consent and ALBERTS wishes to cross-examine the victim on her previous sexual behaviour, with the leave of the court.

In relation to this, which of the following statements is correct?

A Neither ALBERTS nor his legal representative can ask questions about the victim's previous sexual behaviour.

B ALBERTS can ask such questions, provided they relate to behaviour at or about the same time as the incident charged.

C ALBERTS' legal representative can ask questions about the victim's previous sexual behaviour.

D ALBERTS' legal representative can ask such questions provided they relate to sexual behaviour at or about the same time as the incident in question.

Question 5.12

McMAHON is standing trial on a charge of violent disorder, which occurred during a large-scale public disorder situation. The prosecution relied heavily on the evidence of several police officers, some of whom gave evidence that they had seen the accused committing the offence. The officers were cross-examined only in relation to the evidence they had given. McMAHON, whilst giving evidence, accused certain police officers of a conspiracy to fabricate the evidence against him. This was the first time the prosecution had been made aware of the defence's intention to raise this as an issue. The prosecutor wishes to recall the officers to rebut the accusation.

At this stage in the trial, having closed their case, will the prosecution be allowed to call evidence?

A Yes, but only if the defence accepts that there was a misunderstanding between counsel.
B Yes, as they could not reasonably have anticipated this defence.
C No, because this issue was not raised in cross-examination.
D No, because the prosecution must call the whole of their evidence before closing their case—no exceptions.

Question 5.13

WALLACE is a 14-year-old girl who was sexually assaulted. The defendant in the case is about to be tried in the Crown Court and WALLACE will have to give evidence in court. She states that she is likely to be embarrassed about giving evidence in open court, but she is not afraid to give evidence nor is she refusing to give evidence. The prosecution are seeking a special measures direction for the visually-recorded interview the police conducted to be admitted as her evidence-in-chief.

In relation to this application, which of the following is true?

A It *must* be granted as the child is under 17 years of age.
B It may be granted unless the court believes it would not be in the interests of justice to do so.
C It will not be granted as the child is not in fear of giving evidence.
D It will not be granted as the child has not refused to give evidence in open court.

Question 5.14

LAVENDER is appearing at Crown Court charged with stealing a bicycle and is representing himself. The jury are sworn and during the opening of the case by the prosecution LAVENDER states that he wishes to be represented by counsel. The trial takes place and the jury has retired to consider their verdict. LAVENDER decides to change his plea to guilty.

What should the judge direct following this requested change of plea?

A The jury should be dismissed and the judge should record a guilty plea entered.

B The jury should be dismissed and the judge should record a verdict of guilty.

C The jury should be directed by the judge to return a formal verdict of guilty.

D The jury should be allowed to carry on their deliberations; a change of plea is acceptable only up until the jury retire to consider their verdict.

Question 5.15

HUISH is an 81-year-old woman who was allegedly raped by HILL. HUISH also suffers from Alzheimer's disease. A videotape of the complainant's police interview was made. Although her answers were confused, she stated that a man had had sexual intercourse with her against her wishes. Expert evidence indicated that at the time of her interview she was not fit to give evidence in court owing to her dementia.

Which of the following is true in relation to the videotaped evidence?

A Her evidence cannot be admitted as she has impaired intellect and is not a competent witness.

B Her evidence cannot be admitted; she cannot be a competent witness as she is not available to attend court due to dementia.

C Her evidence can be admitted, however the jury must be warned about the reliability of her evidence.

D Her evidence can be admitted, if the court decide her evidence ought to be admitted in the interests of fairness.

Question 5.16

CONVOY is a witness to a theft of petrol committed by her husband, and she is being interviewed by the police who are investigating the theft. They do not tell her that she is not a compellable witness and although she is reluctant she gives a statement. She is called to court but refuses to give evidence against her husband,

and the judge rules she is not compellable. The prosecution seeks to admit the wife's statement under s. 114 of the Criminal Justice Act 2003.

Can her statement be admitted as evidence?

A Yes, as her statement was not obtained fraudulently by the police, she didn't ask if she had to make it.

B Yes as there is no requirement to tell a wife she is not compellable prior to obtaining a statement.

C No, the police are required to tell a witness that they cannot be compelled to give evidence where in law they cannot be so compelled.

D No, as the police are aware that she is reluctant to give a statement they must tell her that she cannot be compelled.

Question 5.17

DYER is appearing at Crown Court on a charge of burglary having originally pleaded not guilty at magistrates' court and electing to be indicted. However fearing a prison sentence he changes his plea to guilty prior to any evidence being adduced. One matter of concern for DYER is that he was accused of stealing a very expensive set of golf clubs. He admits taking them but states they were a very old and cheap set.

What evidence should the prosecution now call?

A Only the accused's criminal record, he has pleaded guilty.

B Only the accused's antecedents and criminal record, he has pleaded guilty.

C The accused's antecedents and criminal record and where necessary evidence to support their version of the facts.

D Evidence that supports their version of events as a previous not guilty plea was entered.

Question 5.18

GRAINGER is 40 years of age and is accused of criminal damage and due to appear at magistrates' court, however he has failed to appear. There is no notice given by GRAINGER as to why he is not there.

In relation to this which of the following is correct?

A The court should inquire as to why GRAINGER is not present; if no satisfactory answer is received it should proceed in his absence.

B The court should consider whether it should issue a warrant for GRAINGER's arrest or issue a summons compelling him to attend.

C The court may proceed in his absence unless it appears to the court to be contrary to the interests of justice do so.

D The court must proceed in his absence unless it appears to the court to be contrary to the interests of justice do so.

ANSWERS

Answer 5.1

Answer **D** — The procedure for a defendant to plead guilty by post is provided by the Magistrates' Courts Act 1980 and applies to proceedings for summary offences started by way of summons (or requisition) in the magistrates' court (s. 12(1)), or in the youth court for persons aged 16 or 17 (s. 12(2)). The summons (or requisition) is served on the defendant together with a 'statement of facts' and a prescribed form of explanation. This allows the defendant an opportunity to plead guilty and put forward any mitigation in their absence. The magistrates' designated officer informs the prosecution of any written guilty plea.

As he is not aged 16 or 17 there is no opportunity to plead guilty by post; answers A and B are therefore incorrect. This restriction is not because he is not an adult, but because he is not aged 16 or 17; answer C is therefore incorrect.

Evidence and Procedure, para. 2.5.2

Answer 5.2

Answer **D** — The Prosecution of Offences (Custody Time Limits) (Amendment) Regulations 1999 (SI 1999/2744) provides for a maximum magistrates' court custody time limit (from first appearance to start of trial) of 56 days in relation to those charged with summary offences. However, this relates only to time for someone in custody. Had MUDGE been in custody trial would have to be within 56 days of first appearance; as this was 21 days ago then 35 days remain before trial. However, MUDGE is not in custody so no specific time limit is imposed; answers A, B and C are therefore incorrect.

Evidence and Procedure, para. 2.5.7.3

Answer 5.3

Answer **D** — Section 174 of the Criminal Justice Act 2003 imposes a general statutory duty on the courts to give reasons for, and explain the effects of, the sentence passed.

The court must explain in non-technical terms its reasons for deciding on the sentence passed, the structure of the sentence, what it requires the offender to do, what will happen if it is not done, and any power which exists to vary or review the sentence (s. 174(1)). In addition, certain specific matters must be dealt with (s. 174(2)). If a custodial or community sentence is being passed, the court must explain why the offence is sufficiently serious to warrant such a sentence. Any reduction for a guilty plea must be mentioned in the reasons, together with any aggravating or mitigating factors which the court regarded as being of particular importance.

This applies to all courts, including magistrates' courts, and includes community sentences; answers A and B are therefore incorrect. The person imposing the sentence must mention any aggravating or mitigating factors that were considered, not just those aggravating factors that may have meant such a sentence was warranted; answer C is therefore incorrect.

Evidence and Procedure, para. 2.5.4

Answer 5.4

Answer **C** — Where an accused fails to appear in the magistrates' court in answer to bail the court may:

- issue a warrant for the accused's arrest under s. 7 of the Bail Act 1976;
- appoint a later time when the accused has to appear in accordance with s. 129(3) of the Magistrates' Courts Act 1980;
- proceed in the accused's absence under s. 11(1) of the Magistrates' Courts Act 1980.

The Criminal Justice and Immigration Act 2008 has made certain amendments to s. 11 of the 1980 Act in relation to magistrates' courts proceeding to trial in the accused's absence. Where an accused is under 18 years of age the court *may* proceed in his or her absence (s. 11(1)(a)), and if the accused has attained the age of 18 the court *must* proceed in his or her absence unless it appears to the court to be contrary to the interests of justice to do so (s. 11(1)(b)); answer D is therefore incorrect.

This matter has been dealt with by the courts in *R (Davies)* v *Solihull Justices* [2008] EWHC 1157 (Admin). After his case had been called on, it was discovered that the accused had been excluded from the court building by the security staff because of disorderly behaviour. The justices ruled that the accused had, by virtue of his conduct, voluntarily absented himself from the hearing of his case, and that he should be tried in his absence. The Court of Appeal disagreed and held that even where the accused had been excluded from the court premises due to his disorderly behaviour, this misbehaviour did not justify excluding him from his own trial; answers A and B are therefore incorrect.

Evidence and Procedure, para. 2.5.6

Answer 5.5

Answer **D** — There is a general rule in English law that 'All people are competent and all competent witnesses are compellable'. The rule was sanctioned by the provisions of s. 53 of the Youth Justice and Criminal Evidence Act 1999. Section 53 states:

> (1) At every stage in criminal proceedings all persons are (whatever their age) competent to give evidence.

Dealing with compellability the law deals with persons who are spouses, the spouse of an accused is competent to give evidence for the accused (Youth Justice and Criminal Evidence Act 1999, s. 53(1)) and shall be compellable to give evidence for the accused (PACE 1984, s. 80(2)), unless also charged in the proceedings (see s. 80(4) and (4A)). The Civil Partnership Act 2004 made ss. 80 and 80A of PACE 1984 applicable to 'civil partners' as well as wives and husbands. Legal civil partners are same-sex couples who have registered their partnership in accordance with the 2004 Act. However cohabitees are not afforded the same concessions as a wife, husband or civil partner in giving evidence against each other (that of being competent but not compellable). In *R* v *Pearce* [2002] 1 WLR 1553 it was held that the position with cohabitees was not in breach of Art. 8 of the European Convention on Human Rights (the right to respect for family life).

That makes the accused here only co-accused as rules relating to spouses do not apply. An accused, however, is not a compellable witness for a co-accused because, under the Criminal Evidence Act 1898, s. 1(1), a person charged in criminal proceedings shall not be called as a witness 'except upon his own application'. An accused who does give evidence for a co-accused may be cross-examined to show his own guilt of the offence charged; answers A, B and C are therefore incorrect.

Evidence and Procedure, para. 2.5.8.6

Answer 5.6

Answer **B** — The Criminal Justice Act 2003 provides for the use of documents and transcripts by witnesses to refresh their memory.

Section 139 of the 2003 Act states:

> (1) A person giving oral evidence in criminal proceedings about any matter may, at any stage in the course of doing so, refresh his memory of it from a document made or verified by him at an earlier time if—

(a) he states in his oral evidence that the document records his recollection of the matter at that earlier time, and
(b) his recollection of the matter is likely to have been significantly better at that time than it is at the time of his oral evidence.

(2) Where—
(a) a person giving oral evidence in criminal proceedings about any matter has previously given an oral account, of which a sound recording was made, and he states in that evidence that the account represented his recollection of the matter at that time,
(b) his recollection of the matter is likely to have been significantly better at the time of the previous account than it is at the time of his oral evidence, and
(c) a transcript has been made of the sound recording, he may, at any stage in the course of giving his evidence, refresh his memory of the matter from that transcript.

However the Court of Appeal made clear that training or coaching witnesses in relation to a forthcoming criminal trial is prohibited (*R* v *Momodou*; *R* v *Limani* [2005] EWCA Crim 177), and the facts of this case mirror this scenario. As it is the courts that prohibit it, not statute, answer A is incorrect. Although training firms do provide this service, those using it would have to be very careful that the training did not so closely resemble the case they were witnesses in to be deemed as coaching; answers C and D are therefore incorrect.

Evidence and Procedure, para. 2.5.11

Answer 5.7

Answer **B** — Section 25(1) of the Youth Justice and Criminal Evidence Act 1999 states that a special measures direction may provide for the exclusion of *any* persons from the court whilst the witness is giving evidence, and answer C is therefore incorrect. This does not include the exclusion of the accused, legal representatives and any interpreter acting for the witness (s. 25(2)), and answer A is therefore incorrect. This direction may be used only where the proceedings relate to a sexual offence, *or* there are reasonable grounds to believe that the witness has been or will be intimidated by any person other than the accused—answer D is therefore incorrect.

Evidence and Procedure, para. 2.5.10.4

Answer 5.8

Answer **D** — The Criminal Justice Act 2003 provides statutory rules that enable witnesses to refer to a document to refresh their memories. This replaces the many authorities and judicial discretion that existed prior to the 2003 Act being enacted. Section 139 of the 2003 Act states:

> (1) A person giving oral evidence in criminal proceedings about any matter may, at any stage in the course of doing so, refresh his memory of it from a document made or verified by him at an earlier time if—
>
> (a) he states in his oral evidence that the document records his recollection of the matter at that earlier time, and
>
> (b) his recollection of the matter is likely to have been significantly better at that time than it is at the time of his oral evidence.

So the officer can refer to her notebook, irrespective of any factors under which such notes were made, if she states it is her recollection, and such recollection is likely to be significantly better than it is now whilst giving evidence-in-chief. Answers A, B and C are therefore incorrect. However the Court of Appeal has made it clear that training or coaching witnesses in relation to a forthcoming criminal trial is prohibited (*R* v *Momodou; R* v *Limani* [2005] EWCA Crim 177).

Evidence and Procedure, para. 2.5.11

Answer 5.9

Answer **C** — A party who fails to cross-examine a witness upon a particular matter in respect of which it is proposed to contradict, tacitly accepts the truth of the witness's evidence-in-chief on that matter; this includes the prosecuting counsel and any counsel for co-accused, so answer B is therefore incorrect. They will not thereafter be entitled to invite the jury to disbelieve the witness in that regard. It is immaterial whether counsel's own client gave evidence or not, what is important is whether they ask questions of a witness: answer D is therefore incorrect. Answer A is incorrect as the fact that the person is alleged to have committed the offence is of no consequence. The proper course is to challenge the witness while he is in the witness box, or at any rate to make it plain to him at that stage that his evidence is not accepted. In *R* v *Bircham* [1972] Crim LR 430, counsel for the accused was not permitted to suggest to the jury in his closing speech that the co-accused and a prosecution witness had committed the offence charged, where the allegation had not been put to either in cross-examination. In *R* v *Bingham* [1999] 1 WLR 598, it was held that a defendant who goes into a witness box exposes himself to cross-examination by the prosecution or any co-accused. This is true even if no evidence-in-chief is offered, or questions asked by defence counsel.

Evidence and Procedure, para. 2.5.16

Answer 5.10

Answer **D** — The procedure for a defendant to plead guilty by post is provided by the Magistrates' Courts Act 1980 and applies to proceedings for summary offences started by way of summons (or requisition) in the magistrates' court (s. 12(1)), or in the youth court for persons aged 16 or 17 (s. 12(2)). The summons (or requisition) is served on the defendant together with a 'statement of facts' and a prescribed form of explanation. This allows the defendant an opportunity to plead guilty and put forward any mitigation in their absence. The magistrates' designated officer informs the prosecution of any written guilty plea.

Where a guilty plea has been received from the defendant, the 'statement of facts' and any mitigation are read out by the magistrates' clerk in open court.

This section is most commonly used for driving offences and provision is made for a printout from the DVLA to be admissible as evidence of previous convictions for traffic offences without the need to give an accused notice of intention to refer to these previous convictions (Road Traffic Offenders Act 1988, s. 13); answers A, B and C are therefore incorrect.

Evidence and Procedure, para. 2.5.2

Answer 5.11

Answer **D** — Section 34 of the Youth Justice and Criminal Evidence Act 1999 states:

> No person charged with a sexual offence may in any criminal proceedings cross-examine in person a witness who is the complainant ...

This means that ALBERTS himself cannot cross-examine the victim about any matters, and answer B is therefore incorrect. Should ALBERTS wish the complainant to be cross-examined, he must, or the court may, appoint a legal representative. Even when this is the case, there are restrictions on questions that can be asked of the victim. Section 41(1) states:

> If at a trial a person is charged with a sexual offence, then, except with the leave of the court—
> (a) no evidence may be adduced, and

(b) no question may be asked in cross-examination, by or on behalf of the accused at the trial, about any sexual behaviour of the complainant.

'On behalf of' would include a legal representative, but there are exceptions, with leave of the court. Section 41(2) of the 1999 Act states:

> The court may give leave only in relation to any evidence or question only on an application made by or on behalf of an accused, and may not give such leave unless it is satisfied— . . .

Section 41(3) states that:

> This subsection applies if the evidence or question relates to a relevant issue in the case and either—
> (a) that the issue is not an issue of consent; or
> (b) it is an issue of consent and the sexual behaviour of the complainant to which the evidence or question relates is alleged to have taken place at or about the same time as the event which is the subject matter of the charge against the accused . . .

So in the facts of the question, consent is in issue and counsel could ask questions, with leave of the court; therefore, answer A is incorrect. The House of Lords have considered the very restrictive phraseology of s. 41(3) of the 1999 Act and a person's right to a fair trial. The overriding theme is that the test of admissibility was whether the evidence, and questioning relating to it, was nevertheless so relevant to the issue of consent that to exclude it would endanger the fairness of the trial under Art. 6 of the European Convention on Human Rights. If that test were satisfied, the evidence should not be excluded (*R* v *A (No. 2)* [2001] UKHL 25, [2001] 3 All ER), but still must be recent; answer C is therefore incorrect.

Evidence and Procedure, paras 2.5.16.2, 2.5.16.4

Answer 5.12

Answer **B** — It is a general rule that all of the evidence on which the prosecution intend to rely should be called before the closure of their case (*R* v *Francis* [1991] 1 All ER 225). There are, however, some exceptions to this general rule, and answer D is incorrect. The three recognised exceptions are:

- evidence not previously available;
- failure to call evidence by reason of inadvertence or oversight; *and*
- evidence in rebuttal of matters arising *ex improviso* (evidence which becomes relevant in circumstances which the prosecution could not have foreseen at the time when they presented their case).

In the facts outlined in the question, only the third exception arises. The principle of *ex improviso* deals with instances where during the case for the defence issues are raised that the prosecution could not have reasonably anticipated when they presented their case. In such instances the judge can allow the prosecution to call evidence in rebuttal of the defence put forward (*R* v *Pilcher* (1974) 60 Cr App R 1). This is true whether the issue is raised during cross-examination or in evidence-in-chief given by a defence witness, and answer C is therefore incorrect. The judge also has discretion to admit evidence of a formal, technical or uncontentious nature, which, by reason of inadvertence or oversight, has not been adduced by the prosecution before the close of their case. In *R* v *Francis*, the prosecution called an identification witness to give evidence that at a group identification he had identified the man standing in position number 20, but failed to call any evidence to prove that the man standing at that position was the appellant. The failure was due to a simple misunderstanding between counsel. The discretion of the judge to admit evidence after the close of the prosecution case is not limited to cases where an issue has arisen *ex improviso*, or where what has been omitted is a mere formality, and *Francis* was one of those rare cases falling outside the two established exceptions. Evidence can be adduced in circumstances where the defence do not accept there was a misunderstanding, and answer A is therefore incorrect.

Evidence and Procedure, para. 2.5.18

Answer 5.13

Answer **B** — Section 27 of the Youth Justice and Criminal Evidence Act 1999 states:

(1) A special measures direction may provide for a video recording of an interview of the witness to be admitted as evidence in chief of the witness.

(2) A special measures direction may, however, not provide for a video recording, or a part of such a recording, to be admitted under this section if the court is of the opinion, having regard to all the circumstances of the case, that in the interests of justice the recording, or that part of it, should not be so admitted.

This section replaces the Criminal Justice Act 1988, s. 32A, and clearly outlines that it is not a matter of course that the court makes this direction, therefore answer A is incorrect. It is a matter for the court to decide in the light of all the available circumstances. As s. 27(2) clearly states, the direction may be given unless the court believes it would not be in the interests of justice to do so. This is the test, and not just fear or refusal to testify; therefore, answers C and D are incorrect.

Evidence and Procedure, para. 2.5.10.6

Answer 5.14

Answer **C** — The judge may allow the accused to change his plea from not guilty to guilty at any stage prior to the jury returning their verdict; answer D is therefore incorrect.

The procedure is that the defence ask for the indictment to be put again; the accused then pleads guilty, and the jury empanelled as a result of the original not guilty plea formally return a verdict. Assuming the change of plea comes after the accused has been put in the charge of a jury, the jury should be directed to return a formal verdict of guilty.

In *R* v *Heyes* [1951] 1 KB 29, the accused pleaded not guilty to charges of stealing and receiving certain property. During the opening of the prosecution case and after advice from counsel who had at that stage been allotted to him, he changed his plea to guilty of receiving. Consequently, where a jury had heard that a prisoner wishes to withdraw his plea of not guilty and admit his guilt, the proper proceeding is to direct it to return a verdict. The judge should not make any announcement of guilt, but direct the jury to return such a formal verdict; answers A and B are therefore incorrect.

Evidence and Procedure, para. 2.5.5

Answer 5.15

Answer **D** — In considering whether a witness is able to give 'intelligible testimony' the Youth Justice and Criminal Evidence Act 1999, s. 55(8) defines this as testimony where the witness is able to:

- understand questions put to him as a witness; and
- give answers to them which can be understood.

Clearly, there is no inherent reason why a person suffering from a mental condition would not make a reliable witness. In *R* v *Barratt* [1996] Crim LR 495, a witness was suffering from a psychiatric condition and the court considered that her evidence was as reliable as that of any other witness save for certain aspects affected by her condition. Answer A is therefore incorrect.

Witnesses suffering from a mental disorder, mental impairment or a learning disability might be allowed 'special measures' to help them with giving evidence in criminal proceedings (s. 16(2) of the 1999 Act). By s. 31 a statement made in a document (including a videotape) was admissible as evidence of any fact of which direct oral evidence by the maker would be admissible if, by reason of his bodily or mental condition, he was unfit to attend as a witness. Answer B is therefore incorrect.

Section 27 of the 1999 Act provided that the statement was not admissible without leave, which the court could not grant unless satisfied that it ought to be admitted in the interests of justice.

However, if the court does admit that evidence the jury will *not* be warned about that witness's reliability, this would be wholly inappropriate. Answer C is therefore incorrect.

Evidence and Procedure, para. 2.5.8.9

Answer 5.16

Answer **B** — A wife, husband or civil partner is only compellable to give evidence on behalf of the prosecution against their spouse or partner (unless jointly charged) in certain circumstances, A charge of theft would not be one of those circumstances—so in this scenario the wife would not be a compellable witness. So should the police have told her this? In *R* v *L* [2008] EWCA Crim 973 the court held that there is no requirement to tell a wife that she was not a compellable witness against her husband before interviewing her about a crime of which her husband was suspected; answers C and D are therefore incorrect. A statement obtained from the wife in such circumstances could be admitted in evidence even though the wife refused to give evidence against her husband, provided it did not lead to an injustice. This is irrespective of whether the wife asks or not; answer A is therefore incorrect.

Evidence and Procedure, para. 2.5.8.6

Answer 5.17

Answer **C** — Trials on indictment take place in the Crown Court, generally before a judge of the High Court, circuit judge or a recorder (see *Evidence and Procedure* para. 2.2.8).

Where there is a 'guilty plea', which must be entered personally by the accused (*R* v *Ellis* (1973) 57 Cr App R 571), the only evidence which the prosecution needs to call are details of the accused's antecedents and criminal record (answer A is therefore incorrect). Where it is necessary, where there is disagreement about the precise facts of the offence, the prosecution may be required to call evidence to support their version of the facts, known as Newton hearings (*R* v *Newton* (1982) 77 Cr App R 13); answer B is therefore incorrect.

Any previous not guilty plea is irrelevant, and certainly is not the precursor to a Newton hearing; answer D is therefore incorrect.

Evidence and Procedure, para. 2.5.5

Answer 5.18

Answer **D** — Where an accused fails to appear in the magistrates' court in answer to bail the court may:

- issue a warrant for the accused's arrest under s. 7 of the Bail Act 1976;
- appoint a later time when the accused has to appear in accordance with s. 129(3) of the Magistrates' Courts Act 1980;
- proceed in the accused's absence under s. 11(1) of the Magistrates' Courts Act 1980.

Where the accused's appearance was by way of summons, the court must be satisfied that the summons was served in the prescribed manner before commencing in the accused's absence (s. 11(2)).

The Criminal Justice and Immigration Act 2008 has made certain amendments to s. 11 of the 1980 Act in relation to magistrates' courts proceeding to trial in the accused's absence. Where an accused is under 18 years of age the court may proceed in his or her absence (s. 11(1)(a) of the 1980 Act), and if the accused has attained the age of 18 the court must proceed in his or her absence unless it appears to the court to be contrary to the interests of justice do so (s. 11(1)(b)); answers B and C are therefore incorrect.

The court is not required to inquire into the reasons for the accused's failure to appear (s. 11(6)); answer A is therefore incorrect, but where it imposes a custodial sentence the accused must be brought before the court before commencing a custodial sentence (s. 11(3A)).

Evidence and Procedure, para. 2.5.6

6 Youth Justice, Crime and Disorder

STUDY PREPARATION

Of all the areas covered by this subject, this one has probably seen the most changes over recent years. Youth justice is a central focus of the Government's overall crime and disorder strategy, and it is therefore a very important area for study.

The overall aims of the Crime and Disorder Act 1998 should be understood, along with the framework for youth justice that it introduced. Reprimands and warnings are important, as are parenting, child safety and curfew orders.

QUESTIONS

Question 6.1

Youth offending teams are a multi-agency approach to the reduction of crime and disorder and are formalised by s. 39 of the Crime and Disorder Act 1998.

Who is responsible (although in cooperation with other persons/bodies) for establishing youth offending teams in their area?

A The chief officer of police.
B The Secretary of State.
C The local authority.
D The local probation board.

Question 6.2

The Youth Court has made an anti-social behaviour order against GILBERT who is 14 years old. The court is considering whether it should also make a parenting order under s. 9 of the Crime and Disorder Act 1998.

In relation to such a parenting order which of the following is correct?

A The court is statutorily bound to make a parenting order in these circumstances.

B The court must make a parenting order if it is satisfied that the relevant condition is fulfilled.

C The court must make a parenting order if it is satisfied that the relevant condition is fulfilled and must state in open court why it is necessary.

D The court may only make a parenting order where a person under the age of 16 is convicted of an offence by the court.

Question 6.3

SEIVRIGHT, who is a youth, pleaded guilty at Youth Court to a minor case of criminal damage. The court made a referral order to the youth offending team. A youth offender panel was formed and they are now considering making SEIVRIGHT pay for the cost of repair to the item he damaged.

Can the youth offender panel take this action?

A Yes, and this can be done without SEIVRIGHT's consent.

B Yes, provided SEIVRIGHT agrees to the proposed programme.

C No, a financial reparation cannot be ordered, but unpaid work can be considered.

D No, the only programme that can be considered is that of mediation.

Question 6.4

A magistrates' court has issued a child safety order under s. 11 of the Crime and Disorder Act 1998 against a 9-year-old child and the child's parents wish to appeal against this decision.

To where, if anywhere, can the parents appeal against the making of this child safety order?

A The Crown Court.

B The High Court.

C The Queens Bench Divisional Court.

D There is no right of appeal against the making of this child safety order.

Question 6.5

Child safety orders were introduced to help prevent children from turning to crime. Such orders are concerned with the child's potential offending behaviour.

Who would make the application for a child safety order?

A The local authority.

B The police.

C The police primarily but they have to show consultation with the local authority.

D The police primarily but they have to show consultation with the local education authority.

Question 6.6

A parenting order has been imposed on the parents of a child who has been involved in anti-social behaviour. As part of this order is a programme of counselling.

For how long can this counselling last?

A 1 month.

B 3 months.

C 6 months.

D 12 months.

Question 6.7

A parenting order is being considered by the court in relation to TODD, who is 10 years of age and has been convicted of a theft, which took place on a Saturday. Part of this order would involve counselling sessions, and the child being escorted to school.

In relation to the proposed parenting order, which of the following statements is true?

A It cannot be made as such orders apply to a child under the age of 10 years only.

B It cannot include the child being escorted to school, as his offence was not committed on a school day.

C The magistrate should specify the amount of counselling needed.

D A member of the youth offending team should specify the amount of counselling needed.

Question 6.8

AUDREY is a particularly unruly 15-year-old, in relation to whom the courts are considering a parenting order. Owing to her misbehaviour at home, AUDREY's uncle and aunt are currently looking after her, but they have no legal guardianship.

Can a parenting order be imposed on AUDREY's uncle and aunt?

A Yes, for the time being, they are caring for AUDREY.

B Yes, provided the court's opinion is that they are caring for AUDREY.

C No, the order can be imposed on the biological parents only.

D No, as they do not have legal guardianship.

Question 6.9

CATHERINE is 13 years old, and has been convicted of an offence at court. The court, however, is not satisfied that the making of a parenting order would be desirable in the interests of preventing the commission of any further offence by CATHERINE.

In relation to the options the court may take regarding the parenting order, which of the following statements is true?

A The court must impose the order as CATHERINE is under 16 (a young person) and has been convicted of an offence.

B The court must impose the order as CATHERINE is under 14 (a child) and has been convicted of an offence.

C The court need not impose the order, but must say in open court why it is not desirable.

D The court need not impose the order as it retains a discretion not to impose an order.

Question 6.10

The Serious Organised Crime and Police Act 2005, Sch. 10, inserted a new section into the Crime and Disorder Act 1998 (s.13A) for the provision of parental compensation orders where parents are ordered to pay compensation for their children's behaviour.

Which of the following is correct in relation to parental compensation orders?

A An order may be made where the child caused damage in excess of £2,500.

B An order may be made where the child caused any damage and the maximum amount of compensation is £2,500.

C An order may be made where the child caused damage in excess of £5,000.

D An order may be made where the child caused any damage and the maximum amount of compensation is £5,000.

Question 6.11

A child can be placed under supervision for a permitted maximum period by the imposition of a child safety order.

How long is that maximum period?

A 3 months.

B 6 months.

C 12 months.

D 15 months.

Question 6.12

AMBROSE, who is aged 6 years, has been responsible for causing alarm, harassment and distress to his neighbours and the magistrates' court is considering a child safety order under s. 11 of the Crime and Disorder Act 1998.

Can a child safety order be issued?

A Yes, on these factors alone a child safety order could be issued.

B Yes, provided he has also committed an offence that had he been aged over 10 or over would have constituted an offence.

C No, a child safety order can only be issued to those who have reached at least 10 years of age.

D No, a child safety order can only be issued to those who have reached at least 8 years of age.

Question 6.13

Constable CORNELIUS is on patrol at 11.30 pm when she finds RICHARD, who is 9 years old, in a public place. RICHARD is in breach of a child curfew scheme that has been imposed.

Which of the following statements is true in relation to Constable CORNELIUS?

A She must take the child to his home and should consider informing the local authority.

B She must take the child to his home and must inform the court which ordered the curfew.

C She may take the child to his home and must inform the local authority.
D She may take the child to his home and must inform the court which ordered the curfew.

Question 6.14

A 16-year-old has been given a youth conditional caution and has failed to comply with the conditions attached to that caution.

Which of the following is correct in relation to this non-compliance with the conditions attached to the caution?

A The youth should be charged with the original offence.
B The youth should be charged with the original offence, unless there is a reasonable excuse for the non-compliance.
C The youth should be given a written warning.
D The youth should be taken back before the youth panel that issued the conditional caution.

Question 6.15

An authority to remove truants to designated premises is in effect and Constable McGIVERN found LAWRENCE, who is of compulsory school age, absent from school with no lawful authority.

What should Constable McGIVERN do?

A LAWRENCE must be returned to his own school.
B LAWRENCE must be returned to any school in the local education authority.
C LAWRENCE can be returned to any place the local authority has nominated.
D LAWRENCE can be returned to any place the local education authority has nominated.

Question 6.16

Constable O'HARA is on foot patrol in the city centre when she comes across a young male who appears to be about 13 years of age. She confirms his age and asks why he is not in school. The young boy states his parents are 'ageing hippies' and they educate him at home on his houseboat.

What should Constable O'HARA do?

A The boy must be returned to his home address.

B The boy must be returned to any school in the local education authority.

C The boy can be returned to any place the local education authority has nominated.

D The boy should be left alone, unless any offences are apparent.

Question 6.17

MULHOLLAND is a youth offender and is being considered for a reprimand under s. 65 of the Crime and Disorder Act 1998.

Which of the following correctly states the burden of proof required before a reprimand can be given?

A There is sufficient evidence to charge the offender with the offence.

B If the offender were prosecuted for the offence it is more likely than not he would be convicted.

C If the offender were prosecuted for the offence on the balance of probabilities he would be convicted.

D No burden of proof is required as the youth has to admit the offence prior to a reprimand being given.

Question 6.18

FENWAY is a youth who has committed a theft. He has had previous reprimands and a previous final warning under s. 65 of the Crime and Disorder Act 1998; that final warning was given three years ago. The officer in the case is not sure whether another final warning can be given to FENWAY or not.

Which of the following is correct?

A Provided the constable considers the offence to be not so serious as to require a charge to be brought or a youth conditional caution to be given.

B Provided the constable considers the offence to be not so serious as to require a youth conditional caution to be given.

C Provided the constable considers the offence to be not so serious as to require a charge to be brought.

D Only one final warning can ever be given; no further final warnings are possible.

Question 6.19

TAYLOR and her parents have been made subject to a parenting order under s. 8 of the Crime and Disorder Act 1998, the terms of which they are not happy about. They wish to have the terms of the order varied.

In relation to this request which of the following is correct?

A They can have the terms varied by any magistrates' court.

B They can have the terms varied by any youth court.

C They can have the terms varied only by the court that made the original order.

D They cannot have the terms varied, only cancelled.

ANSWERS

Answer 6.1

Answer **C** — Youth offending teams are a multi-agency approach to the reduction of crime and disorder and are formalised by s. 39 of the Crime and Disorder Act 1998 which states:

(1) Subject to subsection (2) below, it shall be the duty of each local authority, acting in co-operation with the persons and bodies mentioned in subsection (3) below, to establish for their area one or more youth offending teams.

(2) Two (or more) local authorities acting together may establish one or more youth offending teams for both (or all) their areas; . . .

(3) It shall be the duty of—
   (a) every chief officer of police any part of whose police area lies within the local authority's area;
   (aa) the Secretary of State in relation to his functions under sections 2 and 3 of the Offender Management Act 2007;
   (ab) every provider of probation services that is required by arrangements under section 3(2) of the Offender Management Act 2007 to carry out the duty under this subsection in relation to the local authority; and

to co-operate in the discharge by the local authority of their duty under subsection (1) above.

The responsibility therefore is that of the local authority which is answer C; answers A, B and D are therefore incorrect.

Evidence and Procedure, para. 2.6.3

Answer 6.2

Answer **B** — Parenting orders are about influencing parental responsibility and control. The orders were introduced to give parents more help and support to change the criminal and/or anti-social behaviour of their children by providing a framework where parents participate in their child's supervision. The strategy here is one of prevention in attempting to dissuade a recurrence of criminality or truancy.

Section 9(1) of the Crime and Disorder Act 1998 provides a statutory requirement in favour of making an order where the relevant condition relates to where a child or young person (under 16) is convicted of an offence. A similar duty, and similar exception, applies where the offender has been made subject to an anti-social behaviour order (s. 9(1B)); answer D is therefore incorrect.

There is no statutory binding on the court to make an order, only where the relevant conditions apply can an order be made; answer A is therefore incorrect.

If the court is not so satisfied that an order should be made, it shall state in open court that it is not and why not. This exception is where the court does not consider a parenting order necessary, not where it does deem such an order appropriate; answer C is therefore incorrect.

Evidence and Procedure, para. 2.6.7.4

Answer 6.3

Answer **B** — Sections 23 to 27 of the Powers of Criminal Courts (Sentencing) Act 2000 deal with youth offender contracts. This is a programme of behaviour to prevent re-offending, but it has to be agreed between the offender and the panel (s. 23(5)), and therefore answer A is incorrect. The terms of the programme may include a number of provisions; attendance at mediation sessions is one of them, but is by no means exclusive, and answer D is therefore incorrect. The measures can include unpaid work or service, in addition to financial or other reparation to the victim, and therefore answer C is incorrect.

Evidence and Procedure, para. 2.6.3.1

Answer 6.4

Answer **B** — There is an appeal process for when a child safety order is imposed; answer D is therefore incorrect. The right of appeal is to the High Court against a magistrates' court making a child safety order (s. 13(1) of the Crime and Disorder Act 1998); answers A and C are therefore incorrect.

Evidence and Procedure, para. 2.6.8

Answer 6.5

Answer **A** — Child safety orders were introduced to help prevent children under 10 from turning to crime. Such orders are concerned with the child's potential offending behaviour and in practice are likely to be used in conjunction with parenting orders under s. 8 of the Crime and Disorder Act 1998.

Section 11 of the 1998 Act states:

(1) Subject to subsection (2) below, if a magistrates' court, on the application of a local authority, is satisfied that one or more of the conditions specified in subsection (3) below are fulfilled with respect to a child under the age of 10, it may make an order (a 'child safety order') which—
- (a) places the child, for a period (not exceeding the permitted maximum) specified in the order, under the supervision of the responsible officer; and
- (b) requires the child to comply with such requirements as are so specified.

A local authority with social services responsibilities must make the application for such an order. Although it would probably be the police who first become aware of the misconduct which triggers such an application, however the application is that of the local authority; answers B, C and D are therefore incorrect.

Evidence and Procedure, para. 2.6.8

Answer 6.6

Answer **B** — Parenting orders are defined by s. 8 of the Crime and Disorder Act 1998:

(4) A parenting order is an order which requires the parent—
- (a) to comply, for a period not exceeding twelve months, with such requirements as are specified in the order, and
- (b) subject to subsection (5) below, to attend, for a concurrent period not exceeding three months, such counselling or guidance programme as may be specified in directions given by the responsible officer . . .

As can be seen the period is three months; answers A, C and D are therefore incorrect.

Evidence and Procedure, para. 2.6.7

Answer 6.7

Answer **D** — A parenting order can be imposed on a child or young person. For the purposes of the Crime and Disorder Act 1998, 'child' is someone under the age of 14 and 'young person' is someone of 14 years or over but under 18 (s. 117), and answer A is therefore incorrect. A parenting order is defined by s. 8(4)(a) as an order which requires the parent 'to comply, for a period not exceeding twelve months, with such requirements as are specified in the order'. The requirements provided by s. 8(4)(a) above are not specified, but in drafting the legislation certain examples were given. These included a parent escorting their child to school and a child being supervised by a responsible adult during the evenings (answer B is therefore incorrect). The counselling is defined in s. 8(4)(b) as 'to attend for a concurrent period not exceeding three months and not more than once in any week, such counselling and guidance sessions as may be specified in directions given by the responsible officer'. The responsible officer can be an officer of a local probation board, a social worker of a local authority social services department, a person nominated by a person appointed as chief education officer (under s. 532 of the Education Act 1996) and a member of a youth offending team; answer C is therefore incorrect.

Evidence and Procedure, para. 2.6.7

Answer 6.8

Answer **B** — Under s. 8(2) of the Crime and Disorder Act 1998, a parenting order may be made against:

- one or both biological parents (this could include an order against a father who may not be married to the mother);
- a person who is a guardian.

Therefore, answer C is incorrect.

A guardian is defined as any person who, in the opinion of the court, has for the time being the care of a child or young person (s. 117(1)). It is not a matter of 'legal' guardianship (even if somebody has temporary care and control of a child), as it is the court that will decide who is *in fact* a 'guardian'; therefore, answers A and D are incorrect.

Evidence and Procedure, para. 2.6.7.3

Answer 6.9

Answer **C** — In relation to parenting orders, the court will be required to establish whether or not the making of such an order is 'desirable' in the circumstances of a particular case. This is seen as an entirely subjective test and the court generally retains discretion not to impose an order. Section 9(1)(a) of the Crime and Disorder Act 1998, however, provides a statutory requirement in favour of making an order (unless the court makes a referral order) where the relevant condition relates to where a child or young person (under 16) is convicted of an offence; therefore, answer D is incorrect. If, however, the court is not satisfied that the 'relevant condition' is fulfilled (i.e. that the making of a parenting order would be desirable in the interests of preventing the commission of any further offence by the child or young person under 16), the court must state in open court that it is not so satisfied, and why it is not. There is then some limited discretion where s. 9(1)(a) applies, and therefore answers A and B are incorrect.

Evidence and Procedure, paras 2.6.7.3, 2.6.7.4

Answer 6.10

Answer **D** — Section 13A of the Crime and Disorder Act 1998 Act states:

(1) A magistrates' court may make an order under this section (a 'parental compensation order') if on the application of a local authority it is satisfied, on the civil standard of proof—
   (a) that the condition mentioned in subsection (2) below is fulfilled with respect to a child under the age of 10; and
   (b) that it would be desirable to make the order in the interests of preventing a repetition of the behaviour in question.

(2) The condition is that the child has taken, or caused loss of or damage to, property in the course of—
   (a) committing an act which, if he had been aged 10 or over, would have constituted an offence; or
   (b) acting in a manner that caused or was likely to cause harassment, alarm or distress to one or more persons not of the same household as himself.

So where a child under 10 years of age commits an offence which would in effect be an offence contrary to the Criminal Damage Act 1971, their parents could face paying compensation under the parental compensation scheme. There is no value on the amount of damage caused; answers A and C are therefore incorrect. The amount of compensation specified cannot exceed £5,000 in all (s. 13A(4)); answer B is therefore incorrect.

Collection and enforcement conditions are the same as if the parent had been convicted of an offence (s. 13A(6)).

Evidence and Procedure, para. 2.6.10

Answer 6.11

Answer **C** — The permitted maximum period of supervision of a child safety order is 12 months (s. 11(4) of the Crime and Disorder Act 1998). Therefore answers A, B and D are incorrect.

Evidence and Procedure, para. 2.6.8.1

Answer 6.12

Answer **A** — Before a child safety order under s. 11 of the Crime and Disorder Act 1998 can be issued the court must be satisfied that one or more of three conditions are fulfilled. These are provided by s. 11(3) of the 1998 Act:

(a) that the child has committed an act which, if he had been aged 10 or over, would have constituted an offence;

(b) that a child safety order is necessary for the purpose of preventing the commission by the child of such an act as is mentioned in paragraph (a) above;

(c) . . .; and

(d) that the child has acted in a manner that caused or was likely to cause harassment, alarm or distress to one or more persons not of the same household as himself.

As can be seen although more than one condition may be evident, only one is required; answer B is therefore incorrect.

There is no minimum age for an order; answers C and D are therefore incorrect.

Evidence and Procedure, para. 2.6.8.1

Answer 6.13

Answer **C** — Section 14 of the Crime and Disorder Act 1998 states that it is a local authority, in liaison with the Secretary of State (who needs to confirm it), that makes a child curfew scheme. Therefore, as the courts do not impose a curfew, they do not need to be informed of a breach, and answers B and D are incorrect.

If there has been a contravention of a curfew notice, s. 15 of the 1998 Act states:

(2) The constable shall, as soon as practicable, inform the local authority for the area that the child has contravened the ban.

(3) The constable may remove the child to the child's place of residence unless he has reasonable cause to believe that the child would, if removed to that place, be likely to suffer significant harm.

Informing the local authority who imposed the scheme is mandatory; but taking the child home is not, and therefore answer A is incorrect.

Section 15(3) does not state what a constable should do with a child if he or she does not remove the child to its home. However, it would seem appropriate to use the power under s. 46 of the Children Act 1989 in removing the child to suitable accommodation, i.e. a police station or into the care of social services.

Evidence and Procedure, para. 2.6.9.1

Answer 6.14

Answer **B** — A youth conditional caution is a caution given in respect of an offence committed by a person 10 to 17 years of age, and which has conditions attached to it with which the offender must comply.

If the conditions of the caution are broken, and where there is no reasonable excuse for non-compliance with the conditions (answer A is therefore incorrect), the youth conditional caution can be cancelled and criminal proceedings commenced for the original offence (Crime and Disorder Act 1998, s. 66E).

An authorised person may give a conditional caution to a child or young person, an 'authorised person' for the purposes of s. 66A(1) means a constable, an investigating officer or a person authorised for the purposes of this section (s. 66A(7)), not the youth panel; answer D is therefore incorrect.

A conditional caution is one step up from a written warning, it would be inappropriate to go back down to a written warning where a conditional caution has been imposed; answer C is therefore incorrect.

Evidence and Procedure, para. 2.6.6.4

Answer 6.15

Answer **C** — A local authority is under an obligation by s. 16 of the Crime and Disorder Act 1998 to designate premises in a police area ('designated premises') as premises to which children and young persons of compulsory school age may be removed under this section, and they must notify the chief officer of police for that area of the designation. When an order to remove truants has been issued, if a constable has reasonable cause to believe that a child or young person found by him in a public place in a specified area during a specified period:

- is of compulsory school age; *and*
- is absent from a school without lawful authority,

the constable may remove the child or young person to designated premises, or to the school from which he is absent. He does not *have* to be returned to either his own school, or another school in the local education authority area, so answers A and B are therefore incorrect. Provided a particular place has been designated (or nominated) by the local authority, the child may be returned there. Note, it is the local authority who designates, not the local education authority; answer D is therefore incorrect.

Evidence and Procedure, paras 2.6.11, 2.6.11.1

Answer 6.16

Answer **D** — Section 16 of the Crime and Disorder Act 1998 provides the police powers in relation to dealing with truants:

> (3) If a constable has reasonable cause to believe that a child or young person found by him in a public place in a specified area during a specified period—
> (a) is of compulsory school age; and
> (b) is absent from school without lawful authority,
> the constable may remove the child or young person to designated premises, or to the school from which he is so absent.

The powers apply to those children and young people who are pupils registered at a school. It does not apply to children and young people educated at home who, quite lawfully, are out and about, alone and unaccompanied, during school hours. Therefore there is no power to remove the youth to anywhere; answers A, B and C are therefore incorrect.

Evidence and Procedure, paras 2.6.11, 2.6.11.1

Answer 6.17

Answer **A** — Section 65(1) and (2) of the 1998 Act provides the conditions that must be satisfied in order for a reprimand to be given:

> (a) a constable has evidence that a child or young person ('the offender') has committed an offence;
>
> (b) the constable considers that there is sufficient evidence to charge the offender with the offence;
>
> (c) the offender admits to the constable that he committed the offence;
>
> (d) the offender has not previously been convicted of an offence or given a youth conditional caution in respect of an offence; and
>
> (e) the constable does not consider that the offender should be prosecuted or given a youth conditional caution.

So although the youth has to admit the offence there is still effectively a burden of proof, that there is sufficient evidence to charge the offender with the offence; answer D is therefore incorrect. The other burdens of proof are too high; answers B and C are therefore incorrect.

Evidence and Procedure, para. 2.6.6.1

Answer 6.18

Answer **A** — Section 65(3) of the 1998 Act provides a constable with a power to warn an offender where:

(a) the offender has not previously been warned; or

(b) where the offender has previously been warned, the offence was committed more than two years after the date of the previous warning and the constable considers the offence to be not so serious as to require a charge to be brought or a youth conditional caution to be given;

So provided a period of two years has passed another final warning can be given, even for the same offence as the previous one; answer B is therefore incorrect. There is no requirement for someone to state when giving a final warning that the youth may be suitable for another one; answer C is therefore incorrect.

On this occasion another final warning can be given, although this will be the final 'final' warning; answer D is therefore incorrect.

Evidence and Procedure, para. 2.6.6

Answer 6.19

Answer **C** — Once a parenting order has been made the parent or responsible officer can apply for the discharge or variation of an order and the court can agree to cancel, add or substitute any of its provisions; answer D is therefore incorrect. However, this can only be done by the court making the original order; answers A and B are therefore incorrect.

Evidence and Procedure, para. 2.6.7.5

7 Evidence

STUDY PREPARATION

The subject matter covered in this chapter is at the heart of the whole area of evidence and procedure. As with Chapter 3, most of this chapter is concerned with the fundamentals—what type of evidence can be given by whom to show what. There is a fair amount of complex law in this part, and unfortunately it has to be separated and assimilated.

It is critical to understand the issues of weight and admissibility. It is also critical to understand the different standards of proof, civil and criminal—the latter because it is the only way in which you can prove any criminal liability and the former because it is relevant to issues that the defendant may have to prove. The standard of proof is different from the burden of proof (although they are closely linked), and again it is important to know where the relevant burden lies.

Documentary evidence is increasingly relied upon in criminal trials and this area needs attention.

A further area of great practical importance is the legislation that sets out when adverse inferences can be drawn from silences or failure by the defendant to mention certain things. These are often confused, with some officers getting the various components mixed up; decided cases help to decipher when inferences may and may not be drawn.

QUESTIONS

Question 7.1

ROBINSON is a witness for the prosecution giving evidence in Crown Court. The defence barrister wishes to introduce previous convictions of ROBINSON as they feel it would undermine his credibility.

Which of the following is correct in relation to these previous convictions?

A Any previous conviction may be introduced, provided it is important explanatory evidence.

B Any previous conviction may be introduced, provided all parties agree to it.

C Only previous convictions which materially strengthen the case for the defence.

D Only previous convictions which materially weaken the Crown's case or materially strengthen the case for the defence.

Question 7.2

McDONALD was stopped by police officers and lawfully searched. The officers found 6.79 g of heroin and £200 cash, and McDONALD was arrested for possession of a Class A drug with intent to supply. During his audio-recorded interview, and acting on his solicitor's advice, he made no comment to any of the questions asked. At the conclusion he gave the officers a prepared statement in which he accepted possession of the drugs for his own use, and stated the £200 was obtained by selling designer shirts. At his trial during his evidence-in-chief he stated the £200 was from the sale of designer sunglasses.

Will adverse inferences be drawn from his refusal to answer questions during the police interviews?

A No inferences can be drawn as he was acting on solicitor's advice.

B No inferences can be drawn as he gave evidence at court.

C Inferences can be drawn because he refused to answer questions and handed in a prepared statement.

D Inferences may be drawn because his evidence-in-chief was inconsistent with the statement.

Question 7.3

GOULD is a defendant charged with a number of robbery offences. One of the witnesses has been threatened by friends of GOULD and is petrified of giving evidence against him. The prosecution have tried to persuade the witness to attend court and have offered to use special measures (screens, live links) but the witness has refused all such offers. The witness is a key material eyewitness who identified GOULD; little forensic evidence exists.

Can the statement of the eyewitness be read out in court, given the decisive nature of it?

A Yes, as the witness is clearly in fear of giving evidence the law allows for it to be read out.

B Yes, as the witness is clearly in fear and the prosecution have considered, and tried to use special measures.

C No, this is hearsay evidence and cannot be admitted unless the witness is available to be cross-examined.

D No, although hearsay evidence can be given when a witness is in fear, it cannot be used where it is the sole or decisive evidence against an accused.

Question 7.4

Constable DE MARCO is investigating an assault involving a wounding. The complainant states that WATERS had stabbed him in the arm with a knife in the street outside his house; WATERS then used the knife to cut his hand and rubbed this across the wound he had caused in the complainant's arm. WATERS said 'now you have HIV as well as me'. The officer went to WATERS' address and arrested him, seizing a blood stained knife. During the interview WATERS stated he had cut his hand whilst chopping an onion but said 'no comment' to questions about the knife.

In these circumstances can a special warning under s. 36 of the Criminal Justice and Public Order Act 1994 be given?

A Yes, in relation to the cut on WATERS' hand and also the knife.

B Yes, in relation to the knife only.

C No, the knife was not 'found' at a place at or about the time the offence for which he was arrested is alleged to have been committed.

D No, the cut is not a 'mark' as defined in s. 36 and therefore not subject to a special warning.

Question 7.5

DICKENS makes a complaint to the police about a robbery. During the struggle DICKENS states he bit the perpetrator on the hand, enough to probably leave teeth marks. The police suspect FRENCH and arrest him in the street, and he has bite marks on his hand. A lawfully conducted search of his house finds items stolen from DICKENS. During interview he refuses to answer questions about the property found in his house, and states he was bitten by his girlfriend during sex.

In relation to s. 36 of the Criminal Justice and Public Order Act 1994 can the police give FRENCH a 'special warning'?

A Yes, in relation to the teeth marks only.

B Yes, in relation to the property found only.

C Yes, in relation to both the teeth marks and the property found.

D No, the police cannot give a special warning for either the teeth marks or the property found.

Question 7.6

CHIBA is on trial for an offence of rape, and has been sworn to give evidence. Prosecuting counsel asks him, 'It is true, is it not, that you did have sexual intercourse with Miss DAVIES, and at that time you clearly knew that she did not consent?' CHIBA remains silent, and refuses to answer the question.

Will the jury be entitled to draw any inferences from CHIBA's refusal to answer this question?

A No, CHIBA has a right not to incriminate himself and inferences may not be drawn.

B No, the prosecution have no right to ask such questions, and inferences may not be drawn.

C Yes, CHIBA has refused without good cause to answer the question, and inferences may be drawn.

D Yes, and the inferences drawn from this refusal would be enough to convict.

Question 7.7

NEILSEN is an expert witness, he is an expert in collision investigation and a former police officer, and he has been employed by the defence in a case of causing death by dangerous driving. The car was being driven with six people on board and one was unrestrained in the rear hatchback. During cross-examination NEILSEN is asked if as an ex-road-policing officer he would have considered that carrying an unrestrained passenger would be 'dangerous'. He is aware that if he says 'yes' it would be damaging to the defendant.

Which of the following is correct in relation to expert witnesses?

A The expert witness owes a duty only to the court.

B The expert holds a duty to the court, but firstly to the person from whom he has received instruction.

C The expert holds a duty to the court, but firstly to the person from whom he has received payment.

D The expert only holds a duty to the person from whom he has received instruction.

Question 7.8

AKITA was the driver of a vehicle involved in a fatal road traffic collision, he was taken to hospital where he refused to give a sample of blood under the 'hospital procedure' as set out by s. 9 of the Road Traffic Act 1988 as he has a fear of needles. He was arrested for causing death by dangerous driving and interviewed when deemed fit. Acting on solicitor's advice he remained silent in response to the limited questions asked. Following extensive investigation during which several witnesses claimed AKITA had drunk copious amounts of alcohol and was driving in excess of 90 mph at the time of the collision, he was again interviewed three months after the collision. Again acting on solicitor's advice he remained silent. At his trial AKITA gave evidence that he had drunk very little alcohol and was driving within the speed limit. His counsel argued that no inferences could be drawn on his silence at the first interview due to lack of evidence disclosed by the police to him and no inferences could be drawn on his silence on the second interview as it should not have been held as the police had at that time sufficient evidence to charge.

In relation to whether inferences could be drawn from his silence during his two interviews which of the following is correct?

A No inferences from first interview only as the solicitor advised silence due to lack of disclosure of evidence by the police.

B No inferences from second interview only because the second interview should not have been held; he should have been charged.

C No inferences drawn from either due to lack of disclosure of evidence and that no second interview should have been held; he should have been charged.

D Inferences could be drawn from both interviews as they were both properly conducted.

Question 7.9

SAYERS has been accused of physical assaults (not sexual) on his step-daughter. The prosecution wish to adduce evidence of complaints the girl made to her friend a few weeks after the last assault, and her brother several months after the last assault.

Can the prosecution use these hearsay statements of complaint made by the victim of these assaults?

A Yes, they can use both complaints provided it can be shown that both complaints were made as soon as could reasonably have been expected.

B Yes, but only in relation to the complaint made a few weeks later; as only it could be said to have been made as soon as could reasonably have been expected.

C No, neither complaint has any 'recency' to it, and was not made 'on the first occasion that reasonably offered itself'.

D No, as the assaults do not relate to sexual cases they may not be admitted as hearsay evidence.

Question 7.10

HAYTER was the victim of a serious sexual assault and she is alleging that WILSON raped her. There are no witnesses to the incident and no physical evidence. There is, however, substantial circumstantial evidence. WILSON has denied being the perpetrator, but has been charged and will appear at the Crown Court.

In relation to corroboration, which of the following statements is true?

A In this case corroboration is required in law.

B Although corroboration is not required, the judge must give a corroboration warning to the jury.

C In this case corroboration is not required at all.

D Although corroboration is not required, the judge may choose to give a corroboration warning to the jury.

Question 7.11

SMITHERS is charged with an offence of murder. The circumstances are that he allowed a man, GREY, whom he had met in a nightclub, to stay at his house. At some point a fight took place and GREY was fatally stabbed by SMITHERS. In his defence, SMITHERS has given sworn evidence that he stabbed GREY as a last resort to fight off his continued sexual advances. SMITHERS adduces evidence that he finds homosexuality repugnant. To rebut this, the prosecution wish to introduce SMITHERS' previous convictions; one for buggery with a man, and two for gross indecency in men's public toilets (both offences pre-dating the Sexual Offences Act 2003).

Is the judge likely to allow this evidence to be adduced?

A No, the previous convictions have nothing in common with the offence charged.

B No, as homosexuality is not 'misconduct' and as such is not a propensity to commit misconduct.

C Yes, as this is a matter in issue between the defendant and the prosecution.

D Yes, this will allow the jury to have a clear picture of the defendant and help it to understand the case.

Question 7.12

WADE has been charged with conspiracy to defraud, and an investigation is in progress. The fraud squad has discovered that WADE used to send pager messages to a contact in Switzerland. This was done by contacting the pager company, who wrote down the message on a pad and then transmitted it electronically. Some of these messages show WADE was involved in fraud; however, the operator of the machine had no knowledge of whether the messages were true or not.

Is it likely that the written message pad could be tendered as evidence in a 'business document' under s. 117 of the Criminal Justice Act 2003?

A Yes, it fits the relevant criteria and would be admitted.

B No, the person who made the document has to know the truth of its contents.

C Yes, provided the witness was unavailable to attend court.

D No, as WADE is not the maker of the document it is inadmissible.

Question 7.13

Non-expert witnesses, in certain cases, can give evidence of opinion to the court.

In relation to this, which of the following statements is true?

A Only police officers may give evidence that in their opinion a person is drunk.

B Police officers may identify prohibited drugs only if they are specially trained to do so.

C Police officers can give their opinion as to the speed of a moving vehicle.

D Non-expert witnesses can give only the estimated price of an antique piece of furniture.

Question 7.14

Constable BRIGGS is a road policing officer on duty on the motorway. Whilst dealing with an incident on the hard shoulder a vehicle passes him and he estimates its speed at over 100 mph. He obtains the index number of the vehicle and intends prosecuting the driver. The officer only has his opinion as to the speed, it was not measured. Constable BRIGGS is an advanced police driver and is trained in various speed measurement devices.

Which of the following statements is true in relation to giving evidence to the court about the speed of a moving vehicle?

A The officer could give evidence of his opinion about the speed of the vehicle, as he is a police officer.

B The officer could give evidence of his opinion about the speed of the vehicle, but only because of his training and experience.

C The officer could not give evidence of the speed of the vehicle without any supporting evidence.

D Any person could give evidence in relation to their opinion on the speed of a vehicle.

Question 7.15

STEWART was a witness in a murder trial, and is well known to both co-accused. The defendants had, through an intermediary, arranged to 'warn off' STEWART's wife about giving evidence against them. STEWART fears for his wife's safety and refuses to attend court and give evidence in person. The prosecution wish to have STEWART's statement read out in court instead of him appearing personally.

In relation to this which of the following is correct?

A The statement cannot be read out as it is the defendant's right to examine witnesses against them under the Human Rights Act 1998, Sch. 1, part I, art. 6(3)(d).

B The statement cannot be read out, as the threat that caused the fear was not made to the witness directly.

C The statement can be read out and the evidence is treated as if it had been given in person.

D The statement can be read out and the evidence is treated as if it had been given in person, even if it is unfair to the defence.

Question 7.16

KNIGHT is suspected of being involved in the distribution of internet child pornography. During his police interviews he states that he is a lay preacher and could not be involved in child pornography. KNIGHT is charged and is appearing at the Crown Court; he turns up in clerical collar and is sitting in the dock. The police are aware that he was not ordained as a priest, and is not a lay preacher. KNIGHT is not going to give evidence himself at the trial.

In relation to KNIGHT portraying himself as a religious person, which of the following is correct?

A The jury can be made aware that the way he is dressed is giving a false impression.

B The jury can be made aware that the way he is dressed is giving a false impression *and* that he lied about it during interview.

C The jury can be made aware that he lied about being a lay preacher during interview.

D The jury cannot be made aware of this portrayal as he is not going to give evidence in court that he is a lay preacher.

Question 7.17

FORSYTH has been charged with a robbery, during police questioning he tells them that he could not have possibly committed the offence as the offender had run away and he can hardly walk due to a road traffic collision which occurred whilst he was in the Army. This had left him with a serious leg injury which means he cannot run any distance. This is investigated by the police and they discover he did not have an RTC whilst in the Army, but had a minor injury RTC which did not affect his leg. FORSYTH continues to make this assertion at his trial.

Can the prosecution introduce evidence that shows FORSYTH is not telling the truth about the RTC under the 'bad character' rules?

A Yes, as it shows that the defendant is or has a tendency to lie.

B Yes, as it is evidence to correct a false impression given by the defendant.

C No, as it is not evidence of a previous conviction it cannot be given as 'bad character'.

D No, it is not evidence relating to the offence charged, it would be prejudicial to a fair trial.

Question 7.18

LEWINSKY is a barrister representing HINKS, who is charged with burglary. During her opening speech she tells the jury that HINKS will accept that he was in the area of the factory, but he will deny that he actually committed the burglary. HINKS is horrified, as he did not want his counsel to admit that he was near the factory.

In relation to this admission by counsel, which of the following is true?

A The admission may be admitted as counsel is the accused's agent.

B The admission may be admitted as it appears to be a confession (s. 76 of PACE).

C The admission is not admissible, counsel is not an agent for the accused.

D The admission is hearsay as it is not made by the accused, and is not admissible.

Question 7.19

BROTHERTON is appearing at Crown Court charged with assaulting an off-duty police officer who tried to intervene when BROTHERTON was seen being violent towards his girlfriend in the street. BROTHERTON has called his girlfriend as a defence witness to give evidence that the argument was a tiff, and that they were happily going home when the incident broke out; she claimed that she had been tipsy but had not taken any drugs. The prosecution wish to cross-examine the witness in relation to a previous caution for possession of cocaine.

Is it likely that this previous caution will be admissible under s. 100 of the Criminal Justice Act 2003?

A Yes, as this directly relates to her credibility as a witness and has substantial probative value.

B Yes, as she asserted in her own evidence that she had not taken drugs on that night.

C No, as the caution has no bearing on any issue in this case.

D No, as only evidence of a previous conviction would be admissible to impugn the credibility of the witness.

Question 7.20

HOANG moved to the United Kingdom seven years ago. She had convictions in Holland for offences contrary to their criminal law. Four months ago she received a police caution in relation to a theft offence by shoplifting. She is now appearing in court on another theft offence and wishes to use the fact that she has no UK convictions, and adduce evidence of her good character.

Can she adduce evidence of good character?

A Yes, as she has no previous convictions in this country and cautions do not count as 'bad character'.

B Yes, as she has no previous convictions in this country and cautions are *not* convictions in this context.

C No, she is not entitled to adduce such evidence as she has a recent caution; the foreign convictions, however, are not relevant.

D No, she is not entitled to adduce such evidence as she has a recent caution and a foreign court conviction: both are relevant.

Question 7.21

BRYANT is charged with fraud. Part of the case against him relates to a document that was sent by BRYANT to HM Revenue and Customs which was sent in error. The document is a copy of a letter that was sent to BRYANT from his solicitor warning him that his proposed actions could attract prosecution. As a copy, this document is 'secondary evidence'

In relation to this document which of the following is correct?

A It cannot be used in evidence as it is subject to legal privilege.

B It cannot be used in evidence as it does not fit the best evidence rule.

C It can be used in evidence as copies of legal documents are admissible evidence.

D It can be used in evidence as the content of the letter would not attract legal privilege.

ANSWERS

Answer 7.1

Answer **D** — Section 100(1) of the Criminal Justice Act 2003 sets out the following three conditions where evidence of a non-defendant's previous misconduct can be given in criminal proceedings:

(a) it is important explanatory evidence,

(b) it has substantial probative value in relation to a matter in issue in the proceedings and is of substantial importance in the context of the case as a whole, or

(c) all parties agree to the evidence being admissible.

Section 6 of the Criminal Procedure Act 1865 provides that where a witness is being questioned as to whether they have been convicted of any felony or misdemeanour, and they deny, do not admit or refuse to answer, the cross-examining party may prove such a conviction. Previous convictions may be proved by the production of a certificate of the court of conviction (Police and Criminal Evidence Act 1984, s. 73). The Rehabilitation of Offenders Act 1974 governs those convictions that may properly be put to a witness.

In *HM Advocate* v *Murtagh* [2009] UKPC 36, however, it was held that the accused's right to a fair trial required the disclosure only of such previous convictions as materially weaken the Crown's case or materially strengthen the case for the defence. This is therefore not any previous conviction that can either weaken the prosecution case, **or** strengthen the defence case; answers A, B and C are therefore incorrect.

Evidence and Procedure, para. 2.7.18.1

Answer 7.2

Answer **D** — There have been numerous domestic and European case decisions about failure to advance facts following legal advice to remain silent, and more recent cases have attempted to unravel the difficulties experienced in this area. These cases have accepted that a genuine reliance by a defendant on his or her solicitor's advice to remain silent is not in itself enough to preclude adverse comment; answer A is therefore incorrect. The real question to be answered is whether the defendant remained silent, not because of legal advice, but because there was no satisfactory explanation to give (*R* v *Beckles* [2005] 1 All ER 705 and *R* v *Bresa* [2005] EWCA Crim 1414).

Where an accused, following legal advice, fails to answer questions during interview but presents a prepared statement, no adverse inference can be drawn where the accused's defence does not rely on any facts not mentioned in the interview (*R* v *Campbell* [2005] EWCA Crim 1249); answer C is therefore incorrect.

However, this would not be the case when evidence of facts relied on during the trial were not contained within the pre-prepared statement (*R* v *Turner* [2004] All ER 1025).

Prepared statements can be a dangerous device for an innocent accused who later discovers that something significant has been omitted. In *Turner* it was noted that, as inconsistencies between the prepared statement and the defence at trial do not necessarily amount to reliance on unmentioned facts, the judge must be particularly careful to pinpoint any fact that might properly be the subject of a s. 34 direction. Alternatively, the jury might more appropriately be directed to regard differences between the prepared statement and the accused's evidence as constituting a previous lie rather than as the foundation for a direction under s. 34.

What is important is that the inferences hinge on whether the evidence given in chief varies from that given in interview, and although evidence was given by the accused as to why he had that £200 it varied from the reason given in his prepared statement; answer B is therefore incorrect.

Evidence and Procedure, para. 2.7.6.1

Answer 7.3

Answer **B** — Section 116 of the Criminal Justice Act 2003 deals with the admissibility of evidence where the witness is not available to attend court.

This section provides that a statement not made in oral evidence, which satisfies any of the five conditions set out in the provisions, should be automatically admissible. The five conditions, contained in s. 116(2), are that the relevant person:

(a) is dead;

(b) is unfit because of a bodily or mental condition;

(c) is outside the United Kingdom and it is not reasonably practicable to secure his or her attendance;

(d) cannot be found even though reasonably practicable steps have been taken to find him or her;

(e) through fear, does not give (or continue to give) oral evidence and the court gives leave for the statement to be given in evidence.

A statement may only be admitted under this section where the court considers it is in the interests of justice to do so having regard to the statement's contents, any risk that it may be unfair to any party, that a special measures direction under s. 19 of the Youth Justice and Criminal Evidence Act 1999 could be made for a witness to testify, and any other relevant circumstances (s. 116(4)).

In *Al-Khawaja and Tahery* v *UK* (2009) 49 EHRR 1, the European Court of Human Rights, while generally opposing hearsay as the sole or decisive evidence against an accused, has accepted as a specific exception the case where a witness is absent through intimidation deployed by or on behalf of the accused. This exception was followed in *R* v *Horncastle* [2009] UKSC 14, though the Supreme Court considered that all possible efforts be made to get the witness to court and in cases involving fear the use of special measures (use of screens, live link or video recorded evidence) should be considered.

Evidence and Procedure, para. 2.7.14.7

Answer 7.4

Answer **B** — Section 36 of the Criminal Justice and Public Order Act 1994 provides that inferences can be drawn from an accused's failure to give evidence or refusal to answer any question about any object, substance or mark which may be attributable to the accused in the commission of an offence.

Section 36 states:

(1) Where—
- (a) a person is arrested by a constable, and there is—
  - (i) on his person; or
  - (ii) in or on his clothing or footwear; or
  - (iii) otherwise in his possession; or
  - (iv) in any place in which he is at the time of his arrest,

  any object, substance or mark, or there is any mark on any such object; and
- (b) that or another constable investigating the case reasonably believes that the presence of the object, substance or mark may be attributable to the participation of the person arrested in the commission of an offence specified by the constable; and
- (c) the constable informs the person arrested that he so believes, and requests him to account for the presence of the object, substance or mark; and
- (d) the person fails or refuses to do so ...

In this scenario the cut would be a mark on his person, as mark is not defined in the legislation this could be 'any' mark; answer D is therefore incorrect. However since the suspect has in fact accounted for that mark in accordance with s. 36(1)(c) of the 1994 Act, it could not be subject of a special warning (whether you actually believe the account or not is irrelevant); answer A is therefore incorrect.

'Found by him at a place at or about the time the offence for which he was arrested is alleged to have been committed' relates to the person being found as in s. 37 of the Criminal Justice and Public Order Act 1994, not s. 36. What is important in s. 36 is what is found in the place where he is at the time of his arrest, in this case the knife; answer C is therefore incorrect.

Evidence and Procedure, paras 2.7.6.3, 2.7.6.4

Answer 7.5

Answer **D** — Section 36 of the Criminal Justice and Public Order Act 1994 provides that inferences can be drawn from an accused's failure to give evidence or refusal to answer any question about any object, substance or mark which may be attributable to the accused in the commission of an offence.

Section 36 states:

(1) Where—
- (a) a person is arrested by a constable, and there is—
  - (i) on his person; or
  - (ii) in or on his clothing or footwear; or
  - (iii) otherwise in his possession; or
  - (iv) in any place in which he is at the time of his arrest,

  any object, substance or mark, or there is any mark on any such object; and
- (b) that or another constable investigating the case reasonably believes that the presence of the object, substance or mark may be attributable to the participation of the person arrested in the commission of an offence specified by the constable; and
- (c) the constable informs the person arrested that he so believes, and requests him to account for the presence of the object, substance or mark; and
- (d) the person fails or refuses to do so,

then if, in any proceedings against the person for the offence so specified, evidence of those matters is given, subsection (2) below applies.

The teeth marks are definitely on his person, however he did account for the mark (its believability is irrelevant) and as such cannot be given a special warning for it; answers A and C are therefore incorrect.

The property was not found on his person, nor in the place where he was arrested, so it also cannot be subject to a special warning, even if he refuses to account for them; answers B and C are therefore incorrect.

Evidence and Procedure, para. 2.7.6.3

Answer 7.6

Answer **C** — A jury may draw inferences where a defendant refuses, without good cause, to answer a question properly put. The court must inform the accused that if he or she fails to give evidence, or, being sworn, refuses to answer questions without good cause, the jury may draw such inferences as appear proper from such a failure to give evidence or a refusal to answer any question (*Consolidated Criminal Practice Direction Part IV.44. Defendant's right to give or not give evidence*). Once the defendant becomes a sworn witness, he or she loses the privilege against self-incrimination, and answer A is therefore incorrect. Also, the defendant may be asked questions that tend to incriminate him or her, and answer B is therefore incorrect. So here inferences may be drawn. In *Murray* v *United Kingdom* [1996] 22 EHRR 29 it was held that it would be incompatible with the rights of an accused to base a conviction 'solely or mainly' on their silence, or on their refusal to answer questions or give evidence in person. The Court of Appeal also held that in cases involving directions under s. 34, the burden of proof remained on the Crown despite the fact that the accused chose to make no comment (*R* v *Gowland-Wynn* [2001] EWCA Crim 2715). Answer D is therefore incorrect.

Evidence and Procedure, para. 2.7.6.5

Answer 7.7

Answer **A** — There will be instances in which the issues that the court will need to decide on are beyond its knowledge. In such instances it may be necessary to call on witnesses who, through their own experience or training or both, have the necessary expertise. It is for the judge to decide whether a witness is competent to give expert opinion. The expert witness is only there to assist the court in deciding the facts of the case.

Guidance in respect of expert evidence is provided by *R* v *Harris and Others* [2005] EWCA Crim 1980, where it was emphasised that the duties of an expert witness in a criminal trial are owed to the court and override any obligation to the person from whom the expert has received instructions or by whom the expert is paid. Experts are required to maintain professional objectivity and impartiality at all times. They owe a duty only to the court; answers B, C and D are therefore incorrect.

Evidence and Procedure, para. 2.7.19.2

Answer 7.8

Answer **D** — This question really tests your knowledge of evidence, custody officers procedure and interviews; questions in the national examination also test wide ranging knowledge. So although this question could be in other chapters, it is in this one as it mostly relates to s. 34 of the Criminal Justice and Public Order Act 1994, inferences from silence.

In relation to the first interview consider what evidence the police should have disclosed to the solicitor prior to this interview. There is obviously a statutory disclosure duty after charge, however, this is not necessarily the case at the interview stage of the investigation. There is no specific provision within the Police and Criminal Evidence Act 1984 for the disclosure of any information by the police at the police station, with the exception of the custody record and, in identification cases, the initial description given by the witnesses. Further, there is nothing within the Criminal Justice and Public Order Act 1994 that states that information must be disclosed before an inference from silence can be made. Indeed, in *R* v *Imran* [1997] Crim LR 754 the court held that it is totally wrong to submit that a defendant should be prevented from lying by being presented with the whole of the evidence against him or her prior to the interview.

In *R* v *Argent* [1997] Crim LR 346 the court dismissed the argument that an inference could not be drawn under s. 34 of the Criminal Justice and Public Order Act 1994 because there had not been full disclosure at the interview. However, the court did recognise that it may be a factor to take into account, but it would be for the jury to decide whether the failure to answer questions was reasonable. Consider this though, at this stage of the investigation, a few hours after the collision what actual evidence did the police have? Few, if any, inferences could be drawn, therefore, provided the accused was given an opportunity to give his version of events; answers A and C are therefore incorrect.

In relation to the second interview, Code C of the Police and Criminal Evidence Act 1984 codes of practice provides that as soon as a police officer believes that a prosecution should be brought against a suspect and there is sufficient evidence for it to succeed and that the person has said all that he wishes to say about the offence, he shall without delay bring him before the custody officer who is then responsible for considering whether or not he should be charged. Bearing in mind the accused has had no opportunity to comment on the evidence the police have gathered it would be unfair not to allow them the opportunity to say what they wish about the offence. In any case the phrase in Code C is 'sufficient evidence for it to succeed' not 'sufficient evidence to charge' and if the accused's answers led the police to believe that a prosecution is not likely to succeed then that accused must be given the opportunity to say what they wish; answers B and C are therefore incorrect.

In *R* v *Flynn* [2001] EWCA Crim 1633, the court held that the police are entitled to conduct a second interview with a suspect, having obtained evidence from their witnesses which was not available in the first interview, and adverse inference could be drawn from the suspect's silence.

Evidence and Procedure, para. 2.7.6.1

Answer 7.9

Answer **A** — Section 120 of the Criminal Justice Act 2003 provides circumstances when previous statements of witnesses are admissible as evidence of the truth of their contents. This includes:

- statements which are admitted to rebut a suggestion that the witness's oral evidence is untrue (subs. (2));
- where a witness is refreshing their memory from a written document, if they are being cross-examined on the document and it is received in evidence, the statement will be evidence of any matter contained within it (subs. (3));
- where a witness states that they made the statement and believe it to be true and one of the following conditions is met:
  - the statement describes or identifies a person, place or thing (which includes objects such as a car registration number); or
  - the statement was made when the incident was fresh in the witness's memory and he/she cannot reasonably be expected to remember the matters stated; or
  - the statement consists of a complaint by a victim of the alleged offence which was made as soon as could reasonably be expected after the conduct in question, and the witness gives oral evidence in relation to the matter. The complaint must not have been made as a result of a threat or promise (subss. (4)–(7)).

There is no limit set as to what 'as soon as could reasonably be expected' is; answers B and C are therefore incorrect. Nor does it state that the matter needs to be of a sexual case; answer D is therefore incorrect.

Evidence and Procedure, para. 2.7.17.4

Answer 7.10

Answer **D** — Only treason, perjury and speeding require corroboration in law, and answer A is therefore incorrect. A corroboration warning is no longer a requirement in cases of complaints of sexual offences, and answer B is therefore incorrect. It is a matter of discretion for the judge whether such a warning should be given, and so answer C is therefore incorrect. In *R* v *Makanjuola* [1995] 1 WLR 1348, Lord Taylor LCJ gave guidelines in respect of the exercise of the discretion:

> It is a matter for the judge's discretion what, if any, warning he considers appropriate in respect of such a witness as indeed in respect of any other witness in whatever type of case. Whether he chooses to give a warning and in what terms will depend on the circumstances of the case, the issues raised and the content and quality of the witness's evidence. In some cases, it may be appropriate for the judge to warn the jury to exercise caution before acting upon the unsupported evidence of a witness. This will not be so simply because the witness is a complainant of a sexual offence nor will it necessarily be so because a witness is alleged to be an accomplice. There will need to be an evidential basis for suggesting that the evidence of the witness may be unreliable. An evidential basis does not include mere suggestion by cross-examining counsel.

Evidence and Procedure, para. 2.7.20

Answer 7.11

Answer **D** — Evidence is likely to be admissible if it goes beyond mere evidence of a tendency to commit crime and has a crucial bearing upon the question whether the offence charged was committed by this particular defendant, even 'bad character evidence'.

Part of the definition of bad character in s. 98 of the Criminal Justice Act 2003 directs the court to consider whether the evidence shows a disposition 'towards misconduct', where misconduct means 'the commission of an offence or other reprehensible behaviour'. It would seem unlikely that a homosexual disposition is *per se* 'reprehensible' and therefore not misconduct. However the question is asking about the adducing of previous convictions, not a disposition; answer B is therefore incorrect.

The question here is about the previous convictions of the defendant. The second part of s. 98 has to do with the alleged facts of the offence with which the defendant is charged. Under s. 101, evidence of a defendant's bad character can be entered if it is 'a matter in issue between the defendant and the prosecution'; however s. 103(1)(a) defines this as:

(a) the question whether the defendant has a propensity to commit offences of the kind with which he is charged, except where his having such a propensity makes it no more likely that he is guilty of the offence.

Here the convictions would not show a propensity to commit murder; therefore answer C is incorrect.

That said bad character evidence can be adduced as important explanatory evidence, or evidence to correct a false impression given by the defendant. In both these cases the evidence is likely to be adduced, evidence without which it would be 'impossible or difficult to understand other evidence in the case'. Answer A is therefore incorrect.

Evidence and Procedure, para. 2.7.18.2

Answer 7.12

Answer **A** — Amongst the criteria for admitting a business document under s. 117 of the Criminal Justice Act 2003 are:

- that the information was received in the course of business;
- that the information contained in the document was supplied by a person (whether or not the maker of the statement) who had, or who may reasonably be supposed to have had, personal knowledge of the matters dealt with.

Both these points are contained in the question (note the maker of the document only has to have knowledge of the matters dealt with on the document, not of whether the messages were true or not). Answer B is therefore incorrect. It is immaterial that the accused was not the maker of the document and answer D is therefore incorrect. Also, in relation to business documents, provided the criteria outlined above are fulfilled, it is immaterial whether the witness is able to attend court or not—the document will be admitted and answer C is therefore incorrect.

Evidence and Procedure, para. 2.7.14.9

Answer 7.13

Answer **C** — In relation to non-expert evidence, the courts have allowed the following non-expert opinion evidence from a witness:

- identification of a person or object;
- the speed of a moving vehicle;

- evidence as to temperature or time;
- the value of an item.

Note, however, that non-expert opinion evidence should not be received on the value of less commonplace objects or objects, such as antiques and works of art, the valuation of which calls for expertise; therefore, answer D is incorrect.

One example of non-expert evidence that is likely to be given by police officers is provided by the case of *R* v *Davies* [1962] 1 WLR 1111. In *Davies*, it was held that any competent witness may give evidence that in his or her opinion a person is drunk provided that he or she describes the facts on which his or her opinion is based; therefore, answer A is incorrect. As can be seen, this is not restricted just to police officers, but covers any competent witness.

Although scientific evidence (expert) is not always required to identify a prohibited drug, police officers' descriptions of a drug must be sufficient to justify the inference that it was the drug alleged (*R* v *Hill* (1993) 96 Cr App R 456). As such, they can give non-expert opinion, even though not specially trained; therefore, answer B is incorrect.

Evidence and Procedure, para. 2.7.19.1

Answer 7.14

Answer **D** — The general rule is that the opinion of a witness is inadmissible. However, where it is admissible it can be divided into two groups:

- non-expert evidence;
- expert evidence.

The courts have allowed the following non-expert opinion evidence from a witness:

- identification of a person or object;
- the speed of a moving vehicle;
- evidence as to temperature or time;
- the value of an item (provided it does not require specialist knowledge to estimate the price).

So the non-expert can give evidence of the speed of a moving vehicle (whether a conviction would be achieved without further evidence is debatable) and this is anyone. It is not the preserve of a police officer, even a highly trained one; answers A, B and C are therefore incorrect.

Evidence and Procedure, para. 2.7.19.1

Answer 7.15

Answer **C** — Section 116 of the Criminal Justice Act 2003 deals with the admissibility of evidence where the witness is not available to attend court.

This section provides that a statement not made in oral evidence, which satisfies the five conditions set out in the provisions, should be automatically admissible; answer A is therefore incorrect. The five conditions, contained in s. 116(2), are that the relevant person:

(a) is dead;

(b) is unfit because of a bodily or mental condition;

(c) is outside the United Kingdom and it is not reasonably practicable to secure their attendance;

(d) cannot be found even though reasonably practical steps have been taken to find them;

(e) through fear, does not give (or continue to give) oral evidence and the court gives leave for the statement to be given in evidence.

It is any fear, not necessarily fear caused to the witness; answer B is therefore incorrect.

A statement may only be admitted under this section where the court considers it is in the interests of justice to do so having regard to the statement's contents, any risk that it may be unfair to any party, that a special measures direction under s. 19 of the Youth Justice and Criminal Evidence Act 1999 could be made for a witness to testify, and any other relevant circumstances (s. 116(4)); answer D is therefore incorrect.

Evidence and Procedure, para. 2.7.14.7

Answer 7.16

Answer **A** — Section 105 of the Criminal Justice Act deals directly with 'evidence to correct a false impression' per s. 101(1)(f) of that Act.

(1) For the purposes of section 101(1)(f) —
 (a) the defendant gives a false impression if he is responsible for the making of an express or implied assertion which is apt to give the court or jury a false or misleading impression about the defendant ...

These assertions can be made whilst being questioned under caution about the offence with which they are charged or on being charged with that offence or officially informed that he might be prosecuted for it. However, evidence of the assertion must also be given in the proceedings: as KNIGHT will not give any evidence then this section does not bite. Answers B and C are therefore incorrect.

The accused may be held to have given a false impression by means of conduct and this includes 'dress' (s. 105(4) and (5)). It is unclear how such a provision will operate in practice; however where someone dresses to give the jury a false impression then the prosecution can adduce evidence of bad character, but only going directly to the falsity of the impression. This is so even if the accused does not give evidence themselves, as the court will view the 'dress' itself as an assertion which is apt to give a false impression. Answer D is therefore incorrect.

Evidence and Procedure, para. 2.7.18.2

Answer 7.17

Answer **B** — Section 1(2) of the Criminal Evidence Act 1898 provides that, subject to s. 101 of the Criminal Justice Act 2003 below, a defendant who gives evidence in the proceedings may be asked any questions in cross-examination which tend directly to incriminate him or her.

Section 101(1) of the Criminal Justice Act 2003 sets out those occasions where the defendant's bad character is admissible in evidence in criminal proceedings. These occasions are where:

(a) all parties to the proceedings agree to the evidence being admissible,

(b) the evidence is adduced by the defendant or given in answer to a question asked in cross-examination and intended to elicit it,

(c) it is important explanatory evidence,

(d) it is relevant to an important matter in issue between the defendant and the prosecution,

(e) it has substantial probative value in relation to an important matter in issue between the defendant and a co-defendant,

(f) it is evidence to correct a false impression given by the defendant, or

(g) the defendant has made an attack on another person's character.

As can be seen, the gateways for bad character evidence extend to more than previous convictions; answer C is therefore incorrect. This scenario relates to 'gateway' f.

It is evidence relating to the offence in that it is evidence to counter the assertion that the accused is not the offender; answer D is therefore incorrect.

Evidence that a defendant is lying, or has a tendency to lie, is not one of the gateways, and in any case would lead to a *Lucas* directive by the judge; answer A is therefore incorrect.

Evidence and Procedure, para. 2.7.18.2

Answer 7.18

Answer **A** — An admission made by the agent of an accused person, such as his legal adviser, may be admissible against him (*R* v *Turner* (1975) 61 Cr App R 67); therefore answer C is incorrect. Although at first sight such an admission may appear to be a confession, and thus to be governed by the rules of admissibility in the Police and Criminal Evidence Act 1984, s. 76, this, in fact, is not the case, for the section applies only to a confession made 'by an accused person' and, by s. 82(1) of the 1984 Act, 'confession' includes any statement adverse to 'the person who made it'; answer B is therefore incorrect.

Who is an agent of the accused may be inferred from the circumstances in *Turner*, where it was held that it is permissible to infer from the fact that a barrister makes an admission in court on behalf of and in the presence of his client, that he was authorised to make it. This is hearsay evidence, but is admissible as such and is governed by the relevant sections of the Criminal Justice Act 2003, which place hearsay evidence on a more statutory footing; answer D is therefore incorrect.

Evidence and Procedure, para. 2.7.14.5

Answer 7.19

Answer **C** — Section 100(1) of the 2003 Act sets out the following three conditions where evidence of a non-defendant's previous misconduct can be given in criminal proceedings:

(a) it is important explanatory evidence,

(b) it has substantial probative value in relation to a matter in issue in the proceedings or is of substantial importance in the context of the case as a whole, or

(c) all parties agree to the evidence being admissible.

Section 6 of the Criminal Procedure Act 1865 provides that where a witness is being questioned as to whether he or she has been convicted of any felony or misdemeanour, he or she denies, does not admit, or refuses to answer, the cross-examining party may prove such a conviction. Previous convictions may be proved by the production of a certificate of the court of conviction (s. 73 of the Police and

Criminal Evidence Act 1984). The Rehabilitation of Offenders Act 1974 governs those convictions that may properly be put to a witness.

The previous caution would not fit any of the above criteria and is inadmissible; answers A, B and D are therefore incorrect.

Evidence and Procedure, para. 2.7.18.1

Answer 7.20

Answer **D** — An accused may lay claim to a good character not only where they can adduce positive evidence to that effect, but also where they can truthfully assert that they have no previous convictions (*R* v *Aziz* [1996] AC 41).

However, the jury must not be misled by any claim made by the accused, so where, for example, he or she has recently been cautioned for an offence this cannot simply be ignored (*R* v *Martin* [2000] 2 Cr App R 42), nor can the fact that he or she has been found guilty by a foreign court (*R* v *El Delbi* [2003] EWCA Crim 1767). Answers A, B and C are therefore incorrect.

Evidence and Procedure, para. 2.7.18.3

Answer 7.21

Answer **C** — Secondary evidence is evidence of an inferior kind, e.g. a copy of a document or a copy of such a copy. Such evidence can be admissible (*Butler* v *Board of Trade* [1971] Ch 680) where a copy of a letter from the claimant's solicitor to the claimant had been accidentally included in papers handed over to the Official Receiver. It was held that, although the original letter was privileged, a copy was admissible in the criminal proceedings; answer A is therefore incorrect.

It is whether the document is an original or a copy that is vital as to its legal privilege status, not the content; answer D is therefore incorrect, although it would be safe to assume that the contents would attract privilege.

These days the court is not confined to the best evidence rule but can admit all relevant evidence (*Kajala* v *Noble* (1982) 75 Cr App R 149); therefore answer B is incorrect.

Evidence and Procedure, para. 2.7.12

8 Exclusion of Admissible Evidence

STUDY PREPARATION

There are few more frustrating experiences for police officers than to have brought a person before the court and presented the evidence against them, only to have some of that evidence excluded.

This area of law has grown up partly through the common law decisions of the higher courts and partly through statute. And now there is the additional force of the Human Rights Act 1998, which has focused attention on the defendant's inalienable right to a fair trial and the attendant safeguards under Art. 6 of the European Convention on Human Rights.

Many of the occasions where admissible evidence is later excluded by the courts arise in suspect interviews, or on other occasions where the police officer(s) concerned say or do something that renders any response by the defendant unreliable or its introduction in evidence unfair. Therefore, areas of confessions and oppression are key features in this chapter, as are the practical consequences of an exclusion ruling being made.

QUESTIONS

Question 8.1

WILLIAMS and THOMPSON were jointly charged with possessing stolen property. In his police interview, WILLIAMS admitted that he knew the goods were stolen but stated that THOMPSON had no knowledge of that.

WILLIAMS pleaded guilty. THOMPSON pleaded not guilty and at his trial argued that he did not know that property amounted to stolen goods. WILLIAMS indicated he would be unwilling to give evidence at court on behalf of THOMPSON and was therefore not called by the defence. Instead, the defence sought to rely on WILLIAMS' statements in his police interview.

Will this previous confession by WILLIAMS be admissible in THOMPSON'S trial?

A The statement will be allowed as he is no longer a defendant, he is only a witness.

B The statement will be allowed as a confession made by one accused person can be given in evidence for another person charged in the same proceedings.

C The statement won't be allowed as WILLIAMS is no longer charged in the same proceedings.

D The statement won't be allowed as the confession was from WILLIAMS not from THOMPSON and is therefore inadmissible.

Question 8.2

MARTIN was suspected of an offence and a decision was made to take a hair sample from him for DNA comparison. MARTIN was going bald and asked if the hair could be taken from somewhere other than his head. The officer who was asked to take the sample laughed and grabbed a big handful of hair on the suspect's hand and pulled it out. MARTIN was really upset over his treatment, which was clearly a breach of Code D, para. 6.1 (note 6A) of the Police and Criminal Evidence Act 1984 Codes of Practice. The sample gave a positive DNA result which was to form part of the case against MARTIN.

Is this DNA evidence likely to be excluded due to the breach of the codes of practice when it was obtained?

A Yes, there was a clear breach of the codes of practice, and it was more than a trifling, minor breach and will lead to exclusion.

B Yes, any breach of the codes of practice that was deliberate and malevolent will lead to exclusion of the evidence.

C No, the evidence will be admitted on the basis that the means used to obtain it have done nothing to cast doubt on its reliability and strength.

D No, any physical evidence obtained can never be ruled to be unreliable.

Question 8.3

FRENCH is standing trial at the Crown Court, charged with blackmail. At the *voir dire* the defence make a submission to exclude some of the prosecution evidence and ask that it be excluded using s. 82(3) of the Police and Criminal Evidence Act 1984 which retained the courts' common law power to exclude evidence at its discretion.

In relation to this which of the following is correct?

A The evidence could only be excluded at common law during the trial, not at the *voir dire*.

B Even if evidence is properly obtained it may be excluded by the judge at common law.

C Evidence will be excluded at common law if any breach of any codes of practice has occurred.

D Evidence can only be excluded at common law if its probative value exceeds its prejudicial effect.

Question 8.4

TIMPKINS was arrested for murder. On being told that if he confessed he would be charged with manslaughter only, TIMPKINS stated he had shot the victim in self-defence. TIMPKINS then told the officers where to find the gun, which he had hidden in a hedge. The gun was found, and at a second interview TIMPKINS identified it as the one he had used, again because he believed he would be charged with manslaughter only. Ballistic evidence showed it was the weapon used. TIMPKINS was charged with murder. At TIMPKINS' trial, the judge ruled that the confession obtained at the first interview would be excluded as it was 'unreliable'.

In relation to evidence the police can now give, which of the following statements is true?

A The police can state that TIMPKINS identified the gun, as this was during the second interview, which should be allowed.

B The police can state that they found a gun where TIMPKINS told them to look, and that it was the gun used in the shooting.

C The police may not be able to make a connection between TIMPKINS and the gun.

D The police will be able to state that TIMPKINS said he had used the gun, as this was during the second interview, which should be allowed.

Question 8.5

SKIVINGTON is standing trial for an offence of burglary. During the burglary, where SKIVINGTON pretended to be a meter reader, witnesses noted that the offender spoke with a pronounced stammer, and used the term 'pal' significantly. Whilst being interviewed on audio by police officers, SKIVINGTON stammered and used the word 'pal' 25 times during a 20-minute interview. SKIVINGTON also confessed to the burglary. At the *voir dire* the judge excluded the confession when the defence submitted it had been obtained unfairly. The prosecution seek to have the evidence of the stammer, and the use of the term 'pal', admitted to show the connection between SKIVINGTON and the description obtained from witnesses.

Is it likely that this evidence will be allowed during the trial?

A Yes, as it is evidence properly obtained and admissible for a specific purpose.

B Yes, as it is similar fact evidence and admissible to connect SKIVINGTON to the crime charged.

C No, if the confession is excluded then the entire interview will be excluded.

D No, as it is not one of the 'facts in issue', it will not be admissible.

Question 8.6

Police officers have been carrying out covert surveillance on the home address of MACINTOSH, who is believed to be involved in the supply of class A drugs. During the operation they receive further intelligence that suggests that MACINTOSH may also be involved in the supply of illegal firearms. However, there is absolutely no evidence from the surveillance that this is the case.

Which of the following is true in relation to the attempt to gain evidence of the supply of illegal firearms by HOPES?

A An undercover officer could make a test purchase for drugs as part of the on-going operation, but then ask about the supply of firearms.

B A covert human intelligence source (CHIS) could encourage MACINTOSH to supply firearms while making a drug purchase.

C Any attempt to ask MACINTOSH to supply firearms may well be seen as entrapment and any evidence obtained would be excluded.

D Any attempt to get MACINTOSH to supply firearms would not necessarily be entrapment, but safeguards would have to be observed.

Question 8.7

MORTLOCKE left explicit graffiti messages in a public lavatory, seeking sex with girls aged between 8 and 13 years, and asking them to text his mobile phone number with their details. The police became aware and contacted the text number, with one of their officers sending several messages implying that she was an 11-year-old girl, and interested in meeting him. MORTLOCKE replied, arranging a meeting and describing the various sexual acts he would perform on her. At the meeting, he was arrested and later charged with attempting to incite a child under the age of 13 to engage in sexual activity, contrary to s. 8 of the Sexual Offences Act 2003.

In relation to this which of the following is correct with regards to entrapment?

A MORTLOCKE is guilty as the police provided no more than an opportunity to commit the offence.

B MORTLOCKE is guilty as soon as he left the messages in the toilet, the police action was no more than an attempt to locate and arrest him.

C MORTLOCKE is not guilty, as the officer purporting to be the child was not under 13 years of age, the offence could never be committed.

D MORTLOCKE is not guilty as the police answered the message in the toilet, thereby provoking him into answering and thereby committing the crime.

Question 8.8

COSTELO wished to arrange a contract killing of her husband. In the two years preceding his death, she repeatedly stated that she wanted him killed and asked various witnesses whether they would help her kill him. She associated with SHERD who was a customer of her sandwich shop. SHERD associated with RYRIE. At the trial the prosecution have evidence that SHERD twice sent to RYRIE large amounts of money contained in sandwich bags from COSTELO's shop.

All three are charged jointly with murder, the main evidence being a confession by RYRIE, made to his girlfriend, that he killed COSTELO's husband and that SHERD was the 'middleman'. There is only other circumstantial evidence against SHERD.

In relation to this confession by RYRIE which of the following is correct?

A The confession is not admissible as it was made to a friend and not to the police.

B The confession is not admissible against the co-defendants as confession is relevant and admissible only against its maker.

C The jury can only consider the confession in relation to RYRIE's guilt, not whilst considering the co-defendants' guilt.

D The jury are entitled to take RYRIE's confession into account whilst considering the co-defendants' guilt.

Question 8.9

BRIDGES and JONES were both suspected of committing a murder. During police interviews they exercised their right to silence. There was other evidence and they were charged. The senior investigating officer (SIO) was concerned that the evidence was flimsy and wanted confession evidence from the suspects. Aware that no further interviews were allowed the SIO concocted a ruse where the custody officer argued with the SIO in front of the suspects claiming he had to place them both in the same cell. The SIO apologised to the suspects claiming the custody officer was an 'arse for making you share a cell'. The cell was bugged and the suspects engaged in a conversation which contained a number of damaging admissions, and was recorded.

Considering the evidence obtained during the bugged conversation, which of the following is correct?

A The evidence is admissible as the police did not trick them into making the admissions.

B The evidence will be admissible, but the police will have to re-interview them to allow them to comment upon it.

C The evidence is not admissible as it was obtained after interview and charge.

D The evidence is not admissible as it was obtained by a cheat, where the custody officer clearly lied to the suspects.

Question 8.10

ALBERTS was in custody together with several family members accused of drug dealing. ALBERTS was represented by RITTER and during consultation ALBERTS asked RITTER to establish if the police would release his family members if he confessed to the drug dealing. Although not promising anything the police told RITTER that the case against the other family members was borderline and if at the end of the inquiry there was insufficient evidence they would be released. This information given by the police was correct. ALBERTS confessed, and was even asked leading questions during the police interview by RITTER, in line with his instructions from ALBERTS. At court ALBERTS wishes to have his confession excluded as it was unfairly obtained, even though it was the truth as he was the actual drug dealer.

In relation to this application, which of the following is correct?

A The confession should stand as it was not unreliable.

B The confession should stand as it was true and not gained by oppression.

C The confession should be excluded as it was based on the premise that if given family members would be released.

D The confession should be excluded as RITTER was negligent is assisting ALBERTS confession by asking questions.

Question 8.11

BENTHAM is accused of indecent assault on two male youths. His defence is that the youths' mother put them up to making the allegation after he turned down her sexual advances towards him. He maintains he is heterosexual despite the fact that during a lawfully conducted search of his house several homosexual magazines were found. The defence ask that the magazines be excluded from evidence.

Is it likely that the evidence of the magazines will be admitted?

A Yes, the evidence was obtained by a lawful search of the premises, not unfairly obtained.

B Yes, the evidence is being used to counter an assertion made by the defendant, not as evidence of the offence.

C No, it is not direct evidence and is likely to have an adverse effect on the fairness of the trial.

D No, although it is direct evidence it is likely to have an adverse effect on the fairness of the trial.

ANSWERS

Answer 8.1

Answer **C** — In ensuring that a person has a fair trial the court may exclude evidence, even though the evidence itself is admissible. The court may exclude any evidence in certain circumstances and has additional powers in relation to evidence obtained by confession. The courts' powers to exclude evidence come generally from s. 78 of the Police and Criminal Evidence Act 1984 (and specifically in relation to confession evidence from s. 76(2) of that Act), although the courts also have common law powers to exclude evidence.

This is supported by s. 76A of the Police and Criminal Evidence Act 1984 which states that as long as it has not been excluded by the court under s. 76A (which makes similar provisions for exclusion as those under s. 76), in any proceedings where a confession was made by one accused person it may be given in evidence for another person charged in the same proceedings (a co-accused); answer D is therefore incorrect.

The key part of this subsection is that the co-accused must be 'charged in the same proceedings', for instance in *R* v *Finch* [2007] EWCA Crim 36 where one suspect pleaded guilty the House of Lords held that he was no longer a person charged or accused in the trial, accordingly s. 76A of the 1984 Act did not apply and what he said to the police was not admissible; answer B is therefore incorrect.

It is correct to say that he is a witness, however he would have to give evidence-in-chief, and a previous confession made on tape would NOT be admissible as outlined in *Finch*; answer A is therefore incorrect.

Evidence and Procedure, para. 2.8.1

Answer 8.2

Answer **C** — Section 78 of the Police and Criminal Evidence Act 1984 states:

> (1) In any proceedings the court may refuse to allow evidence on which the prosecution proposes to rely to be given if it appears to the court that, having regard to all the circumstances, including the circumstances in which the evidence was obtained, the admission of the evidence would have such an adverse effect on the fairness of the proceedings that the court ought not to admit it.

The important question here is, what is the actual evidence obtained? The answer is that it is the DNA obtained from the hair, not the hair itself. So although the officer's actions clearly breached the Police and Criminal Evidence Act 1984 Codes of Practice (and are reprehensible) the obtaining of the actual evidence (DNA) did not breach the codes. If a sample of hair is obtained by an assault and not in accordance with ss. 63 and 65 of the 1984 Act and is then used to prepare a DNA profile which implicates the accused, the evidence will be admitted on the basis that the means used to obtain it have done nothing to cast doubt on its reliability and strength (see *R* v *Cooke* [1995] 1 Cr App R 318); answers A and B are therefore incorrect.

Any physical evidence found should be excluded, however, where there is a real risk that the improper means used to obtain it have affected its reliability, and therefore the fairness of the trial, for example a case involving a complete flouting of Code B in which the accused claims that the property allegedly found must have been planted; answer D is therefore incorrect.

Evidence and Procedure, para. 2.8.3.1

Answer 8.3

Answer **B** — Section 82(3) of the Police and Criminal Evidence Act 1984 retained the courts' common law power to exclude evidence at their discretion.

For evidence to be excluded at common law the court will not so much concern itself with how evidence is obtained, but rather the effect that the evidence will have at trial. Evidence can be excluded at common law at any time during the trial, including pre-trial submissions (*voir dire*); answer A is therefore incorrect.

The court can exclude evidence at common law where the prejudicial effect of the evidence on the defendant greatly outweighs its probative value, not the other way round as stated in answer D which makes it incorrect.

In these cases the courts are looking at the trial process itself, as opposed to the investigation. Evidence obtained in breach of codes of practice may be excluded, but not at common law; answer C is therefore incorrect.

Evidence and Procedure, para. 2.8.3.3

Answer 8.4

Answer **C** — This question shows what could happen where vital evidence is lost due to police impropriety (i.e. a clear inducement to confess), particularly where a false pretence has been used. The first interview was rightly excluded, and for the same reasons it is more than likely that the second interview would also be excluded. Answers A and D are therefore incorrect. In this case, it will not be possible to show any connection between the suspect and the weapon and, unless there is some other evidence to link the weapon to the suspect, the case may fail. The reason is that it would not be possible to say that the police went to the location where the weapon was hidden without at least implying that the suspect had indicated that it was there when interviewed, and answer B is therefore incorrect. All that can be said is that the weapon was found at the particular location, which could be accessible to any number of people, and that the scientific evidence shows it to be the murder weapon.

Evidence and Procedure, para. 2.8.2.6

Answer 8.5

Answer **A** — Dealing with answer D first, one of the 'facts in issue' in any case is that of identification. Clearly the peculiar voice patterns go towards proving the identification of the offender. They are a physical feature of the defendant and not affected by anything that may have been done or said which rendered the *content* of the interview inadmissible, and as such would be allowed (answer D is therefore incorrect).

Even where a confession on audio is excluded, it may still be admissible for other matters, such as the fact that the accused speaks in a certain way, or writes or expresses himself or herself in a particular fashion. In such a case it will only be that part of the confession which is necessary to prove the point that will be admissible, and answer C is therefore incorrect. Similar fact evidence relates to evidence of previous convictions or actions which may suggest that the accused has committed the offence charged. This is not the case here and answer B is therefore incorrect.

Evidence and Procedure, para. 2.8.2.6

Answer 8.6

Answer **D** — In cases where officers are trying to obtain evidence of offences yet to be committed, the key question as to the admissibility of evidence is whether the actions of those involved in the 'trap' amount to entrapment.

The issues surrounding entrapment are considered by some to be an infringement of a person's human rights. In *Teixeira de Castro* v *Portugal* (1998) 28 EHRR 101, the European Court of Human Rights (subject to the following two qualifications) held that the use of undercover agents is not incompatible with Art. 6 of the European Convention (right to a fair trial). Those qualifications were that:

- their use must be restricted and safeguards observed to prevent abuse;
- their actions must not exceed passive surveillance.

This is an area where the substantive criminal law overlaps with evidence and procedure.

Evidential factors to consider in running an operation that involves forms of entrapment include:

- The nature of the offence, as some offences are difficult to detect otherwise. Therefore, the more difficult the offence is to detect without intrusive inducement from the police, the more such intrusion will be justifiable.
- What suspicion officers have that an offence of that kind would be committed in the locality. For example, the setting up of a van containing cigarettes to see if someone takes the opportunity to steal them (*Williams and O'Hare* v *DPP* (1994) 98 Cr App R 209). 'If the trick had been the individual enterprise of a policeman in an area where such crime was not suspected to be prevalent, it would have been an abuse of State power' (Lord Hoffmann in *Attorney General's Reference (No. 3 of 2000)* [2001] 1 WLR 2060).

In this scenario there was no evidence obtained by surveillance that firearms supply was going on in that premises. Therefore any attempt to 'trick' the suspect using either officers or CHIS would be likely to be entrapment; answers A and B are therefore incorrect.

The key question is whether the suspects voluntarily applied themselves to 'the trick' and that they were not enticed or provoked into committing a crime which they would otherwise have not committed. In this case there could be evidence obtained covertly, however the safeguards would have to be put in prior to that evidence being obtained; answer C is therefore incorrect.

Evidence and Procedure, para. 2.8.3.4

Answer 8.7

Answer **A** — The issue of entrapment falls into two categories: that is to say, trying to obtain evidence relating to offences that have already been committed; and those cases where evidence is obtained of offences yet to be committed. In relation to offences yet to be committed the key question is whether the suspects voluntarily applied themselves to 'the trick' and that they were not enticed or provoked into committing a crime which they would otherwise have not committed. In *R* v *Jones* [2007] EWCA Crim 1118 the police had received reports of graffiti being written in black marker on the toilets of trains and stations seeking girls of 8 to 13 years old for sex, offering payment and leaving a contact number. Police began an undercover operation using an officer posing as a 12-year-old girl. The undercover officer exchanged several texts with the suspect which clarified her age and arrangements for a meeting, the defendant sent the officer further text messages of an explicit nature including various sexual acts that he expected he would be able to perform on her. The Court of Appeal held that the police did not incite or instigate a crime but merely provided the opportunity for the defendant to commit a similar offence and provide evidence for a conviction; answer D is therefore incorrect. The officer did no more than pretend to be a child of a particular age. The police did not behave improperly in choosing the age of 12. It was Jones who had asked the officer for her age, and he therefore believed that he was inciting penetrative sexual activity with a child under 13.

MORTLOCKE is charged with an attempt to commit the offence, and the message in the toilet would not be 'more than merely preparatory'; however the police action is certainly more than an attempt just to locate him, and is part of evidence gathering, for these reasons answer B is incorrect. As the offence charged is 'attempt' it is irrelevant that the actual offence could not have been committed; answer C is therefore incorrect.

Evidence and Procedure, para. 2.8.3.4

Answer 8.8

Answer **D** — Section 82(1) of the Police and Criminal Evidence Act 1984 makes it clear that the law is no longer concerned with whether a confession was made to a person in authority, such as a police or customs officer, and that the statutory test for admissibility is equally applicable to, for example, an informal admission to a friend or colleague. Answer A is therefore incorrect.

When the case against a defendant in a joint trial depended on the prosecution proving the guilt of a co-defendant, and the evidence against the co-defendant consisted solely of their own out-of-court confession, then that confession would be admissible against the defendant but only insofar as it went to proving the co-defendant's guilt. At the end of the prosecution case the defendant would have a case to answer, because the jury could properly find, first, that the co-defendant was guilty on the basis of their own confession, and then go on to find that the fact of the co-defendant's guilt coupled with any other evidence incriminating the defendant was sufficient to prove the latter's guilt.

This was the finding by a 3:2 majority judgment in the House of Lords in *R* v *Hayter* [2005] UKHL 6, despite the general principle that confession is relevant and admissible only against its maker. Therefore answers B and C are incorrect.

Evidence and Procedure, para. 2.8.2

Answer 8.9

Answer **A** — So what have the police done? They lied to the suspects that they had to be put into the same cell. Although this was an untruthful act by the police did it lead directly to any evidence being obtained because of those lies?

In *R* v *Bailey*; *R* v *Smith* [1993] Crim LR 681 a blatant piece of play acting was approved. The investigating officers and the custody officer played out a conversation in front of the defendants, in which the custody officer, appearing to act against the wishes of the investigating officers, insisted in placing the two defendants in the same cell. In fact, the investigating officers wanted the defendants together, as the cell was bugged. The defendants, lulled into a false sense of security, engaged in a conversation which contained a number of damaging admissions, and was recorded. The Court of Appeal found nothing wrong in what the police had done, even though it was clearly a means of circumventing the fact that they could not question the defendants further (because they had both already been charged). The court held that the fact the defendants could not, under Code of Practice C, properly have been subjected to further questioning did not mean that they had to be protected from the opportunity to speak incriminatingly to one another if they chose to do so. It was acknowledged to appear odd that, alongside the 'rigorously controlled legislative regime' for questioning it should be considered acceptable for 'parallel covert investigations' legitimately to continue, but, provided such strategems were used only in grave cases and that there was no suggestion of oppression or unreliability, there was nothing unfair about admitting the evidence obtained in consequence.

The evidence will be adduced; answers B, C and D are therefore incorrect.

Evidence and Procedure, para. 2.8.3.1

Answer 8.10

Answer **A** — Section 76(2) of the Police and Criminal Evidence Act 1984 gives the courts a responsibility to exclude confessions where they have been obtained by oppression (s. 76(2)(a)), or where the court considers they are unreliable (s. 76(2)(b)). There is also a general power (under s. 78 of the 1984 Act and at common law) to exclude any evidence that the court considers would be detrimental to the fairness of the trial if allowed, which can also be applicable to the exclusion of confessions. When looking at whether a confession is reliable, the court will consider the circumstances as they actually were at the time and not as they were believed to be. The circumstances are that the family members would be released if there was no evidence against them. This was not a condition of a confession; answer C is therefore incorrect.

In relation to s. 76(2), the court is more concerned about the circumstances in which the confession was obtained than the truthfulness of what was said. So even though it is the truth and not gained by oppression, if the court feels that the way the confession was gained was unfair it may exclude it; answer B is therefore incorrect.

It is the duty of a solicitor to give rational help and advice to their client, and to carry out their instructions. Their client can hardly cry foul if the solicitor follows this edict; answer D is therefore incorrect.

Evidence and Procedure, para. 2.8.2.2

Answer 8.11

Answer **C** — The question that is important here is what is the charge? In this case, it is indecent assault, so any evidence adduced by the prosecution must relate to the facts in issue. Such facts will include:

- the identity of the defendant;
- the *actus reus*;
- the *mens rea*.

In what way will the magazines assist here? The fact is they don't and their prejudicial effect is likely to far outweigh their probative value, particularly as their probative value seems to be little if anything (taking the facts in issue into account).

The court may refuse to allow evidence on which the prosecution proposes to rely if it appears to the court that, having regard to all the circumstances, including the circumstances in which the evidence was obtained, the admission of the evidence would have such an adverse effect on the fairness of the proceedings that the court ought not to admit it.

This is all the circumstances not just those in which the evidence was obtained, so although it was not unfairly obtained it may still be excluded; answer A is therefore incorrect.

Just because a defendant makes an assertion in their defence does not allow the prosecution to adduce evidence to counter that, the prejudicial/probative test will always be applied; answer B is therefore incorrect.

The magazines do not represent direct evidence of the crime charged; answer D is therefore incorrect.

Of course whether evidence is excluded is a matter for the court, however you were asked if it was likely it would be admitted. In this case, it is unlikely as the scenario mirrors *R* v *B (RA)* [1997] Crim LR 440 where the evidence was excluded.

Evidence and Procedure, para. 2.8.3

9 Disclosure of Evidence

STUDY PREPARATION

Once again, this is an area that began life as a common law development through the courts, being later encapsulated in statute—the Criminal Procedure and Investigations Act 1996 (as amended by the Criminal Justice Act 2003).

Although most of the specific responsibilities under the Act fall on the disclosure officer, the general duties of the disclosure system are important to all police officers and others involved in the gathering of evidence.

As well as understanding the main principles of the Criminal Procedure and Investigations Act—and the code that accompanies it—you should also understand the practical aspects of disclosure schedules, defence statements and retention of materials.

QUESTIONS

Question 9.1

Constable STEYN was investigating a fraud case, and had taken several statements. He spoke to one particular witness, ROGERS, who claimed that another witness, MURPHY, may not possibly have seen what she said she had seen. ROGERS claims MURPHY did not like the defendant as she had been rude to her previously. However there is no evidence that MURPHY is lying in his statement and it's only ROGERS' opinion. The officer recorded this in her pocket notebook. All the statements taken indicate that the defendant passed cheques fraudulently and it was captured on CCTV.

In relation to disclosure which of the following is correct in relation to the officer's pocket notebook note?

A As there is no evidence that MURPHY may be mistaken in what she saw, the note does not have to be disclosed.

B As there is other compelling evidence, including CCTV, this note does not have to be disclosed.

C The note would have to be disclosed as it relates to the investigation and has been recorded.

D The note would have to be disclosed as it indicates a possible motive for lying by a witness.

Question 9.2

Police officers have received intelligence to suggest that an armed robbery will take place at a local post office. They set up lawful surveillance on a post office, but after a day that is withdrawn as they have intelligence to suggest that HOUSE is the suspect and the surveillance moves on to him.

Regarding the surveillance at the post office, which of the following is correct in relation to material obtained during that surveillance in line with the Criminal Procedure and Investigations Act 1996 and its definition of 'criminal investigation'?

A All the material from the investigation/operation would need to be retained and disclosed if necessary, including the location of the surveillance.

B All the material from the investigation/operation would have to be reviewed to see if it is relevant to the defence case.

C All the material from the investigation/operation is not relevant as at that time a crime had not been committed.

D All the material from the investigation/operation is not relevant as at that time a suspect had not been identified.

Question 9.3

Police officers have been carrying out covert surveillance in relation to the large-scale supply of class A drugs. They have used under cover officers and a CHIS (covert human intelligence source) and these people are clearly visible on the recorded footage. The defence have asked for this material, which was deemed to be sensitive by the prosecutor, to be made available to them.

In relation to this which of the following is correct?

A The court would decide if 'public interest immunity' applied, if it did, the material need not be disclosed.

B As the material has been considered to be sensitive, it can only be disclosed if the 'public interest immunity' test fails or with the express written approval of the Attorney General.

C As the material has been considered to be sensitive, it can only be disclosed if the 'public interest immunity' test fails or with the express written approval of the Director of Public Prosecutions.

D As the material has been considered to be sensitive, it need not be disclosed, unless the prohibitive value of it to the defence outweighed the prejudicial effect it would have on the person seen in it.

Question 9.4

KENDAL has been charged with murder, and is awaiting committal to the Crown Court.

In relation to the unused evidential material held by the prosecution, how much, if any, needs to be disclosed prior to committal to ensure KENDAL's right to a fair trial?

A All of the unused material must be disclosed, or the case may be halted as an abuse of process.

B Some of the material should be disclosed at an early stage (e.g. information to assist a bail application).

C None of the material, as the Criminal Procedure and Investigations Act 1996 requires disclosure after committal only.

D Most of the material should be disclosed, except that material which has been deemed to be 'sensitive'.

Question 9.5

BROWNLOW has been charged with an indictable offence and has been committed to Crown Court. Despite requests from the prosecution the defence has not provided a defence statement that outlines what defence he will rely on.

What level of disclosure is placed upon the prosecution?

A The proceedings may be adjourned in order that the defence statement is properly served.

B The jury at the trial may draw such inferences as appear proper in deciding the guilt or innocence of the accused.

C This will have no effect on the trial as failing to comply with rules of disclosure only affect the prosecution case.

D This will have no effect as the defence statement does not have to outline what defence the accused will rely on.

Question 9.6

By virtue of s. 5 of the Criminal Procedure and Investigations Act 1996, when a case is committed to the Crown Court, the accused must give a defence statement to the prosecutor.

What information should be contained in that statement?

A Only the defence case in general terms.

B The exact nature of the defence case.

C The defence case in general terms and areas where they take issue with the prosecution.

D The defence case in general terms and areas where they take issue with the prosecution, and why.

Question 9.7

LICARI is giving evidence at the Crown Court as a prosecution witness. During LICARI's evidence-in-chief, she gives evidence which is materially inconsistent with the first statement she made earlier to the police. In her first statement to the police LICARI stated that she had seen the accused at the place where the crime was committed about 3 hours before the crime was committed. This statement was contained in the schedule of unused material, but was not disclosed by the prosecution as it did not undermine their case. It is on her second statement to the police, which was disclosed, that she is now giving evidence.

What should the prosecution now do in relation to the first statement?

A Nothing, as disclosure rules ceased to apply when the trial began.

B Nothing, as the statement only supports the prosecution case, it does not undermine it.

C The prosecution should ensure it is retained in case of any future appeal.

D The prosecution should disclose it immediately so that the defence can use it in cross-examination to discredit the testimony of the witness.

Question 9.8

Detective Sergeant BARRY was the disclosure officer on a particularly complex fraud case; unfortunately he broke his leg playing rugby and is unable to continue in his role as disclosure officer on the case. The case is nearing the stage where secondary disclosure is to be made.

At this stage who is responsible for assigning a new disclosure officer?

A Detective Sergeant BARRY's first line manager.

B Detective Sergeant BARRY's first line manager, or the police officer in charge of the investigation.

C Detective Sergeant BARRY's first line manager, or the police officer in charge of the investigation in consultation with the Crown Prosecution Service.

D The prosecutor from the Crown Prosecution Service who is in direct charge of the investigation.

Question 9.9

During a police investigation into a street robbery, a key eyewitness provides a statement outlining in detail the description of the attacker. When the robber is eventually captured, he admits the offence on audio-recorded interview and there is ample supporting evidence to show he is guilty. The key eyewitness's description, however, is completely different from the actual appearance of the accused.

Which of the following is true in relation to whether this statement should be included on the schedule and disclosed?

A The prosecution should disclose it if the disclosure officer considers it undermines the prosecution case.

B The prosecution should disclose it only if the prosecutor considers it undermines the prosecution case.

C The prosecution should disclose it only if the prosecutor and the disclosure officer agree it undermines the prosecution case.

D The prosecution should disclose it even if no one involved in the process considers it undermines the prosecution case.

Question 9.10

Constable GUZMAN is engaged in inquiries into an allegation of assault against BANDRICK. Constable GUZMAN obtains a statement from a witness that indicates that BANDRICK was not the person responsible for the assault.

What action best outlines Constable GUZMAN's responsibility as an investigator in relation to this witness statement as required by the Code of Practice under the Criminal Procedure and Investigations Act 1996?

A He should retain the statement and include it on the relevant sensitive material schedule.

B He should retain the statement and disclose it himself as it undermines the prosecution case.

C He should carry out further investigation to gather more evidence that would assist the defence.

D He should inform the prosecutor and seek guidance as to the correct procedure to follow.

Question 9.11

Constable DIMECH received anonymous information that stolen vehicles were being hidden in a garage. She attended the area one evening with Detective Constable COLE in an unmarked police vehicle, which they used to keep observation on the garage. They saw PARNIS pull up in a Range Rover and they approached him to question him about the car. On seeing them, he sped off and was lost. PARNIS was traced 2 days later and was lawfully arrested. This was witnessed by NEACHELL. Constable DIMECH became the disclosure officer, and subsequently discovered that Detective Constable COLE was under investigation by the complaints department for giving false evidence in court in a recent case.

In relation to material that needs to be disclosed to the defence, which of the following is correct?

A A statement would have to be obtained from NEACHELL and disclosed to the defence.

B The investigation against Detective Constable COLE may have to be disclosed, even though he has not been convicted.

C The details of the police vehicle used for the observation would not need to be disclosed.

D As the anonymous information is inadmissible as evidence, the fact of its existence does not need to be conveyed to the prosecutor.

Question 9.12

The Criminal Procedure and Investigations Act 1996 outlines what statements should be disclosed in cases that involve complaints against police officers. MOTHERSOLE is the father of a youth who has made a complaint of assault against a police officer. He is aware that the police have obtained several witness statements.

In relation to these statements which of the following is correct?

A MOTHERSOLE is entitled at any time to have those statements disclosed to him.

B MOTHERSOLE is entitled at any time to have those statements disclosed to him, at the earliest at the conclusion of the investigation.

C MOTHERSOLE is not entitled to any disclosure as he is not the actual complainant.

D MOTHERSOLE is only entitled to disclosure if criminal charges are raised against the police officer.

Question 9.13

Police have been investigating drug supply and as such have been using a disused office premises nearby as an observation post. During the trial the defence ask that the jury be taken to the observation post to test what the officers could see and as such they are seeking to have the location of the observation post disclosed.

In relation to this which of the following is correct?

A The location would have to be disclosed as there are no grounds to withhold it.

B The location would have to be disclosed as it is not a private house.

C The location need not be disclosed if there is fear or threat of violence.

D The location need not be disclosed if there is fear or threat of harassment.

Question 9.14

EAST appeared in Crown Court as a defendant for an offence of robbery. Before the trial, EAST's solicitor served a defence statement on the prosecution, outlining an alibi for the offence, which the police were able to negate. EAST elected to give evidence on his own behalf during the trial and, under cross-examination, he put forward a different alibi to the offence. As a result, the prosecuting barrister sought permission from the court to examine EAST about the contents of his defence statement.

Could the prosecution's request be granted in these circumstances?

A No, under no circumstances may a defendant be cross-examined in relation to a defence statement.

B Yes, the request may be granted in these circumstances.

C No, a defendant may be cross-examined in relation to a defence statement only when he or she is accused of an offence of perjury.

D Yes, a defendant may be cross-examined in relation to a defence statement on every occasion.

Question 9.15

PRODAN has been charged with attempted rape and has been committed for trial. The disclosure officer, Detective Constable LANE, has discovered a previous allegation of crime made against the complainant in the attempted rape case, which indicated that she was a prostitute and that she had stolen from the male who had made this complaint. Detective Constable LANE discovered that the male who made this previous allegation had given false details and could not be traced; this crime had in fact been 'no crimed'.

Should this previous unsubstantiated crime complaint be disclosed under the Criminal Procedure and Investigations Act 1996?

A This should be disclosed as it is relevant material.

B This should be disclosed as it undermines the prosecution case.

C This should not be disclosed as it was a false allegation.

D This should not be disclosed as it was not recorded as a crime and is not therefore relevant material.

Question 9.16

ROGERS and BARBU were jointly charged with fraud relating to counterfeit computer software from a major software company. The prosecutor was aware that there was material in the hands of the major software company that may be prejudicial to the prosecution case; however, as the company is American they cannot get hold of the material, and the company is refusing to supply it.

What is their liability in relation to disclosure of this material to the defence?

A The prosecutor must obtain the material, or risk the prosecution being stayed.

B The prosecutor must disclose to the defence why they think the material may be prejudicial.

C The prosecutor is under no duty to disclose material that has not come into their hands.

D The prosecutor can apply to have a witness summons served against the company, but the defence cannot do so.

Question 9.17

VESELY has been charged with an offence of causing death by dangerous driving. The prosecution has given primary disclosure, the defence did not provide their defence statement until 20 days after receipt of the primary disclosure.

Which of the following is correct in relation to what the prosecution must now do?

A Consider the statement to see if secondary disclosure is required, the defence statement was served in time.

B Consider the statement to see if secondary disclosure is required, although technically it is late it is still within the 7-day leeway allowed by the court.

C Consider the statement to see if secondary disclosure is required, even though it is late.

D Consider the statement, but as it is late they are no longer under an obligation to provide secondary disclosure, that is now voluntary.

ANSWERS

Answer 9.1

Answer **D** — Primary or initial disclosure by prosecutor is covered by s. 3 of the Criminal Procedure and Investigations Act 1996. This section talks about material which 'might undermine the prosecution case against the accused'. The courts are likely to consider this to include material which has an adverse effect on the strength of the prosecution case, not just material that at some stage in the investigation has been recorded somewhere; answer C is therefore incorrect. Section 3 was amended by the Criminal Justice Act 2003, so for cases where the investigation commenced after 4 April 2005 the requirement is wider in that it covers material that might reasonably be considered capable of undermining the case for the prosecution against the accused, or of assisting the case for the accused. This introduces a more objective test and in effect incorporates the previous secondary disclosure test at this earlier stage. Clearly there is a need to guess what the defence case may be in considering what should be disclosed but this can be further reviewed after the defence disclosure.

In *Tucker* v *Crown Prosecution Service* [2008] EWCA Crim 3063, the prosecution never revealed to the defence the record containing important information as to a possible motive for a witness lying about the defendant's involvement in the offence, which led to the conviction being overturned. This was clearly material that undermined the prosecution case as it raised questions over the value of the witness's evidence. There does not need to be compelling evidence of this and the fact there is other evidence supporting the prosecution case does not undermine this duty; answers A and B are therefore incorrect.

Evidence and Procedure, para. 2.9.6.2

Answer 9.2

Answer **B** — The Criminal Procedure and Investigations Act 1996 is primarily concerned with the disclosure of material which does not form part of the prosecution case resulting from a criminal investigation (i.e. 'unused material'). A criminal investigation is defined by s. 1(4) of the 1996 Act and para. 2.1 of the Code of Practice. In order to satisfy the disclosure requirements police officers should consider recording and retaining material in the early stages of an investigation. This will include:

- investigations into crimes that have been committed;
- investigations the purpose of which is to ascertain whether a crime has been committed, with a view to the possible institution of criminal proceedings; and
- investigations which begin in the belief that a crime may be committed,

for example when the police keep premises or individuals under observation for a period of time, with a view to the possible institution of criminal proceedings; answer C is therefore incorrect.

In these cases the investigation may well have started some time before the defendant became a suspect; answer D is therefore incorrect. In such cases all the material from the investigation/operation would have to be reviewed to see if it is relevant to the defence case. In cases where there is a surveillance operation or observation point, it may be that the details of the observation point and the surveillance techniques would not be revealed but it would be necessary to retain material generating from it; answer A is therefore incorrect.

Evidence and Procedure, para. 2.9.3.3

Answer 9.3

Answer **A** — This is material which the investigator believes is not in the public interest to disclose. While the general principle that governs the 1996 Act and Art. 6 of the European Convention is that material should not be withheld from the defence, sensitive material is an exception to this. In *Van Mechelen* v *Netherlands* (1997) 25 EHRR 647, the court stated that in some cases it may be necessary to withhold certain evidence from the defence so as to preserve the fundamental rights of another individual or to safeguard an important public interest; this is the test and although prohibitive value/prejudicial effect are factors the public interest test extends beyond this; answer D is therefore incorrect. However, only such measures restricting the rights of the defence which are strictly necessary are permissible under Art. 6. It should be noted that the court did recognise that the entitlement of disclosure of relevant evidence was not an absolute right but could only be restricted as was strictly necessary. In *R* v *Keane* [1994] 1 WLR 746 Lord Taylor CJ stated that:

> the judge should carry out a balancing exercise, having regard both to the weight of the public interest in non-disclosure and to the importance of the documents to the issues of interest, present and potential, to the defence, and if the disputed material might prove a defendant's innocence or avoid a miscarriage of justice, the balance came down resoundingly in favour of disclosure.

Decisions as to what should be withheld from the defence are a matter for the court and where necessary an application to withhold the material must be made to the court (*R* v *Ward* [1993] 1 WLR 619). The application of public interest immunity was considered by the House of Lords in *R* v *H* [2004] UKHL 3. In this case the defendants were charged with conspiracy to supply a class A drug following a covert police investigation, and sought disclosure of material held by the prosecution relating to the investigation. The prosecution resisted the disclosure on grounds of public interest immunity. The court held that if the material did not weaken the prosecution case or strengthen the defence, there would be no requirement to disclose it. Only in truly borderline cases should the prosecution seek a judicial ruling on the disclosability of material in their hands. In considering any disclosure issue the trial judge had constantly to bear in mind the overriding principle that derogation from the principle of full disclosure had always to be the minimum necessary to protect the public interest in question and must never imperil the overall fairness of the trial. Once material is considered to be sensitive then it should be disclosed only if the pubic interest application fails (unless abandoning the case is considered more appropriate) or with the express written approval of the Treasury Solicitor; answers B and C are therefore incorrect (CPS Disclosure Manual, Chapters 33/34).

Evidence and Procedure, para. 2.9.6.6

Answer 9.4

Answer **B** — There has always been an ethical dimension to the duty to disclose, and the decision in *R* v *DPP, ex parte Lee* [1999] 1 WLR 1950 is an indication that it survives the introduction of the Criminal Procedure and Investigations Act 1996. In *Lee*, the Divisional Court considered whether the prosecution had a duty to disclose unused material in indictable-only offences prior to committal. The statutory framework for disclosure set out in the 1996 Act is silent as to any such duty until after committal. But there may well be reasons why it would be helpful to the defence to know of unused material at an earlier stage. For example, the following circumstances were considered by the court:

- the previous convictions of the alleged victim when they might be expected to help the defence in a bail application;
- material to help an application to stay proceedings as an abuse of process;
- material to help the defendant's arguments at committal;
- material to help the defendant prepare for trial, e.g. eyewitnesses whom the prosecution did not intend to use.

Kennedy LJ said that a responsible prosecutor might recognise that fairness required that some of this material might be disclosed. Therefore, only some of the material should be disclosed, and answers A, C and D are therefore incorrect.

Evidence and Procedure, para. 2.9.4.3

Answer 9.5

Answer **B** — Compliance with the rules of disclosure, by both the defence (answer C is therefore incorrect) and prosecution, is essential if the Criminal Procedure and Investigations Act 1996 is to have any real value. Failure to comply with the disclosure rules has implications for the defence. Where the prosecution fails to comply proceedings can be stayed; obviously this is not a sanction available where the defence fail to disclose (although the defence would not object to such a stay!). So what is the correct course of action? In cases where the defence is obliged to make disclosure to the prosecution, failure to do so may lead to the court or jury drawing such inferences as appear proper in deciding the guilt or innocence of the accused (s. 11(5) of the Criminal Procedure and Investigations Act 1996). Proceedings will not be adjourned, adverse inferences will instead be made; answer A is therefore incorrect. The defence statement should set out particulars of the matters of fact on which the defendant intends to rely, this means they will need to disclose a factual narrative of their case; answer D is therefore incorrect.

Evidence and Procedure, paras 2.9.3.4, 2.9.4.5

Answer 9.6

Answer **D** — The defence statement should outline the defence case in general terms. In addition, those issues, relevant to the case, which the accused disputes with the prosecution must be set out with reasons. This requirement to give reasons is intended to stop the defence going on a 'fishing expedition' to look speculatively at material in order to find some kind of defence. Because the defence statement must outline more than just a case in general terms, answer A is incorrect. The defence statement need not go so far as to set out the exact nature of the defence case (e.g. its oral cross-examination), and answer B is therefore incorrect. Note that the defence must outline where they are in dispute with the prosecution *and* state the reasons why, and answer C is therefore incorrect.

Evidence and Procedure, para. 2.9.4.5

Answer 9.7

Answer **D** — The duty is on the prosecution to continue to review the disclosure of prosecution material right up until the case is completed (acquittal, conviction or discontinuance of the case), and answer A is therefore incorrect. Material must be disclosed if the prosecutor forms the opinion that there is material which might undermine the prosecution case, or might reasonably be expected to assist the accused's defence. Even if the information did not undermine the prosecution case, the material might have to be disclosed, and answer B is therefore incorrect. It is worth asking a number of pertinent questions: Would the previous statement bring the witnesses' credibility into question? Would this then assist the accused's defence? If the answer to both these questions is 'yes', the prosecutor would have to do more than just retain the information: it would have to be disclosed immediately to allow the defence an opportunity effectively to cross-examine the witness, and answer C is therefore incorrect.

Evidence and Procedure, para. 2.9.4.9

Answer 9.8

Answer **B** — In all cases there must be an officer in charge of the case (OIC) and a disclosure officer.

In the Criminal Procedure and Investigations Act 1996 Code of Practice at para. 3.7 it is outlined that if, during a criminal investigation, the officer in charge of an investigation or disclosure officer for any reason no longer has responsibility for the functions falling to him, either his supervisor or the police officer in charge of investigations within the police force concerned must assign someone else to assume that responsibility. That person's identity must be recorded, as with those initially responsible for these functions in each investigation.

So it can be either the supervisor *or* the police officer in charge of criminal investigations for the police force concerned that has responsibility for reassigning the role, and there is no need to consult the CPS on this matter; answers A, C and D are therefore incorrect.

Evidence and Procedure, para. 2.9.5.11

Answer 9.9

Answer **D** — Where disclosure is required, the first task is to create a schedule of all *non-sensitive material* which may be relevant to the investigation, and which has been retained by the police but which does not form part of the prosecution case. Once the schedules have been completed, the disclosure officer must decide what material, if any (whether listed on the schedules or not), might undermine the prosecution case. The disclosure officer must draw this information to the attention of the prosecutor and the reasons why he or she believes that the material undermines the prosecution case. In addition to the schedules and copies of material which undermine the prosecution case, the Codes of Practice to the 1996 Act require the disclosure officer to provide a copy of any material, whether or not he or she considers it to undermine the prosecution case.

One example of this would be a record of the first description of a suspect given to the police by a potential witness, whether or not the description differs from that of the alleged offender. Irrespective of any person's opinion, this material would have to be disclosed, and answers A, B and C are incorrect.

Evidence and Procedure, para. 2.9.5.4

Answer 9.10

Answer **C** — Paragraph 3.4 of the Code of Practice to the Criminal Procedure and Investigations Act 1996, requires investigators to pursue all reasonable lines of inquiry, *whether these point towards or away from the suspect.* Although the officer must retain the statement, it would not fit the definition of sensitive material (i.e. material which the investigator believes it is not in the public interest to disclose). Thus, sensitive material does not mean evidence which might harm the prosecution case, and answer A is therefore incorrect. It is the prosecutors' job to disclose the statement, not the police officers', and answer B is therefore incorrect. Answer D is avoiding the clear responsibility outlined in the Code of Practice and is therefore incorrect.

Evidence and Procedure, para. 2.9.5.9

Answer 9.11

Answer **B** — What is relevant to the offence, and needs to be disclosed, is a question of fact. In *DPP* v *Metten*, [1999] EWHC Admin 49, the court held that the actual arrest for an offence was not relevant to the case as it did not fall within the definition of an investigation in s. 2(1) of the Criminal Procedure and Investigations Act 1996, and answer A is therefore incorrect.

Material obtained during an investigation does not have to be admissible in court for it to undermine the prosecution case (*R* v *Preston* (1994) 98 Cr App R 405), and therefore the anonymous information should form part of the schedule sent to the prosecutor and answer D is incorrect. Where officers have used an unmarked police vehicle for observation, information relating to the surveillance and the colour, make and model of the vehicle should not be withheld (*R* v *Brown and Daley* (1987) 87 Cr App R 52), and answer C is therefore incorrect. Disclosure of previous convictions and other matters which affect the credibility of the witness, might undermine the prosecution case. Some guidance is given by the case of *R* v *Guney* (1998) 2 Cr App R 242. In *Guney*, the court said that the defence are not entitled to be informed of every occasion when any officer has given evidence 'unsuccessfully', or whenever allegations are made against him or her. However, in this case the court felt that disclosure should have been made. It will therefore be a question of fact in each case, and consultation with the Crown Prosecution Service is advisable if there is any doubt.

Evidence and Procedure, para. 2.9.6.1

Answer 9.12

Answer **B** — Statements made by witnesses during an investigation of a complaint against a police officer are disclosable, however the timing of the disclosure may be controlled; answer A is therefore incorrect. This is the case even if criminal charges are not raised; answer D is therefore incorrect.

In *R* v *Police Complaints Authority, ex parte Green* [2002] EWCA Civ 389, the Court of Appeal stated that there is no requirement to disclose witness statements to eyewitness complainants during the course of an investigation. The evidence of such complainants could be contaminated and, therefore, disclosure would risk hindering or frustrating the very purpose of the investigation. A complainant's legitimate interests were appropriately and adequately safeguarded by his or her right to a thorough and independent investigation, to contribute to the evidence, to be kept informed of the progress of the investigation and to be given reasoned conclusions on completion of the investigation. However, a complainant had no right to participate in the investigation as though he or she were supervising it. The general rule was that complainants, whether victims or next of kin, were not entitled to the disclosure of witness statements used in the course of a police investigation until its conclusion at the earliest. Note that disclosure can be made to next of kin; answer C is therefore incorrect.

Evidence and Procedure, para. 2.9.6.5

Answer 9.13

Answer **A** — This question relates to what is known as the *Johnson* ruling. In *R* v *Johnson* [1988] 1 WLR 1377, the appellant was convicted of supplying drugs. The only evidence against him was given by police officers, who testified that, while stationed in private premises in a known drug-dealing locality, they had observed him selling drugs. The defence applied to cross-examine the officers on the exact location of the observation posts, in order to test what they could see, having regard to the layout of the street and the objects in it. In the jury's absence the prosecution called evidence as to the difficulty of obtaining assistance from the public, and the desire of the occupiers, who were also occupiers at the time of the offence, that their names and addresses should not be disclosed because they feared for their safety.

The judge ruled that the exact location of the premises need not be revealed. This extended the rules established in *R* v *Rankine* [1986] QB 861 (police protecting sources of information) and is based on the protection of the owner or occupier of the premises, and not on the identity of the observation post. Thus, where officers have witnessed the commission of an offence as part of a surveillance operation conducted from an unmarked police vehicle, information relating to the surveillance and the colour, make and model of the vehicle should not be withheld (*R* v *Brown and Daley* (1987) 87 Cr App R 52).

As the observation post was disused, *Johnson* does not apply and no protection can be given (protection could be given even if the premises were business premises, provided there were occupiers); answers B, C and D are therefore incorrect.

Evidence and Procedure, para. 2.9.6.8

Answer 9.14

Answer **B** — This issue was examined in the case of *R* v *Lowe* [2003] EWCA Crim 3182. It was held in this case that there may be occasions where the defence statement is allowed to be used in cross-examination, namely when it is alleged that the defendant has changed his or her defence, or in re-examination to rebut a suggestion of recent invention. Answer A is therefore incorrect.

Such a request will not be granted on every occasion, therefore answer D is incorrect. There is no requirement for the defendant to be facing a charge of perjury, therefore answer C is incorrect.

Evidence and Procedure, para. 2.9.4.4

Answer 9.15

Answer **A** — The Criminal Procedure and Investigations Act 1996 is concerned with the disclosure of material which is obtained during the course of a criminal investigation and which may be relevant to the investigation. Material can be in any form and should be widely interpreted. This applies to any material coming to the knowledge of officers involved in the case at any stage of the investigation or even after a suspect has been charged. This is material which the investigator, officer in charge of the case (OIC) or disclosure officer consider has some bearing on any offence being investigated or any people being investigated for those offences or any of the surrounding circumstances. The material will be relevant whether it is beneficial to the prosecution case, weakens the prosecution case or assists the defence case. It is not only material that will become 'evidence' in the case that should be considered; any information, record or thing which may have a bearing on the case can be material for the purposes of disclosure. The way in which evidence has been obtained in itself may be relevant.

The unsubstantiated crime may not undermine directly the prosecution case, but it is relevant material and ought to be disclosed; answer B is therefore incorrect. In *R* v *Bourimech* [2002] EWCA Crim 2089 the Court of Appeal held that material concerning false allegations in the past may be relevant material. Indeed in *Bourimech*, where a similar crime complaint was disclosed in a large clip of other documentation (albeit two days before trial) to the defence, and the defence failed to notice it, the appellant's conviction was quashed. The Court held that failure to previously disclose the material did amount to an unfairness in the proceedings; answers C and D are therefore incorrect.

Evidence and Procedure, para. 2.9.6.9

Answer 9.16

Answer **C** — There may be occasions in an investigation where a third party refuses to hand over material in their possession and/or allow it to be examined. Where access to the material is declined or refused by the third party and it is believed that it is reasonable to seek production of the material before a suspect is charged, the investigator should consider making an application under Sch. 1 to the Police and Criminal Evidence Act 1984 (special procedure material). Where the suspect has been charged and the third party refuses to produce the material, application will have to be made to the court for a witness summons (such an application can also be made by the defence). Answer D is therefore incorrect. The third party can then argue at court that it is not material, or that it should not be disclosed on grounds of public interest immunity.

In *R* v *Alibhai and others* [2004] EWCA Crim 681, the Court of Appeal held that the obligation to disclose third party material only arises if and when that material has come into the possession of the prosecutor and, at this early stage, when, in the opinion of the prosecutor, it might undermine the prosecution's case. However, the Attorney General requires the prosecutor to take steps to secure such material. The prosecutor enjoys a margin of consideration in relation to what are reasonable steps.

Clearly the court cannot issue summonses outside its jurisdiction and the prosecution cannot be asked to 'guess' what material the third party had or why he felt it may be prejudicial. Answers A and B are therefore incorrect.

Evidence and Procedure, para. 2.9.6.9

Answer 9.17

Answer **C** — The duty on the defence, whether the accused is represented or not, is to provide a defence statement to the court and the prosecutor within 14 days of the prosecution making primary disclosure. Although this period can be extended by the courts, there is no 'leeway' as such; answers A and B are therefore incorrect. However the courts have held that even if the defence statement is outside the 14 days the prosecution must still consider the impact of the statement in terms of the need for any further disclosure (*Murphy* v *DPP* [2006] EWHC 1753 (Admin)); answer D is therefore incorrect.

Evidence and Procedure, para. 2.9.4.7

10 Custody Officers' Duties

STUDY PREPARATION

The duties imposed by the Police and Criminal Evidence Act 1984 on custody officers are many and various, and, once again, there is no substitute for knowing them in detail. This is a big area, both in terms of its volume and its importance. The need to have custody officers at certain police stations, along with the exceptional circumstances when they will not be needed, are key areas; so too are the basic entitlements of anyone when arrested and brought to a police station.

You will need to know the occasions and grounds on which some of a suspect's entitlements can be delayed and, of course, you will have to know the highly examinable areas of clocks, relevant times and time limits. A complex scenario containing different times, days and locations can often induce panic! However, once you have got the formula for working out the relevant times clear in your mind, detention periods and reviews are very straightforward and questions on them should represent 'easy marks'.

Reviews both before and after charge should be known, as should the areas of searching prisoners, seizing property and the treatment of people in police detention.

QUESTIONS

Question 10.1

Inspector WILKINSON is on duty at a designated police station. There are no sergeants in the custody unit and no other sergeant in the police station is readily available.

In relation to who can perform custody duties in these circumstances which of the following is correct?

A Only an officer of the rank of sergeant may perform the role of custody officer.

B Only an officer of the rank of sergeant may perform the role of custody officer or a constable if a sergeant is not readily available to perform them.

C Inspector WILKINSON can always perform the role of custody officer.

D Inspector WILKINSON can perform the role of custody officer if a sergeant is not readily available to perform them.

Question 10.2

FORTEY has been arrested for an offence of theft and placed before the custody officer. Her details are obtained and items of property are taken from her, she is shown a copy of the property taken from her and asked to sign to indicate that this is a true record. She refuses to sign.

What do the Police and Criminal Evidence Act 1984 Codes of Practice state the custody officer should record?

A The fact she refused to sign should be recorded.

B The fact she refused to sign and the time she refused should be recorded.

C The fact she refused to sign should be recorded, also any reason, if given, for the refusal.

D The fact she refused to sign and the time she refused should be recorded, also any reason, if given, for the refusal.

Question 10.3

Constable PETROV has arrested HIGGINS for criminal damage at the inquiry office of a non-designated police station, where she works alone. Constable PETROV intends dealing with HIGGINS at her own station, as he is likely to be in custody only for an hour. Constable PETROV has called for assistance from Constable FRY, who works in a neighbouring station.

Would it be appropriate for Constable PETROV to act as custody officer for HIGGINS in these circumstances?

A Yes, provided she informs an on-duty inspector of her intention.

B No, she is the officer in the case and must await the arrival of Constable FRY, who should act as custody officer.

C Yes, provided she informs an inspector at a designated station of her intention.

D No, HIGGINS may not be dealt with at a non-designated station.

Question 10.4

LEEMAY is in police detention suspected of committing an assault. He was arrested at 3 pm on Monday, he arrived at the police station at 3.30 pm and his detention was authorised at 3.45 pm. Following questioning it has been decided to seek CPS advice as to whether he should be charged, this decision was made at 6 pm.

Given that the police wish to seek CPS advice, when should LEEMAY be released from custody?

A Immediately, there is no power to detain pending CPS advice.
B As soon as advice has been given, but before 3.30 pm on Tuesday.
C As soon as advice has been given, but before 3.45 pm on Tuesday.
D As soon as advice has been given, but before 6 pm on Tuesday.

Question 10.5

FORSYTHE was detained for robbery, and on his arrival at the police station his girlfriend was informed of his arrest. FORSYTHE was wanted for another offence of robbery in another police area, and the custody officer intended to transfer him there when the inquiries were complete in relation to the first offence.

What does Code C say about FORSYTHE's entitlement to have someone informed of his detention, as he will be transferred to another station?

A His girlfriend must be informed of his transfer before he is moved to another station.
B He will be entitled to have someone informed of his detention on arrival at the second station.
C His girlfriend must be informed of his transfer after he has been moved to another station.
D He has no further entitlement to have someone informed of his detention as his girlfriend has been informed.

Question 10.6

BAKER has been arrested for the theft of a radio from a motor vehicle. BAKER was arrested near the vehicle and he was accompanied by another person, who escaped the police. On his arrival at the custody office, BAKER asked the custody officer, Sergeant HOSKINS, if he could make a telephone call. The arresting officer asked for this right to be delayed, as he believed BAKER might try to alert his accomplice of his arrest.

Who would be able to authorise a delay of BAKER's right to a telephone call in these circumstances?

A An inspector may authorise such a delay.

B Only a superintendent may authorise such a delay.

C Nobody, BAKER has an absolute entitlement to make a phone call.

D The custody officer may authorise such a delay.

Question 10.7

DEYLON has been arrested for an offence of murder and arrives at the designated police station at 10 am. Due to a queue his detention was not authorised until 10.30 am. At 10.40 am the officer in charge of the investigation asks that the right to have someone informed of the arrest is withheld and gives lawful grounds for that request.

By what time, assuming the maximum time allowed is used, will this delay of rights end?

A 10 am the following day.

B 10.30 am the following day.

C 10 pm the following day.

D 10.30 pm the following day.

Question 10.8

O'REILLY has been arrested for armed robbery of a building society, where £50,000 was stolen. The officer in the case has proposed that O'REILLY be denied his right to have someone informed of his arrest, as it may alert his accomplice, who has not yet been arrested. The duty inspector is engaged at a firearms incident, but she can be contacted by mobile phone.

Would it be lawful for the inspector to authorise a delay to O'REILLY's rights over the telephone in these circumstances?

A Yes, but the decision must be recorded in writing within 24 hours.

B No, the authorisation must be given by an officer not below the rank of superintendent.

C Yes, but the decision must be recorded in writing as soon as practicable.

D No, the authorisation must be made in person.

Question 10.9

BOUCHE was arrested for the kidnap and murder of a young girl. On his way to the police station, BOUCHE made an unsolicited comment to Detective Constable STEPHENSON that he had kidnapped another girl that day and that she was being held at a friend's house. On arrival at the station, BOUCHE asked for a solicitor. Detective Constable STEPHENSON requested an interview to be authorised immediately, in order to discover the whereabouts of the child.

If Detective Constable STEPHENSON's request were granted, what should the custody officer do if BOUCHE's solicitor were to arrive during the interview?

A The solicitor may be allowed access, unless this would cause a risk to the kidnapped girl.

B The authorisation will mean that the solicitor will automatically be excluded from the interview.

C The solicitor must be allowed access to BOUCHE as soon as he or she arrives.

D An interview may not be authorised without a solicitor being present in these circumstances.

Question 10.10

PRINCE was arrested at 10 am in Reading for an offence of theft. PRINCE arrived at the police station at 10.15 am, when it was discovered that she was wanted for an offence of theft in Bristol. PRINCE was interviewed and charged with theft, and at 3 pm the same day she was taken to Bristol to be interviewed, arriving at the custody office at 4.30 pm.

What would PRINCE's 'relevant time' be, in relation to her detention in Bristol?

A 10 am.

B 3 pm.

C 10.15 am.

D 4.30 pm.

Question 10.11

Constable WISLICKI has arrested a person under s. 5 of the Prevention of Terrorism Act 2005 in order that a control order can be served against him; this control order imposes obligations on him for purposes connected with protecting members of the public from a risk of terrorism. Constable WISLICKI takes the person to the designated place.

How long can this person be kept at the designated place?

A Initially for 48 hours, which can be extended by a further 48 hours.

B Initially for 36 hours, which can be extended by a further 48 hours.

C Initially for 48 hours, which can be extended by a further 36 hours.

D Initially for 36 hours, which can be extended by a further 36 hours.

Question 10.12

PACE Code C gives guidance as to what a custody officer must record on a custody record when detaining a person with or without charge.

What details should be recorded on the custody record in these circumstances?

A The grounds for detention in the person's presence, unless it is apparent that he or she would not understand what was being said.

B The grounds for detention in the person's presence, regardless of his or her condition.

C The grounds for the person's detention which can be recorded at any time.

D The grounds for detention in the person's presence if it is practicable to do so.

Question 10.13

BROWN, MOTHERSOLE and ROBERTS have been arrested for criminal damage to a shop window. A witness saw one person from the group throwing a stone through the window, but was not able to identify the exact person who caused the damage. BROWN has been interviewed by Constable KEANE, and the officer has asked the custody officer for him to be detained until the other two suspects are interviewed.

Under what circumstances may the custody officer detain BROWN further in these circumstances?

A BROWN may be detained if the custody officer has reasonable grounds to believe it is necessary to preserve evidence.

B BROWN should be released as there is insufficient evidence against him to secure a conviction.

C BROWN may be detained if the custody officer has reasonable cause to suspect it is necessary to preserve evidence.

D BROWN may be detained until the investigation is complete against all three defendants.

Question 10.14

Constable DEAR has attended at a large department store to deal with a person suspected of theft. The officer arrests the person at 3.15 pm and decides to release them on street bail in accordance with s. 30 of the Police and Criminal Evidence Act 1984.

The person is bailed at 3.30 pm to attend at police station 'A' at 6 pm. Unfortunately the person misunderstands the instructions and arrives at police station 'B' which is nearer their home; they arrive at 6 pm.

They are re-directed to police station 'A' arriving at that police station front counter at 6.45 pm in accordance with their bail. They are taken through to the custody unit and detention is authorised at 7.20 pm.

What is the 'relevant time' as outlined in the Police and Criminal Evidence Act 1984?

A 3.30 pm, the time they were bailed.

B 6 pm, the time of arrival at the first police station in that force area.

C 6.45 pm, the time of arrival at the police station to which the notice of bail states they must attend.

D 7.20 pm, the time their detention is authorised.

Question 10.15

STIRLING has been arrested for a summary offence. At 10 pm, Detective Constable MUTKI approached the custody officer, stating that he was not in a position to charge STIRLING and that a vital witness had been identified who would not be available until 9 am the following day. Detective Constable MUTKI asked if a superintendent could authorise STIRLING's continued detention beyond 24 hours in order to speak to the witness. STIRLING has been in custody for 14 hours.

Could a superintendent authorise such a request at this stage of STIRLING's detention?

A Yes, but only after he has been in custody for at least 15 hours.

B No, not until he has been in custody for 24 hours.

C Yes, but only after an inspector has conducted a second review.

D No, as BOWYER has not been arrested for an indictable offence.

Question 10.16

Under ss. 43 and 44 of the Police and Criminal Evidence Act 1984, where a person has been in custody for 36 hours without being charged, the police must apply to a magistrate to extend that person's detention beyond that time.

What is the total amount of detention time that can be authorised by magistrates beyond the original 36 hours, before a person must be charged or released? (Do *not* consider offences under the Terrorism Act 2000.)

A 3 days.
B 72 hours.
C 36 hours.
D 60 hours.

Question 10.17

WILCE has been in custody for 26 hours, having been detained under the Terrorism Act 2000. A warrant of further detention has been applied for and granted by a magistrate, and WILCE has returned to the custody office.

At what intervals should WILCE now be reviewed in relation to his detention, and who should conduct the reviews?

A There is no requirement to conduct further reviews.
B Reviews should be conducted at least every 12 hours by an inspector.
C Reviews should be conducted at least every 9 hours by an inspector.
D Reviews should be conducted at least every 12 hours by a superintendent.

Question 10.18

CROCKER was charged and acquitted of a charge of murder by the Crown Court. Following further inquiries he was arrested under the Criminal Justice Act 2003 for that same murder and is in custody at the police station; CROCKER is not precluded from further prosecution by virtue of s. 75(3) of that Act.

Who is responsible for determining whether there is sufficient evidence to charge CROCKER with murder again?

A The custody officer.
B An officer of at least the rank of superintendent.
C An officer of at least the rank of assistant chief constable (commander in the Metropolitan Police).
D The Director of Public Prosecutions (DPP).

Question 10.19

DE LACY has been arrested for an indictable only offence (the relevant time is 11 pm on Monday) and is in custody at the city centre police station. The superintendent of that police station will be on leave from 1 pm on Tuesday and after that time there will be a rota outlining who the force 'on call' superintendent will be. DE LACY's detention clock will terminate at 11 pm on Tuesday and the officer in charge of the investigation considers that an extension of the detention clock is required; the second review is due at 2 pm on Tuesday.

What must the officer in charge of the investigation do to ensure an extension is granted?

A The superintendent responsible for the city centre police station must authorise the extension prior to terminating duty.

B The superintendent responsible for the city centre police station must authorise the extension prior to terminating duty, so the second review will have to be brought forward.

C The on call superintendent can authorise the extension at any time up to 11 pm on Tuesday.

D The on call superintendent can authorise the extension up to 11 pm on Tuesday but only after the second review.

Question 10.20

WILSON was arrested for a breach of the peace following a domestic dispute. After being in custody for 6 hours he is charged with the offence and at his solicitor's request WILSON is granted bail with conditions not to re-enter the marital home. An hour later police are called to the house and WILSON is there, the officers arrest him for breach of bail and are now before the custody officer.

What action should the custody officer now take?

A Charge WILSON with a breach of the bail conditions and consider bail again.

B Charge WILSON with a breach of bail and refuse bail due to the previous breach.

C Release WILSON as bail conditions cannot be attached to a charge of breach of the peace, only bail without conditions.

D Release WILSON as he has committed no criminal offence and therefore should not have been arrested.

Question 10.21

KEY was arrested for affray, and on his arrival at the custody suite he was violent towards the custody officer. KEY was taken to a cell because of his behaviour and, because he had not been searched, the custody officer ordered him to be searched in the cell. The arresting officer, who was female, was present in the cell when KEY was searched by the male custody staff.

Have the provisions of s. 54 of the Police and Criminal Evidence Act 1984 (searching of detained persons) been complied with in these circumstances?

A Yes, a female officer may search a male prisoner, provided it is not an intimate search.

B Yes, provided the female officer did not conduct the search.

C No, the female officer should not have been present at the search.

D Yes, a female officer may search a male prisoner, provided it is not a strip search.

Question 10.22

MURTAGH was arrested and interviewed in relation to a terrorist offence and there is sufficient evidence to charge him. During the interviews MURTAGH was denied access to a solicitor and the charging officer is considering how MURTAGH should be cautioned when charged.

What should the words of this caution be?

A You do not have to say anything. But it may harm your defence if you do not mention now something which you later rely on in court. Anything you do say may be given in evidence.

B You do not have to say anything. But it may harm your defence if you do not mention when questioned something which you later rely on in court. Anything you do say may be given in evidence.

C You do not have to say anything, but anything you do say may be given in evidence.

D You do not have to say anything, but anything you do say will be noted down, and may be given in evidence.

Question 10.23

KENWRIGHT was arrested and taken to the custody office of a designated police station. The arresting officer told the custody officer that KENWRIGHT had a warning signal on Police National Computer (PNC) that, while in custody previously, she had concealed razor blades in her mouth and had used them to cause injury to herself. The custody officer decided that KENWRIGHT's mouth should be searched for objects which she might use to harm herself.

Which of the following is true in relation to the search?

A The custody officer can authorise this search at the custody office.
B Only a superintendent can authorise this search at the custody office.
C An inspector can authorise this search at medical premises.
D Only a superintendent can authorise this search at medical premises.

Question 10.24

GOODEY was arrested for deception and was accompanied at the time by her boyfriend, BEDFORD. When he was interviewed at the station, BEDFORD admitted that GOODEY was in possession of a stolen credit card, which she had concealed in her vagina. GOODEY admitted possession of the credit card, but refused to submit to a search.

Could GOODEY be subjected to an 'intimate search' in these circumstances?

A Yes, but this could not be done by force.
B Yes, she is in possession of stolen property.
C Yes, and this may be done, if necessary, by force.
D No, an intimate search may not be authorised in these circumstances.

Question 10.25

WILKINSON is arrested for murder and is interviewed several times. At the end of the day WILKINSON is placed in a rest period, and after 3 hours his solicitor requests that he be allowed to speak to his client to obtain fresh instructions.

In relation to this which of the following is correct?

A The rest period can only be interrupted at the request of the detainee, not his legal representative.
B A full 8-hour rest period must be given at the end of the consultation requested.
C At the end of the consultation requested the rest period the accused is entitled to will now be 5 hours long.
D A rest period can only be interrupted where there is a risk of harm to people or serious loss of, or damage to, property so the consultation will not be allowed.

Question 10.26

In relation to the treatment and welfare of a detained person, the PACE Codes of Practice, Code C, para. 8.6 describes how many meals a detainee should be offered whilst in custody.

How many meals should be offered to a detained person in any period of 24 hours?

A At least one light meal and at least two main meals.

B At least one light meal and at least one main meal.

C At least two light meals and at least one main meal.

D At least two light meals and at least two main meals.

Question 10.27

JOHNSON is employed as a civilian detention officer by his local police authority.

In relation to duties that he can perform, which of the following is correct?

A He may take a non-intimate sample, but he may not use force to do so.

B He may take a non-intimate sample and may use force to do so where necessary.

C He may take fingerprints and photographs, but may not take non-intimate samples.

D He may take photographs, but may not take fingerprints or non-intimate samples.

Question 10.28

PATCH, aged 21, was arrested for theft and taken to the custody office, where she asked for her father to be informed of her detention. When the custody officer spoke to PATCH's father, he informed her that PATCH was suffering from a mental disorder, which would make it difficult for her to understand questions being put to her about the offence. PATCH's condition was not apparent to either the custody officer or the arresting officer.

In relation to PATCH's detention, what action should the custody officer now take?

A The custody officer must contact an appropriate adult, based on the information received from PATCH's father.

B The custody officer must contact a medical practitioner to seek advice on PATCH's condition before she is interviewed.

C The custody officer may decide whether or not an appropriate adult should be called, based on her own observations.

D The custody officer must contact a medical practitioner or a social worker to seek advice on PATCH's condition before she is interviewed.

Question 10.29

MELFORD has been arrested for an offence of assault and has been given his rights under PACE. He has opted to speak with his solicitor on the phone, but wants to do so privately.

In relation to this request, which of the following statements is correct?

A He should be allowed to speak to his solicitor, but in private only if this is practicable.

B He should be allowed to speak to his solicitor privately, and such a facility should normally be provided.

C He is allowed to consult with his solicitor privately only if this is done in person.

D He should be allowed to consult with his solicitor, but this must be done whilst the custody officer can hear the conversation.

Question 10.30

FELICE was arrested for an offence of theft, but will not be charged as there was insufficient evidence. Police wish to take FELICE's photograph for future use whilst she is still in police detention.

In relation to taking the photograph, which of the following is correct?

A The photograph can be taken without FELICE's consent and used for identification procedures.

B The photograph can be taken, but only if FELICE gives her permission.

C The photograph can be taken without FELICE's consent, but cannot be used for identification procedures.

D The photograph cannot be taken, as FELICE has not been charged or reported for a recordable offence.

Question 10.31

HURTY was stopped while driving his vehicle on a Saturday morning in Margate. The officer who stopped him, Constable DICKINSON, conducted a Police National

Computer (PNC) check and discovered that HURTY was wanted for an offence of burglary in the Newcastle area. Constable DICKINSON arrested HURTY at 10 am and took him to the nearest designated station in Margate, where they arrived at 10.30 am. Constable DICKINSON contacted the police in Newcastle; however, they had no officers available to attend until later that day. The escorting officers finally arrived in the early hours of the next morning, and left with HURTY at 4 am on the Sunday. They transported HURTY to Newcastle, arriving in that force area at 11.10 am; they eventually arrived at Newcastle Police Station at 11.30 am on the Sunday.

What would HURTY's 'relevant time' be, in relation to his detention in Newcastle, if he was not interviewed for the offence in Margate?

A 10.30 am on the Saturday.

B 10 am on the Sunday.

C 11.10 am on the Sunday.

D 11.30 am on the Sunday.

Question 10.32

Constable MOLE arrested WOOD at 3 pm on a Saturday for an offence of theft. Constable MOLE radioed through to her station, but discovered that the custody office could not accept her prisoner at that time, as they were too busy. She decided to utilise her powers under s. 30A of the Police and Criminal Evidence Act 1984, to bail WOOD to the police station the next day. WOOD was released on bail by the officer at 3.30 pm on the Saturday. WOOD was due to answer bail at 2 pm on the Sunday, but he was late and arrived there at 2.30 pm. His detention was authorised by the custody officer at 2.50 pm.

From which time on the Sunday would WOOD's 'relevant time' be calculated, under s. 41 of the Police and Criminal Evidence Act 1984?

A 2.50 pm, the time he appeared before the custody officer on the Sunday.

B 2.20 pm, taking into account the time he was detained by the officer the previous day.

C 2.30 pm, the time he arrived at the police station on the Sunday.

D 2 pm, the time he was due to answer bail on the Sunday.

Question 10.33

Authorisation to search detainees and examine them to ascertain their identity under s. 54A of the Police and Criminal Evidence Act 1984 must be obtained by the custody officer.

Who, out of the following, can correctly give such authorisation?

A An officer of at least the rank of superintendent only, either orally or in writing, provided it is confirmed in writing as soon as practicable.

B An officer of at least the rank of inspector before charge, or a custody officer after charge, either orally or in writing, provided it is confirmed in writing as soon as practicable.

C An officer of at least the rank of inspector, either orally or in writing, provided it is confirmed in writing as soon as practicable.

D An officer of at least the rank of inspector, and permission may only be given in writing.

Question 10.34

WHITE is 14 years of age and has been arrested on suspicion of raping a girl his own age. The witness has described a distinguishable tattoo that the attacker had on his chest, and WHITE has agreed to have a photograph of a tattoo on his chest taken for identification purposes. WHITE was photographed by a male police officer in the medical room and no other people were present. WHITE was made to remove only his shirt, and the tattoo on his chest was photographed. This was done without the presence of an appropriate adult, as WHITE had signified that he did not want one present.

Did the search and photographing of the tattoo comply with the codes of practice, in respect of dealing with juvenile detainees?

A Yes, as WHITE had signified that he did not want an appropriate adult present.

B No, there must *always* be at least one other person present, even if an appropriate adult does not have to be present.

C Yes, because the officer was not photographing intimate parts of the body, the presence of an appropriate adult was not necessary.

D No, because an appropriate adult should have been present in the above circumstances.

Question 10.35

DING was arrested for being found drunk in a public place. He was so intoxicated that, when he arrived at the station, he was placed in a cell after being searched and fell asleep immediately. DING had nothing in his property which would have assisted in identifying him, therefore the arresting officer asked the custody officer whether DING could be examined without his consent, while he was asleep, to establish if he had any tattoos that might assist in identifying him.

Could an examination be authorised without DING's consent, under s. 54A of the Police and Criminal Evidence Act 1984, in these circumstances?

A Yes, because it was not practicable to obtain his consent.

B No, an examination may be conducted without a detainee's consent only where that person has refused to give consent.

C No, an examination may be conducted without consent only in cases of urgency.

D No, because the officer was not attempting to establish whether DING was a person who had been involved in the commission of an offence.

Question 10.36

MORRISON was arrested for shoplifting and taken to the custody office. On MORRISON's arrival, the custody officer noticed that he was intoxicated. MORRISON was detained for interview and placed in a cell to allow him time to sober up. While he was asleep, MORRISON's sister contacted the custody officer to advise that MORRISON was an alcoholic and might get the shakes while in custody. When he was sober, MORRISON was interviewed and returned to his cell pending preparation of charges. He displayed no symptoms of the shakes, and did not complain of an illness. Unfortunately, while he was in his cell, MORRISON died from asphyxiation. MORRISON was not medically examined while in custody.

Would the police have any liability in relation to the custody officer's failure to act on the information given by MORRISON's sister, and not arranging for him to be medically examined?

A No, as MORRISON's sister is not a registered health care professional or doctor.

B Yes, a custody officer should act on any information relating to a detainee's health care, no matter what the source.

C No, since MORRISON displayed no symptoms of his illness and did not ask to see a doctor.

D Yes, but only if MORRISON's sister informed the custody officer that he was taking medication or seeking medical help for his condition.

Question 10.37

Code C, para. 2.1A of the PACE Codes of Practice defines when a detained person will be deemed to be 'at a police station' for the purposes of detention.

Which of the following statements most accurately describes when a detained person will be 'at a police station' according to this code of practice?

A When the person first arrives within the confines of the custody office, whether or not the custody officer is ready to receive them.

B When the person is first brought before the custody officer, within the confines of the custody office.

C When the person first arrives inside a police station, whether this is the custody office or another part of the building.

D When the person first arrives within the confines of the police station, whether this is inside the building or in an enclosed yard which is part of the police station.

Question 10.38

BRAITHWAITE is 13 years of age and was arrested for an offence of aggravated vehicle taking. On his arrival at the custody office, BRAITHWAITE declined legal advice and stated that neither of his parents would attend the police station to act as an appropriate adult. BOYCE works for the local Youth Offending Team (YOT) and attended to act as appropriate adult. On arrival at the custody office, BOYCE told the custody officer that it was their policy that all juveniles represented by the YOT must also be represented by a solicitor. BOYCE insisted on a solicitor being called.

Would BOYCE be able to overrule BRAITHWAITE's decision, and ensure that he seeks legal advice?

A Yes, as BOYCE was acting in BRAITHWAITE's best interests.

B No, BOYCE had no right to ask for a solicitor to attend once BRAITHWAITE had declined legal advice.

C Yes, because BRAITHWAITE is under 14 and it is in his best interests.

D No, the decision remains with BRAITHWAITE, who does not have to speak to the solicitor.

Question 10.39

Code C, para. 3.4 of the PACE Codes of Practice requires the custody officer to note on the custody record any comment the detainee makes in relation to the arresting officer's account.

According to this code of practice, which of the following statements is correct in relation to who may give the account of the arrest?

A The account may only be given by the arresting officer, but this may be done from a remote location.

B The account may be given from a remote location by the arresting officer, or through another officer accompanying the detainee.

C The arresting officer must be present to give the account in order for any comments to be admissible.

D The officer giving the account must be at the custody office, whether it is the arresting officer or another officer.

Question 10.40

A person may be detained without charge when they are suspected of having committed an offence under the Terrorism Act 2000.

What is the maximum period they may be detained for?

A 96 hours.

B 7 days.

C 28 days.

D 21 days.

Question 10.41

DAWLISH has been interviewed about a large-scale fraud offence. The officers have concluded their investigation but ask that DAWLISH be bailed without charge for further consultation with the National Fraud Office to take place. The officers intend seeking CPS advice on charging when DAWLISH returns on bail. The custody officer is going to release DAWLISH on bail under s. 37(7)(b) of the Police and Criminal Evidence Act 1984 as she believes there is sufficient evidence to charge DAWLISH but is releasing him to allow for further inquiries to be made. The investigating officers, however, are concerned DAWLISH may try to leave the country and ask that as a condition of bail he surrenders his passport.

In relation to this request which of the following is correct?

A The custody officer can impose bail conditions as s. 47 of the Police and Criminal Evidence Act 1984 allows normal powers to impose conditions of bail where a custody officer releases a person on bail under s. 37.

B The custody officer can impose bail conditions as s. 47 of the Police and Criminal Evidence Act 1984 allows normal powers to impose conditions of bail where a custody officer releases a person on bail under s. 37 and CPS advice will be sought when bail is answered.

C The custody officer cannot impose conditions of bail where the custody officer considers that there is sufficient evidence to charge.

D The custody officer cannot impose conditions of bail where a person is released under s. 37 unless that the person is released for the purpose of a CPS referral.

Question 10.42

BAILLON has been arrested for an offence of kidnapping and the relevant time began at 10 am on Tuesday. Unfortunately he became ill and had to go to hospital; he left the custody unit at 4 pm arriving at the hospital at 4.30 pm. He remained at the hospital until 9.30 pm and arrived back in custody at 10 pm. Throughout his time in hospital officers remained with him hoping to interview him regarding the whereabouts of the yet unfound victim. However the casualty doctors refused to allow any questioning of BAILLON.

At what time will BAILLON's detention time end (assuming no extensions are applied for or granted)?

A 10 am on Wednesday; the hospital time counts as officers were present intending to interview BAILLON.

B 3 pm on Wednesday; standard detention time excluding the time spent in hospital.

C 3.30 pm on Wednesday; standard detention time excluding the time spent in hospital and travelling to hospital.

D 4 pm on Wednesday; standard detention time excluding the time spent in hospital and time travelling to and from hospital.

ANSWERS

Answer 10.1

Answer **D** — Section 36 of the Police and Criminal Evidence Act 1984 requires that one or more custody officers must be appointed for each designated police station. However, in *Vince* v *Chief Constable of Dorset* [1993] 1 WLR 415 it was held that a chief constable was under a duty to appoint one custody officer for each designated police station and had a discretionary power to appoint more than one but this duty did not go so far as to require a sufficient number to ensure that the functions of custody officer were always performed by them.

The provision of the facility of a custody officer must be reasonable. Section 36(3) states that a custody officer must be an officer of at least the rank of sergeant. However, s. 36(4) allows officers of *any* rank to perform the functions of custody officer at a designated police station if a sergeant is not readily available to perform; answer A is therefore incorrect. This means that, as unlikely as it seems, officers higher in rank than a sergeant can perform custody duties and not just constables; answer B is therefore incorrect. However this is only where a sergeant is not readily available to perform them; answer C is therefore incorrect.

The effect of s. 36(3) and (4) is that the practice of allowing officers of any other rank to perform the role of custody officer where a sergeant (who has no other role to perform) is in the police station must therefore be unlawful.

Evidence and Procedure, para. 2.10.5

Answer 10.2

Answer **B** — If a person is requested to sign an entry on a custody record in accordance with the Police and Criminal Evidence Act 1984 Codes of Practice and refuses, this too should be recorded, as should the time the detained person refused (Code C, para. 2.7); answer A is therefore incorrect. There is no requirement for the person to give reasons for their refusal, nor for this reason to be recorded; answers C and D are therefore incorrect.

Evidence and Procedure, para. 2.10.5

Answer 10.3

Answer **C** — Section 30 of the Police and Criminal Evidence Act 1984 states that an arrested person should be taken to a designated station as soon as practicable after arrest, unless he or she has been bailed prior to arrival at the police station. Section 30A of the Police and Criminal Evidence Act 1984 allows a constable to release on bail a person who is under arrest. However, an arrested person may be dealt with at a non-designated station, provided the person is not likely to be detained for longer than six hours. Answer D is therefore incorrect.

Where a person is taken to a non-designated station, s. 36(7) states that an officer of any rank not involved in the investigation should perform the role of custody officer. However, if no such person is at the station, the arresting officer (or any other officer involved in the investigation) may act as custody officer. Answer B is therefore incorrect.

Where a person is dealt with in a non-designated station in the circumstances described, an officer of at least the rank of inspector at a *designated station* must be informed. Answer A is therefore incorrect.

Evidence and Procedure, para. 2.10.5

Answer 10.4

Answer **B** — The relevant time is the time the person arrives at the police station, or 24 hours after arrest (whichever is earlier). So normally speaking the person in this case should be released by 3.30 pm on Tuesday.

Previously where a case is referred to the Crown Prosecution Service to determine whether proceedings should be instituted (and if so on which charge), it was the case that if the decision to charge was not made at the time the detained person had to be released on police bail with or without conditions, however the Police and Justice Act 2006 has amended PACE, s. 37 and the person can now be kept in police detention pending the decision; answer A is therefore incorrect.

However this change is still subject to the normal time limits for detention, and the person will still have to be released by 3.30 pm on Tuesday; answers C and D are therefore incorrect.

Evidence and Procedure, para. 2.10.6.8

Answer 10.5

Answer **B** — A person in police detention is entitled to have one friend or relative or person known to him/her or who is likely to take an interest in his/her welfare informed of his or her whereabouts as soon as practicable (PACE Code C, para. 5.1).

Code C, paras 3.1 and 5.3 outline that this is a continuing right that applies every time a person is brought to a police station under arrest. This means that a person may have another person (or the same person) informed of his or her detention at the second station. Answer D is therefore incorrect. Note it is the detained person's right; no one has the right to be told of detention without the detained person's permission.

There is no specific requirement for the custody officer to re-contact the person who was originally informed of the detention, either before or after the prisoner has been moved. Answers A and C are therefore incorrect.

Evidence and Procedure, para. 2.10.6.2

Answer 10.6

Answer **A** — Detained people are entitled to speak to a person on the telephone for a reasonable time, or send letters. The right can be denied or delayed when a person has been arrested for an indictable offence. Answer C is incorrect for this reason.

PACE Code C, para. 5.6 states that an officer of the rank of *inspector* or above may authorise the delay if he or she has reasonable grounds for believing, amongst other things, that by allowing the person to exercise his or her right, it will alert other people suspected of having committed such an offence but not yet arrested for it. A superintendent may authorise the delay as well as an inspector, and therefore answer B is incorrect. A custody officer may not authorise such a delay (unless of course the custody officer is an inspector). Answer D is therefore incorrect.

Evidence and Procedure, para. 2.10.6.2

Answer 10.7

Answer **C** — Section 56 of the Police and Criminal Evidence Act 1984 provides that a person arrested and held in custody at a police station or other premises may, on request, have one friend or relative or person known to him/her or who is likely to take an interest in his/her welfare, informed at public expense of his/her whereabouts as soon as practicable (PACE Code C, para. 5.1). This right can only be delayed if the offence is 'an indictable offence' and an officer of the rank of inspector or above (whether or not connected to the investigation) authorises the delay. The delay can only be for a maximum of 36 hours (48 hours in cases involving terrorism), and the 36-hour period is calculated from the 'relevant time', that is the time of arrival at the police station, i.e 10 am. So the maximum time is 36 hours, add that to 10 am and that is 10 pm the following day – answer C, making answers A, B and D incorrect.

Evidence and Procedure, para. 2.10.6.2

Answer 10.8

Answer **C** — First, the inspector must be satisfied that O'REILLY is in custody for an indictable offence (which is the case in the scenario). Also, the inspector must have reasonable grounds for believing that if O'REILLY were to exercise his right to have someone informed of his arrest, it might alert other people suspected of the offence but not yet arrested.

PACE Code C, Annex B states that the grounds for action under this Annex shall be recorded and the person informed of them as soon as practicable. The authorisation can initially be made orally, either in person or by telephone, but must be recorded in writing as soon as practicable. Answer D is therefore incorrect.

The decision must be recorded in writing *as soon as practicable*; therefore, answer A is incorrect.

The authorising officer for delaying rights under Code C, para. 5 was reduced from superintendent to inspector by virtue of s. 74 of the Criminal Justice and Police Act 2001; therefore answer B is incorrect.

Evidence and Procedure, para. 2.10.6.2

Answer 10.9

Answer **A** — A superintendent must be satisfied that BOUCHE is in custody for an indictable offence (which is the case in the scenario). Also, the superintendent must have reasonable grounds for believing that to delay an interview will involve an *immediate* risk of harm to people (PACE Code C, para. 6.6(b)(i)). Again, given the circumstances in the question, this is a reasonable assumption, and answer D is incorrect for this reason.

If an interview is authorised in these circumstances (sometimes this is called an 'urgent interview'), it does not mean that the solicitor will be automatically excluded on his or her arrival, and answer B is therefore incorrect.

When an interview has been started without the solicitor being present, he or she must be allowed to be present when he or she arrives, *unless* para. 6.6(b)(i) applies (i.e. the delay will involve an immediate risk of harm to people). Answer C is incorrect because of this exception.

Evidence and Procedure, para. 2.10.6.6

Answer 10.10

Answer **D** — Under s. 41(2) of the Police and Criminal Evidence Act 1984, a person's 'relevant time' is calculated from the time he or she arrives at the police station, or 24 hours after he or she was arrested, whichever is earlier. Since most detainees arrive at the station well within 24 hours, their relevant time is generally when they first arrive at the station.

There are several variations contained within s. 41 of the 1984 Act, and the circumstances covered in the question are to be found in s. 41(5). Section 41 states:

> (5) If—
> (a) a person is in police detention in a police area in England and Wales ('the first area'); and
> (b) his arrest for an offence is sought in some other police area in England and Wales ('the second area'); and
> (c) he is taken to the second area for the purposes of investigating that offence, without being questioned in the first area in order to obtain evidence in relation to it,
> the relevant time shall be—
> (i) the time 24 hours after he leaves the place where he is detained in the first area; *or*
> (ii) the time at which he arrives at the first police station to which he is taken in the second area,
> whichever is the earlier.

Note that under s. 41(5), the detainee has, in effect, two detention clocks running. It is important to note that the second clock will start earlier if the detained person is questioned about the offence under investigation in the other police area. However, in the scenario PRINCE was *not* questioned about the offence in the first station, and she arrived at the second station *less than 24 hours* after her departure from the first station. Her relevant time is, therefore, her time of arrival at the second station (i.e. 4.30 pm). Answers A, B and C are therefore incorrect.

Evidence and Procedure, para. 2.10.6.8

Answer 10.11

Answer **A** — The Prevention of Terrorism Act 2005 allows a control order to be served against an individual that imposes obligations on him/her for purposes connected with protecting members of the public from a risk of terrorism.

Section 5 of the 2005 Act allows a constable to arrest a person to ensure that the order can be served on that person. Section 5(2) requires the constable who has arrested an individual to take him/her to the designated place (which is the same as the Terrorism Act 2000) that the constable considers most appropriate as soon as practicable after the arrest.

An individual taken to a designated place under this section may be detained there until the end of 48 hours from the time of his or her arrest unless:

- he or she has become bound by a derogating control order made against him/her on the Secretary of State's application; or
- the court has dismissed the application.

If the court considers that it is necessary to do so to ensure that the individual in question is available to be given notice of any derogating control order that is made against him, it may, during the 48 hours following his arrest, extend the period for which the individual may be detained under this section by a period of no more than 48 hours (Prevention of Terrorism Act 2005, s. 5).

So this is initially 48 hours, which can be extended by a further 48 hours which is answer A; therefore answers B, C and D are incorrect.

Evidence and Procedure, para. 2.10.7.7

Answer 10.12

Answer **D** — Under PACE Code C, para. 3.23, a custody officer should record the grounds for detention in the person's presence if it is practicable to do so. Therefore, in cases such as when a person is drunk or violent, it may not be practicable to record the grounds in his or her presence. Answer B is therefore incorrect. This recording of the grounds must, by virtue of Code C, para. 3.4, be before that person is questioned about any offence; answer C is therefore incorrect.

Answer A is incorrect. If a person cannot understand what is being said, it may be 'impracticable' to record the grounds for detention in his or her presence; however, it is not written as such in the Codes of Practice.

Evidence and Procedure, para. 2.10.6.9

Answer 10.13

Answer **A** — If the custody officer has determined there is insufficient evidence to charge, the person must be released unless the custody officer has *reasonable grounds for believing* that the person's detention is necessary to preserve or to obtain evidence by questioning the person (s. 37 of the Police and Criminal Evidence Act 1984). Answer C is incorrect as 'reasonable grounds for believing' requires a greater amount of evidence than 'reasonable cause to suspect'.

Although the person may ultimately be detained until all the suspects are interviewed in these circumstances, each case must be considered on its own merit, against the above criteria. Answer D is therefore incorrect.

Where the suspicion rests with several suspects, it may be appropriate to hold all suspects until they are all interviewed before deciding whether there is sufficient evidence to warrant a charge against any or all of them. This continues provided suspicion on that individual has not been dispelled in the interim and the questioning is not unnecessarily delayed (*Clarke* v *Chief Constable of North Wales*, Independent, 22 May 2000); answer B is therefore incorrect.

Evidence and Procedure, para. 2.10.6.12

Answer 10.14

Answer **C** — The 'relevant time' is worked out according to the relevant circumstances.

Where a person is arrested and bailed at a place other than a police station the time of arrival at the police station to which the notice of bail states he or she must attend is the relevant time. In this particular case then the relevant time is 6.45 pm, no account is taken of the time they are bailed, or the time they arrived at the wrong police station (irrespective of the fact it is in the same police area); answers A and B are therefore incorrect.

The time of detention relates to the review clock, not the 'relevant time'; answer D is therefore incorrect.

Evidence and Procedure, para. 2.10.6.8

Answer 10.15

Answer **D** — An officer of at least the rank of superintendent can authorise a person's continued detention, beyond 24 hours, up to a maximum of 36 hours. The period can be shorter, but if a shorter period is granted, this can be extended up to the 36-hour limit.

The superintendent must be satisfied that an offence being investigated is an 'indictable offence' and that there is not sufficient evidence to charge, *and* the investigation is being conducted diligently and expeditiously, *and* that the person's detention is necessary to secure and preserve evidence or obtain evidence by questioning (s. 42 of the Police and Criminal Evidence Act 1984).

The extension of a person's detention must be made *within 24 hours* of the relevant time. Also, the extension cannot be granted before *at least two reviews* have been carried out by the reviewing inspector.

Although reviews are normally carried out after six and nine hours, they can be conducted earlier. Section 42(4) is deliberately worded, so that the focus is not on the length of time a person has been in custody, but on how many reviews have been conducted.

A superintendent could authorise an extension in these circumstances, but would have to wait until a second review had been conducted.

As BOWYER was arrested for a summary offence no extension beyond the 24-hour period of initial detention can be made; answers A, B and C are therefore incorrect.

Evidence and Procedure, para. 2.10.7.4

Answer 10.16

Answer **D** — A superintendent may authorise a person's detention without charge to a maximum of 36 hours (s. 42 of the Police and Criminal Evidence Act 1984). Any further periods of detention must be authorised by a magistrate.

A magistrate may initially authorise detention for 36 hours (s. 43). However, this period may be extended by 24 hours upon further application (s. 44), which means that a magistrate may authorise a maximum detention period of 60 hours. A person may not be detained for longer than 96 hours in total without being charged or released. Answers A, B and C are therefore incorrect.

Evidence and Procedure, para. 2.10.7.5

Answer 10.17

Answer **A** — Where a person is in custody for an offence under the Terrorism Act 2000, the first review should be conducted as soon as reasonably practicable after his or her arrest and then at least every 12 hours; after 24 hours it must be conducted by an officer of the rank of superintendent or above. Once a warrant of further detention has been obtained there is no requirement to conduct further reviews. Section 14 of Code H of the Police and Criminal Evidence Act 1984 codes of practice provides guidance on terrorism reviews and extensions of detention.

Answer D would be correct only if the person was in custody prior to going to court for the warrant of further detention hearing. Answer B would be incorrect in any circumstances; once a person has been in custody for longer than 24 hours, having been arrested under the 2000 Act, his or her detention must be reviewed by a superintendent. Answer C is incorrect as reviews of people detained under the 2000 Act must be conducted every 12 hours, following the first review.

Evidence and Procedure, para. 2.10.7.7

Answer 10.18

Answer **B** — When a person is arrested under the provisions of the Criminal Justice Act 2003, which allow a person to be re-tried after being acquitted of a serious offence which is a qualifying offence specified in sch. 5 to that Act and not precluded from further prosecution by virtue of s. 75(3) of that Act, the detention provisions of PACE are modified and make an officer of the rank of superintendent or above who has not been directly involved in the investigation responsible for determining whether the evidence is sufficient to charge; answers A, C and D are therefore incorrect.

Evidence and Procedure, para. 2.10.9.1

Answer 10.19

Answer **D** — Under s. 42(1) of the Police and Criminal Evidence Act 1984, detention can only be authorised beyond 24 hours and up to a maximum of 36 hours from the relevant time if:

- an offence being investigated is an 'indictable offence'; and
- an officer of the rank of superintendent or above who is responsible for the station at which the person is detained (referred to here as the authorising officer); and
- that senior officer is satisfied that:
  - — there is not sufficient evidence to charge; and
  - — the investigation is being conducted diligently and expeditiously; and
  - — that the person's detention is necessary to secure or preserve evidence relating to the offence or to obtain such evidence by questioning that person.

The grounds for this continuing detention are the same as those when the custody officer made the initial decision to detain, with the additional requirements that the case has been conducted diligently and expeditiously. It is suggested that Art. 5 of the European Convention requires this to be a consideration at all times of detention as a person's right to freedom is one of his or her human rights and any unnecessary periods of detention might be considered actionable. To be able to satisfy the senior officer of this, it will be necessary for the custody record to be available for inspection and details of what inquiries have been made, and evidence that the investigation has been moving at a pace that will satisfy the senior officer that the inquiries should not already have been completed. Code C, para. 15.2A outlines issues to be considered before extending the period of juveniles and mentally vulnerable persons.

The authorising officer (which here must be an officer of the rank of superintendent or above who is responsible for the station at which the person is detained) can authorise detention up to a maximum of 36 hours from the 'relevant time' of detention. The period can be shorter than this and can then be further authorised by that officer or any other officer of the rank of superintendent or above who is responsible for the station at which the person is detained to allow the period to be further extended up to the maximum 36-hour period (s. 42(2)). Code C, Note 15E gives guidance as to which officers this would include. This section outlines that the officer responsible for the station holding the detainee includes a superintendent or above who, in accordance with their force operational policy or police regulations, is given that responsibility on a temporary basis whilst the appointed long-term holder is off duty or otherwise unavailable. So although the superintendent in charge of the city centre police station is clearly the person defined by this section, Note 15E allows for eventualities where they are absent. It would be wrong to bring forward reviews and authorise extensions some time before the clock runs out to accommodate someone going on leave; answers A and B are therefore incorrect.

The extension of a person's detention by a superintendent or above must be made within 24 hours of the relevant time and cannot be made before at least two reviews have been carried out by a review officer under s. 40 of the 1984 Act (i.e. those normally carried out by an inspector) (s. 42(4)) (Code C, para. 15.2); answer C is therefore incorrect.

Evidence and Procedure, para. 2.10.7.4

Answer 10.20

Answer **D** — If the person is charged then the custody officer has to decide whether the person is going to be bailed to appear at court (and any conditions of bail) or whether bail will be refused and the person kept in custody until the next available court. This is a review of the person's detention and therefore the person or his/her solicitor should be given an opportunity to make representations to the custody officer.

However this relates to criminal proceedings only. In *Williamson* v *Chief Constable of West Midlands* [2004] 1 WLR 14, the Court of Appeal clarified the point that breach of the peace is not a criminal offence. Consequently, as there is no power in the Bail Act 1976 to grant bail except in criminal proceedings, no power exists to grant bail for breach of the peace; answer C is therefore incorrect. This means that if the person is bailed, there is no power to arrest the person or obtain a warrant for his/her failure to appear at court under the Bail Act 1976 or if they breach their conditions of that bail.

Hopefully the custody officer will now not compound their earlier mistake by selecting options A and B as they are incorrect.

Evidence and Procedure, para. 2.10.10

Answer 10.21

Answer **B** — Under s. 54(9) of the Police and Criminal Evidence Act 1984, the constable carrying out a search must be of the same sex as the person searched. Section 54 does not prohibit a constable of the opposite sex from being present at a search, provided it is not a strip search or an intimate search. Answer C is therefore incorrect.

Because of the prohibition referred to above, under s. 54(9), a constable may *not* search a person of the opposite sex, whether during an ordinary search, a strip search or an intimate search. Answers A and D are therefore incorrect.

Evidence and Procedure, para. 2.10.11.8

Answer 10.22

Answer **C** — If a decision is taken to charge the detained person, Code C, para. 16 sets out the procedures to be followed by the custody officer. When a detained person is charged with or informed that he/she may be prosecuted for an offence, para. 16.2 requires him/her to be cautioned. The caution varies slightly from that when arrested or interviewed and is as follows:

> You do not have to say anything. But it may harm your defence if you do not mention now something which you later rely on in court. Anything you do say may be given in evidence.

The above caution should not be used in circumstances where the detained person has been denied access to a solicitor in which case the following cautions should be used:

> You do not have to say anything, but anything you do say may be given in evidence.

This is answer C; answers A, B and D are therefore incorrect.

Evidence and Procedure, para. 2.10.9.4

Answer 10.23

Answer **A** — An intimate search may be authorised by an inspector and consists of the physical examination of a person's bodily orifices *other than the mouth*. The physical examination of a person's mouth is *not* classed as an intimate search, and may be authorised by a custody officer for the same reasons as a strip search. Answers B and C are incorrect as the search in the scenario does not amount to an intimate search.

An *intimate search* may be conducted only by a medical practitioner (or registered nurse) at medical premises, where the purpose of the search is to discover a Class A drug. Other *intimate searches* may be conducted at the custody office by police officers (provided all the criteria are met). Answer D is therefore incorrect for this reason.

Evidence and Procedure, para. 2.10.10.12

Answer 10.24

Answer **D** — An intimate search may be authorised by an inspector and consists of the physical examination of a person's bodily orifices other than the mouth. The search may be authorised *only* when the authorising officer has reasonable grounds for believing that the person has concealed an article which could be used to cause physical injury, or has concealed a Class A drug which he or she intended to supply to another or export.

Since the search may be authorised only for the above purposes, answers A, B and C are incorrect. Where an intimate search is authorised correctly, reasonable force may be used (s. 117 of the Police and Criminal Evidence Act 1984). However, in these circumstances, the use of force is not permitted.

Evidence and Procedure, para. 2.10.10.12

Answer 10.25

Answer **C** — PACE Code C, para. 12.2 provides that a detained person must have a continuous 8-hour 'rest period' while he or she is in detention; this period should normally be at night. The period should be free from questioning, travel or any interruption by police officers in connection with the case. The period may not be interrupted or delayed, except:

(a) when there are reasonable grounds for believing not delaying or interrupting the period would:
  (i) involve a risk of harm to people or serious loss of, or damage to, property;
  (ii) delay unnecessarily the person's release from custody;
  (iii) otherwise prejudice the outcome of the investigation;
(b) at the request of the detainee, their appropriate adult or legal representative; [answer A is therefore incorrect]
(c) when a delay or interruption is necessary in order to:
  (i) comply with the legal obligations and duties arising under s. 15;
  (ii) to take action required under s. 9 or in accordance with medical advice.

As can be seen interruptions can be requested, in which case there is no requirement for there to be any of the requirements of (a) above to be in force; answer D is therefore incorrect.

If the period is interrupted in accordance with (a), a fresh period must be allowed.

Interruptions under (b) and (c) do not require a fresh period to be allowed; answer B is therefore incorrect.

Evidence and Procedure, para. 2.10.10.17

Answer 10.26

Answer **C** — At least *two light meals* and *one main meal* shall be offered in any period of 24 hours. Answers A, B and D are therefore incorrect. Drinks should be provided at meal times and upon reasonable request between meal times (PACE Code C, para. 8.6). Meals should so far as practicable be offered at recognised meal times (Code C, Note 8B).

Evidence and Procedure, para. 2.10.10.17

Answer 10.27

Answer **B** — Sections 38 and 39 of the Police Reform Act 2002 provide certain police powers for police authority employees. This recognises that many of the functions that were traditionally carried out by police officers are now performed by accredited (and trained) staff, and gives statutory footing to their actions. Part of this group are detention officers, and they are given power to carry out most of the functions that were previously given only to police officers. It includes taking non-intimate samples; answers C and D are therefore incorrect. By virtue of s. 38(8) of the Police Reform Act 2002, detention officers have the same power to use *reasonable* force that is given to police officers in the execution of the same duties; answer A is therefore incorrect.

Evidence and Procedure, para. 2.10.3.2

Answer 10.28

Answer **A** — Code C, Note 1G defines 'mentally vulnerable' as applying to any detainees who, because of their mental state or capacity, may not understand the significance of what is said, of questions or of their replies. 'Mental disorder' is defined by the Mental Health Act 1983, s. 1(2) (as amended by the Mental Health Act 2007, s. 1), as 'any disorder or disability of the mind'. Code C, para. 1.4 provides further guidance, if there is any doubt, the detained person should be treated as if they are mentally vulnerable. There is no room for interpretation, and the custody officer must contact an appropriate adult in these circumstances. Answer C is therefore incorrect.

Although a custody officer may contact a medical practitioner or a social worker for advice as to how to deal with a person suffering from a mental disorder, Code C, para. 1.4 makes it clear that the information given by PATCH's father is sufficient to ensure that a person is treated as such in these circumstances. Answers B and D are therefore incorrect.

Evidence and Procedure, para. 2.10.13

Answer 10.29

Answer **B** — Code C, Note 6J clearly outlines that whenever a detainee exercises his or her right to legal advice by consulting with or communicating with a solicitor, he or she must be allowed to do so in private; therefore, answer D is incorrect. This means both personal consultations and those done via the telephone; answer C is therefore incorrect.

Although this may well present practical difficulties in a busy custody unit, Note 6J makes it clear that the normal expectation is that such a facility *will* be available, and a private consultation should be allowed; answer A is therefore incorrect.

Evidence and Procedure, para. 2.10.6.6

Answer 10.30

Answer **A** — Section 64A of the Police and Criminal Evidence Act 1984 has been amended by the Serious and Organised Crime and Police Act 2005. This means that a person who is detained at a police station or elsewhere than at a police station may be photographed with his or her consent; or if it is withheld or it is not practicable to obtain it, without his or her consent (guidance is provided in Code D, paras 5.12 to 5.18). This applies to all persons who are in police detention, and not just those charged or reported for an offence; therefore answer D is incorrect.

Code D para. 5.12 sets out the circumstances where a person who is not detained at a police station may be photographed.

Photographs can be taken with or without consent (although consent should be asked for). Code D, paras 5.12 to 5.18 outline these requirements. As photographs can be taken without consent, answer B is incorrect. A photograph taken under s. 64A may be used by, or disclosed to, any person for any purpose related to the prevention or detection of crime, the investigation of an offence or the conduct of a prosecution or the enforcement of a sentence. Code D, Note 5B gives examples where such photographs may be of use. The use of the photograph is for any conduct which constitutes a criminal offence (whether under UK law or in another country). This therefore allows the photograph to be used in the preparation of any identification procedure that is being arranged involving the suspect (Code D, para. 3.30); answer C is therefore incorrect.

Evidence and Procedure, para. 2.10.11

Answer 10.31

Answer **B** — Questions relating to relevant times can appear daunting, but they can be solved using fairly constructed formulas. In the scenario, HURTY has not been arrested for a 'local offence' so the last part of the table 4 at para. 2.10.7.3 *Evidence and Procedure* applies, therefore the relevant time is the time he arrived at a police station in the police area where he was wanted (not just the time he arrived in that force's area; therefore answer C is incorrect) *or* 24 hours after arrest, whichever is the earliest. He was arrested at 10 am on Saturday, and arrived at the station at 11.30 am on the Sunday, therefore the relevant time is 10 am on the Sunday (by applying the formula, and noting that 10 am is in fact earlier than 11.30 am!). Answer D is therefore incorrect. Had HURTY been questioned by Margate police about the burglary, the relevant time would have been 10.30 am on the Saturday (time of arrival at local station); but as he was not questioned, answer A is incorrect.

Evidence and Procedure, para. 2.10.6.8

Answer 10.32

Answer **C** — Section 41(2)(ca) of the Police and Criminal Evidence Act 1984 takes into account police officers' powers to bail people from the scene of their arrest. Where a person has been bailed under s. 30A of the Act, his or her relevant time will be the time that he or she arrives at the station (2.30 pm in the scenario). Answers A, B and D are incorrect for this reason.

Evidence and Procedure, para. 2.10.6.8.

Answer 10.33

Answer **C** — The authority to search detainees and examine them to ascertain their identity is contained in s. 54A of the Police and Criminal Evidence Act 1984. An officer of at least the rank of inspector may authorise a person to be searched or examined in order to ascertain if the person has any mark that would tend to identify him or her as a person involved in the commission of an offence, or any mark that would assist to identify him or her (including showing that he or she is not a particular person). Answers A and B are therefore incorrect. Authority may be given either orally or in writing, provided it is confirmed in writing as soon as practicable (see Code D, para. 5.2). Answer D is therefore incorrect.

Evidence and Procedure, para. 2.10.11.1

Answer 10.34

Answer **D** — The authority to search detainees and examine them to ascertain their identity is contained in s. 54A of the Police and Criminal Evidence Act 1984 and governed by Code D, paras 5.1 to 5.11. Note that this power can be authorised by an inspector where consent is absent, although where consent is given it must be proper consent. For a juvenile aged 14 or over this must be his or her consent, and that of the appropriate adult. The search, if it involves the removal of more than the person's outer clothing, will be conducted in accordance with Code C, Annex A, para. 11 (strip searches). Paragraph 11(c) states that except in cases of urgency, where there is a risk of serious harm to the detainee or others (which is not the case in the scenario), a search of a juvenile may take place in the absence of an appropriate adult only if the juvenile signifies in the presence of the appropriate adult that he or she does not want the adult to be present during the search, and the appropriate adult agrees; therefore answer A is incorrect. Thus, even though the officer was not photographing intimate parts of the body, because this case involved a juvenile, the consent of both the detainee and the appropriate adult must be obtained; answer C is therefore incorrect. If an appropriate adult is not present without appropriate consent, there need to be at least two people present during the search only where intimate parts of the body may be exposed; answer B is therefore incorrect.

Evidence and Procedure, para. 2.10.11.1

Answer 10.35

Answer **D** — The authority to search detainees and examine them to ascertain their identity is contained in s. 54A of the Police and Criminal Evidence Act 1984 and Code D, para. 5. An officer of at least the rank of inspector may authorise a person to be searched or examined for two general purposes, namely, in order to ascertain if the person:

- has any mark that would tend to identify him or her as a person involved in the commission of an offence (para. 5(1)(a)); *or*
- has any mark that would assist to identify him or her (including showing that he or she is not a particular person) (para. 5(1)(b)).

The detainee in the scenario would fall within para. 5(1)(b) above. Searches and examinations may be conducted without the person's consent in order to identify him or her for either of the above reasons. However, the requirements are different, depending on the paragraph concerned. A search or examination under para. 5(1)(a) above may be carried out without the person's consent only when consent is withheld, or it is not practicable to obtain consent. A search or examination under para. 5(1)(b) above (which is applicable to the scenario) may be carried out without the person's consent only when the detainee has refused to identify himself or herself, or the authorising officer has reasonable grounds for suspecting that the person is not who he or she claims to be.

Returning to the scenario, the detainee had not been given the opportunity to refuse to identify himself, therefore a search under this section could not take place at this time. As can be seen above, the search could not be authorised because it was not practicable to obtain his consent, because this requirement only applies to detainees who fall within para. 5(1)(a) above. Answer A is therefore incorrect.

Answer B is incorrect because, as can be seen above, an examination may be conducted without a detainee's consent for reasons other than where a person has simply refused to give consent.

Lastly, an examination without a detainee's consent may be authorised for any of the reasons listed above. There is no mention in the Codes of Practice of 'urgent' cases. Answer C is therefore incorrect.

(Note that reasonable force may be used, if necessary, to carry out a search or examination under this section.)

Evidence and Procedure, para. 2.10.11.1

Answer 10.36

Answer **B** — Any information that is available about the detained person should be considered in deciding whether to request a medical examination. In *R* v *HM Coroner for Coventry, ex parte Chief Constable of Staffordshire Police* (2000) 164 JP 665 the detained person had been drunk on arrest and was detained to be interviewed. The detained person made no complaint of his condition but his sister called the police to advise them that he would get the shakes. It was clear at interview and the following morning that he did have the shakes but no complaint was made and no doctor was called. A verdict of accidental death aggravated by neglect was an option in the case, as the deceased had died whilst in police custody. The court considered the facts, such as the deceased's withdrawal and the warning as to his condition, from which a properly directed jury could have concluded that had certain steps been taken it was at least possible that the deceased would not have died. In this case a verdict of accidental death aggravated by neglect was left open to the jury, even though a doctor at the inquest gave evidence that he doubted whether calling a doctor would have made any difference to the eventual outcome.

The clear message from this case is that the custody officer must take into account *any* information about a person's health, whether it comes from the detainee, the arresting officer or any other source. Answer A is therefore incorrect. Whether or not the detainee displayed symptoms of illness is immaterial and therefore answer C is incorrect. Also, the fact that the detainee's sister failed to mention whether or not the person was taking medication or seeking medical help is also immaterial and answer D is therefore incorrect.

Evidence and Procedure, para. 2.10.10.18

Answer 10.37

Answer **D** — According to the PACE Codes of Practice, Code C, para. 2.1A:

> A person is deemed to be 'at a police station' for these purposes if they are within the boundary of any building or enclosed yard which forms part of that police station.

This definition is far wider than merely inside a police station (and answer C is incorrect) or within the confines of a custody office (and answer B is incorrect). It is important to note this addition to the Codes of Practice, because the time the person arrives at the police station forms the basis of a detainee's relevant time and could have an effect later in the person's detention when investigating officers are seeking extensions. It should also be noted that since many custody offices have CCTV cameras fitted, the accuracy of such information is crucial in case of challenges. Answer A is completely wrong, as a person may be waiting in a police vehicle in a yard outside a busy custody office for some time and this will count towards their overall detention time.

Evidence and Procedure, para. 2.10.5

Answer 10.38

Answer **D** — The situation in this question is covered by Code C, para. 6.5A of the PACE Codes of Practice, which states:

> In the case of a juvenile, an appropriate adult should consider whether legal advice from a solicitor is required. If the juvenile indicates that they do not want legal advice, the appropriate adult has the right to ask for a solicitor to attend if this would be in the best interests of the person. However, the detained person cannot be forced to see the solicitor if he is adamant that he does not wish to do so.

As can be seen from this paragraph, a juvenile cannot be made to speak with a legal representative, even if this is in his or her best interests, regardless of his or her age or the local YOT's policy. Answers A and C are therefore incorrect. The appropriate adult *does* have the right to ask for a solicitor to attend if it is in the best interests of the detainee (and answer B is incorrect); however, this right does not extend to forcing the juvenile to speak to the solicitor once he/she has arrived at the custody office.

Evidence and Procedure, para. 2.10.6.6

Answer 10.39

Answer **B** — The PACE Codes of Practice, Code C, para. 3.4 states that the custody officer shall:

> note on the custody record any comment the detainee makes in relation to the arresting officer's account but shall not invite comment. If the arresting officer is not physically present when the detainee is brought to a police station, the arresting officer's account must be made available to the custody officer remotely or by a third party on the arresting officer's behalf. If the custody officer authorises a person's detention the detainee must be informed of the grounds as soon as practicable and before they are questioned about any offence.

Answer A is correct in the sense that the information regarding a person's arrest may be given from a remote location; however, it is incorrect as the information may also be given by another officer accompanying the detainee. Answer C is incorrect, as the arresting officer need not be present when giving the information, and answer D is incorrect as para. 3.4 above clearly states that the information may be given from a remote location.

Evidence and Procedure, para. 2.10.6.9

Answer 10.40

Answer **C** — The maximum period a person may be detained without charge under PACE is 96 hours, following the granting of an extension by the magistrates' court. However, when a person is in police detention and is suspected of having committed an offence under the Terrorism Act 2000, the *maximum* period is 28 days. Answers A, B and D are therefore incorrect.

Evidence and Procedure, paras 2.10.7, 2.10.7.5

Answer 10.41

Answer **D** — Where the custody officer considers there is sufficient evidence to charge and the person is bailed after charge or bailed without charge and on bail for the purpose of enabling the CPS to make a decision regarding case disposal, the custody officer may impose conditions on that bail; answer C is therefore incorrect.

Section 47 of the Police and Criminal Evidence Act 1984 states:

> (1A) The normal powers to impose conditions of bail shall be available to him where a custody officer releases a person on bail under section 37 above or section 38(1) above (including that subsection as applied by section 40(10) above) but not in any other cases.

However, where a person is bailed under s. 37 for a purpose other than a CPS referral, as is the case in the question scenario, then conditions cannot be applied to that bail; answer A is therefore incorrect.

The bail must be for CPS advice, it is irrelevant that CPS advice will be sought when bail is answered; answer B is therefore incorrect.

Evidence and Procedure, para. 2.10.9.3

Answer 10.42

Answer **D** — The standard detention time is 24 hours from the relevant time, so all things being equal the detention time will end at 10 am Wednesday.

If a detained person is taken to hospital for medical treatment, the time at hospital and the period spent travelling to and from the hospital does not count towards the relevant time unless the person is asked questions for the purpose of obtaining evidence about an offence. This applies only where questions are actually asked not intended; answer A is therefore incorrect. Also note that the clock would effectively be 'off' from the moment travelling to the hospital begins until it ends. In this scenario that is from 4 pm to 10 pm. This is 6 hours off the clock, effectively 6 hours added to 10 am, making it 4 pm on Wednesday; answers A, B and C are therefore incorrect.

Where questioning takes place, this period would count towards the relevant time and therefore the custody officer must be informed of it (s. 41(6) PACE).

Evidence and Procedure, para. 2.10.7.3

11 Identification

STUDY PREPARATION

The area of identification was regulated by the Police and Criminal Evidence Act 1984 and principally Code D of the Codes of Practice. This is the starting point. However, identification is a very fertile area for defence lawyers and, not surprisingly, case law in this area has extended or restricted the legislation—depending on your viewpoint. One thing is certain—the case law has complicated the subject for those who are trying to study it.

The law regulating the various methods of identification (e.g. witness testimony, ID parades, DNA samples and fingerprints) should be known, and you should be able to recognise the relevant circumstances and authorisation levels that must exist.

QUESTIONS

Question 11.1

Officers in London are investigating a robbery at a bank and have obtained colour CCTV of the robbers leaving the premises. Other officers have been asked to view the CCTV to identify the as yet unknown suspects and Constable DEVONISH has attended to view the CCTV. The officer watches the footage, and during the first showing he fails to recognise anyone. The officer is shown the footage a second time and whilst watching the footage he says, 'the first one out the door could be Jimmy McGOWAN, as he has a pronounced limp like McGOWAN, he is also wearing a West Ham football scarf to cover his face, and McGOWAN also wears a West Ham scarf all the time, but it might not be him'.

In relation to what the officer says, which of the following is correct in relation to what should be recorded about this identification?

A The only fact that should be recorded is 'it might not be him' as this undermines the identification.

B The only fact that should be recorded is that the officer was shown the footage twice.

C Everything relating to the identification should be recorded, however the factors that triggered identification need not be recorded.

D Everything relating to the identification should be recorded, including the factors that triggered identification.

Question 11.2

Constable HASSEL was off duty when she witnessed a robbery; she tried to tackle the robbers but was knocked unconscious. Constable HASSEL regained consciousness 6 hours later, and 2 hours after this she was interviewed by detectives. She gave a description of one of the suspects, but named the other as MACKONICY, a well-known local criminal.

Which of the following statements is true?

A Constable HASSEL's description of the suspects is not 'a first description' as it was given several hours after the incident.

B Constable HASSEL may be shown photographs to help identify both suspects.

C Constable HASSEL may *not* be shown photographs to help identify the suspects, as she is a police officer.

D Constable HASSEL's description of the suspects would be 'a first description' even though it was given several hours after the incident.

Question 11.3

DICKINS was involved in a fight, and Constable KHAN tried to arrest him. DICKINS escaped and Constable KHAN circulated his description. Constable KHAN resumed driving the police van. A short time later Constable KHAN was called to transport a prisoner. The prisoner was placed in the van and Constable KHAN was asked to identify the suspect as DICKINS, who had escaped earlier. This was because the arresting officer recognised DICKINS from the description circulated by Constable KHAN. Constable KHAN identified DICKINS as the person who had escaped, which DICKINS strongly denied.

Is this identification of DICKINS procedurally correct?

A Yes, provided Constable KHAN recorded the first description he gave.

B Yes, as the confrontation was unavoidable.

C No, DICKINS should have been kept away from Constable KHAN and an identification procedure arranged.

D No, as Constable KHAN should not have been asked if he recognised DICKINS.

Question 11.4

Inspector GOULD is carrying out an identification procedure and has a copy of the first description of the suspect as obtained from a witness. The suspect is represented by a solicitor.

What should the Inspector do with this record?

A The Inspector must give it to the solicitor prior to the identification procedure taking place.

B The Inspector must give it to the suspect or their solicitor prior to the identification procedure taking place.

C The Inspector must, where practicable, give it only to the solicitor prior to the identification procedure taking place.

D The Inspector must, where practicable, give it to the suspect or their solicitor prior to the identification procedure taking place.

Question 11.5

Constable MEMORY was on mobile patrol and was accompanied by a colleague from the Dutch police. Whilst stationary at traffic lights a car pulled alongside them. Constable MEMORY recognised the driver as NANCARROW whom she knew was a disqualified driver. In the vehicle was NANCARROW's wife, who the officer also recognised. The vehicles were next to each other for no more than 30 seconds, and NANCARROW's vehicle made off and was not traced. NANCARROW was arrested some time later and denied being the driver and demanded an identification parade. The Dutch officer is now with another force several hundred miles away.

In relation to identification procedures which of the following is correct?

A An identification must be held with Constable MEMORY as a witness, it is not practical to hold one for the Dutch officer.

B An identification procedure should be held with the Dutch officer as a witness, there would be no useful purpose in having Constable MEMORY as a witness.

C An identification procedure should be held with both Constable MEMORY and the Dutch officer as witnesses.

D An identification procedure need not be held as it is it is not practical to hold one for the Dutch officer and there would be no useful purpose in having Constable MEMORY as a witness.

Question 11.6

PRYCE was approached by three men and robbed of his wallet. The three men then ran off, whilst PRYCE flagged down a passing police car. An area search found the three men about 900 m away from the scene of the crime and they were arrested. They denied being involved in the robbery but accepted they were at the location where they were arrested.

In these circumstances should an identification procedure be held?

A Yes, this is an issue of identification and it is disputed; a procedure should be held.

B Yes, even though this is only an issue of participation a procedure should be held.

C No, the youths do not deny their presence at the scene; a procedure need not be held.

D No, as they were arrested in the vicinity of the crime, a procedure need not be held.

Question 11.7

Police officers are dealing with a murder inquiry during which there was significant publicity to identify a suspect. The suspect has been identified and an identification procedure is being considered by the police.

What is the requirement on the police in relation to material released by them to the press for publicity purposes?

A The material need only be retained and disclosed in accordance with the relevant codes of the Criminal Procedure and Investigations Act 1996.

B The material must be shown to either the suspect or their solicitor prior to any identification procedure taking place.

C The material must be shown, where practicable, to either the suspect or their solicitor prior to any identification procedure taking place.

D The material need not be retained by the police or shown to either the suspect or their solicitor as it has already been in the public domain.

Question 11.8

An armed robbery had taken place at a post office involving a suspect wearing a mask to hide his features. The suspect demanded money, and this was recorded on video, which had a voice track. The post office worker who received the verbal threat, thought he recognised the voice as belonging to BLAKE, who was a regular customer and had a distinctive speech impediment.

In relation to voice identification, which of the following is true?

A The witness can give identification evidence of the voice, based on what he heard at the time.

B The witness can give identification evidence of the speech impediment only, based on what he heard at the time.

C The jury should be allowed to hear the recording and compare it to the suspect's voice in court.

D Only an expert witness can give voice identification evidence, based on the voice recording on the video.

Question 11.9

CURBISHLEY was arrested on suspicion of burglary, as fingerprint identification from the scene of the crime was available. CURBISHLEY initially denied the offence, and the taking of his fingerprints was authorised to prove or disprove his involvement in the offence and taken for that purpose. Following further comparison and further interviews, CURBISHLEY admitted the offence. CURBISHLEY has been charged and the officer in charge of the case wishes to take his fingerprints. CURBISHLEY refuses this request.

Which of the following statements is true?

A As CURBISHLEY has been charged, his fingerprints can be taken without his consent.

B As CURBISHLEY has been charged, his fingerprints can be taken only *with* his consent.

C As CURBISHLEY has refused, an inspector's authority, in writing, is required.

D As CURBISHLEY has refused, an inspector's authority, which can be oral or written, is required.

Question 11.10

SIDOLI was charged with an assault and had her fingerprints taken. At court, she was found not guilty of the offence, and she has no previous convictions.

What should now happen to SIDOLI's fingerprints held on file?

A The fingerprints must be destroyed as soon as practicable.

B The fingerprints must be destroyed upon application by SIDOLI.

C The fingerprints can be retained and may be used in future police investigations.

D The fingerprints can be retained, but may not be used for future evidential purposes.

Question 11.11

HAVARD has been charged with driving whilst disqualified, and when interviewed he made no comment at all. The police have on record a person with the same name who was also disqualified in the same year that HAVARD is suspected of being disqualified, and identification of HAVARD as the actual disqualified driver has not been made. The Crown Prosecution Service (CPS) propose to call HAVARD's solicitor; in addition to currently representing HAVARD she was present in court when the male known as HAVARD was disqualified. The CPS only intend asking questions for the purpose of solely identifying the person disqualified from driving at the original court hearing.

Can the solicitor be called to identify HAVARD as the disqualified driver?

A The solicitor cannot be called, as this would breach legal professional privilege.

B The solicitor cannot be called, as this would breach HAVARD's right to be represented by a lawyer of his choice.

C The solicitor can be called, as she was a person present when HAVARD was originally disqualified.

D The solicitor should not ordinarily be called, but can be called and this should only be entertained as a last resort.

Question 11.12

GUILLETTE is standing trial for rape, and DNA evidence will be an issue for the jury.

In relation to DNA evidence against GUILLETTE, which of the following is true?

A The DNA evidence will be sufficient to prove GUILLETTE was the assailant.

B The DNA evidence must be supported by other direct evidence.

C The DNA evidence can be supported only by other identification evidence.

D The DNA evidence can be supported by mere circumstantial evidence.

Question 11.13

Section 62 of the Police and Criminal Evidence Act 1984 allows for the taking from a suspect of intimate and non-intimate samples. Police officers wish to take a penile swab from a suspect in custody.

Is this penile swab an intimate sample?

A Yes, this is an intimate sample even though it is not a body orifice.

B Yes, as the legislation states that the penis is in effect a body orifice.

C No, as intimate samples are samples of blood, semen, or any other tissue fluid, urine or pubic hair.

D No, as a non-intimate sample is described as a swab taken from any part of a person's body including the mouth but not any other body orifice.

Question 11.14

McGREGOR is a 16-year-old boy who has been arrested following an allegation of rape against him. When he was brought into custody a member of social services was called to act as appropriate adult, however they left when the police said the interviews would be held in several hours' time. The officer in charge of the investigation now wants to take an intimate sample which would require the removal of the suspect's clothing. McGREGOR agrees to give the sample and states he does not want the social worker to be present. The social worker is phoned and agrees that she does not need to be present when the juvenile's clothes are removed.

Can the police now lawfully remove the juvenile's clothes to obtain an intimate sample?

A Yes, the suspect has agreed and indicated he does not wish to have an appropriate adult present.

B Yes, the suspect has agreed and indicated he does not wish to have an appropriate adult present, and the appropriate adult agrees.

C No, as the appropriate adult was not present with the juvenile when he elected not to have an appropriate adult present.

D No, as an appropriate adult would have to be present at all times when an intimate sample is taken, provided they are the same sex.

Question 11.15

KEETING was charged with an offence of theft and a non-intimate sample (mouth swab) was obtained on 21 March. KEETING pleaded guilty and was convicted on 28 March. On 2 April the laboratory informed the officer in the case that the sample obtained after charge was 'insufficient' for analysis.

In relation to obtaining another sample, which of the following is true?

A Another sample can be obtained only with the consent of KEETING.

B Another sample can be obtained, but the requirement to attend the police station must be made before 2 May.

C Another sample can be obtained, but the requirement to attend the police station must be made before 28 April.

D Another sample can be obtained, but the requirement to attend the police station must be made before 21 April.

Question 11.16

Intimate samples may be taken from persons in police detention or, in certain circumstances, from persons who are not in police detention.

In relation to the authority needed for the taking of such samples, which of the following is true?

A Inspector's authority in detention; superintendent's authority not in detention.

B Inspector's authority irrespective of whether the person is in detention or not.

C Superintendent's authority irrespective of whether the person is in detention or not.

D Superintendent's authority in detention; inspector's authority not in detention.

Question 11.17

WILTORD was arrested by Detective Constable COLE for an assault. He was released on bail for an identification procedure and his fingerprints were taken prior to his release. On the day that he was due to answer bail, WILTORD's brother, who was similar in appearance, attended the station instead of WILTORD, in an attempt to confuse witnesses. However, after the brother had been booked in by the custody officer, Detective Constable COLE suspected that he was not the person who had been released on bail. Detective Constable COLE contacted the duty inspector by telephone and asked for permission to obtain fingerprints from WILTORD's brother because of his suspicions.

Would the duty inspector be able to authorise such a request in these circumstances?

A No, this power is only given to a court, when a person has been charged with an offence.

B No, this power is only given to an inspector where a person has been charged with an offence.

C Yes, but the fingerprints may be taken only when the inspector has provided written authority.

D Yes, and the fingerprints may be taken immediately.

Question 11.18

WINSLETT is aged 16 and is in police detention, having been given a reprimand for an offence of theft. She is accompanied at this time by her parent. The officer in the case is wondering if there is power to take WINSLETT's fingerprints, and whose consent is required before they could be taken.

Can fingerprints be taken, and whose consent is required?

A Yes, they can be taken and only WINSLETT's consent is required.

B Yes, they can be taken and both the consent of WINSLETT and her parent is required.

C No, fingerprints can only be taken where a person has been convicted of a recordable offence, not reprimanded.

D No, fingerprints can only be taken where a person has been convicted of or given a final warning for a recordable offence, not reprimanded.

Question 11.19

Samples can be defined as 'intimate' or 'non-intimate'.

Which of the following will be classed as 'non-intimate' within the definition outlined in Code D, para. 6.1 of the PACE Codes of Practice?

A A skin impression other than a fingerprint.

B A sample of urine.

C A blood sample.

D A dental impression.

Question 11.20

A person who has been detained under the Terrorism Act 2000 may have their fingerprints taken without their consent, in order to ascertain their identity. This may take place when the person has refused to identify himself or herself, or where there are reasonable grounds for suspecting that the person is not who they claim to be.

Who may authorise fingerprints to be taken in these circumstances?

A An officer of at least the rank of inspector.
B An officer of at least the rank of superintendent.
C An officer of at least the rank of assistant chief constable or commander.
D An officer of at least the rank of superintendent, or, in cases of urgency, an inspector.

Question 11.21

MURPHY is 16 years of age and in police detention, having been arrested on suspicion of rape. Authorisation has been given to take samples of MURPHY's pubic hair, which will involve the removal of his clothing. MURPHY has agreed to the provision of the samples and has signed the custody record accordingly. MURPHY's mother was at the custody office earlier for the interviews, but has now gone to work. She will not be available to return to the custody office for another 3 hours.

Would the police need to consult with MURPHY's mother before taking the sample of pubic hairs in these circumstances?

A No, he does not want his mother there and has signed the custody record; this is sufficient.
B Yes, because MURPHY's mother was not present when he made the decision.
C No, because MURPHY's mother has left the station and is not readily available.
D No, because MURPHY is over 14, he may make such a decision for himself.

Question 11.22

Constable CANALE is the first officer to arrive at the scene of a robbery. The officer is given a first description of the suspect by the victim.

How should the officer record this description?

A The officer can only record it in their pocket notebook and it must be in a visible and legible form.

B The officer can only record it in their pocket notebook and in note form provided it will be in a visible and legible form in a s. 9 statement.

C The officer can record it on any paper-based record provided it is in a visible and legible form.

D The officer can record it electronically or on any paper-based record provided it is in a visible and legible form.

ANSWERS

Answer 11.1

Answer **D** — The showing of a CCTV film used for security purposes is addressed at para. 3.28 of Code D.

Videos or photographs can be shown to the public at large through the national or local media, or to police officers for the purposes of recognition and tracing suspects. However, when such material is shown to potential witnesses (including police officers) it should be shown on an individual basis so as to avoid any possibility of collusion, and the showing shall, as far as possible, follow the principles for video identification if the suspect is known (paras 3.28, 3.29 and Annex A) or identification by photographs if the suspect is not known (see paras 3.3, 3.4 and Annex E).

It is important that where pictures or film are shown to specific police officers to try to identify suspects this must be done in a controlled way. In *R* v *Smith (Dean) and others* [2008] EWCA Crim 1342, the court held that a police officer who was asked to view a CCTV recording to see if he could recognise any suspects involved in a robbery was not in the same shoes as a witness asked to identify someone he had seen committing a crime. However, safeguards that Code D was designed to put in place were equally important in cases where a police officer was asked to see whether he could recognise anyone in a CCTV recording. Whether or not Code D applied, there had to be in place some record that assisted in gauging the reliability of the assertion that the police officer recognised an individual. It was important that a police officer's initial reactions to viewing a CCTV recording were set out and available for scrutiny. Thus if the police officer failed to recognise anyone on first viewing but did so subsequently those circumstances ought to be noted. If a police officer failed to pick anybody else out that also should be recorded, as should any words of doubt. Furthermore, it was necessary that if recognition took place a record was made of what it was about the image that was said to have triggered the recognition. This is all the factors in our scenario; answers A, B and C are therefore incorrect as they limit what should be recorded.

Evidence and Procedure, para. 2.11.2.9

Answer 11.2

Answer **D** — PACE Code D requires that a first description provided of a person suspected of a crime (regardless of the time it was given) must be recorded (para. 3.1). This was the first description as given by Constable HASSEL and it should be recorded in accordance with Code D. How strong the evidence would be, given the circumstances of the officer's head injury, would be a matter for the court, but Code D must be complied with, and answer A is therefore incorrect. As far as showing photographs is concerned, one of the suspects is 'known', and therefore showing the officer photographs to identify both would be a breach of the Codes, and answer B is therefore incorrect. Showing photographs of the accomplice, who is merely described, may be appropriate if the suspect is 'not known'. Code D provides for witnesses (including police officers) to be shown photographs, or be taken to a place where the suspect might be for the purpose of identification (paras 3.2 and 3.3), and answer C is therefore incorrect.

Evidence and Procedure, paras 2.11.2.2, 2.11.2.3

Answer 11.3

Answer **C** — It is essential that once a person becomes a 'known suspect', he or she is afforded the rights and protection provided by PACE Code D. In this case the second officer stated he recognised DICKINS from the description given by Constable KHAN and, by Code D, para. 3.4, this makes the suspect 'known'. It is important that any witnesses, *including police officers*, who might be used at an identification process, are kept apart from the suspect. As this was not the case, the Codes were breached, and therefore answers A and B are incorrect. As *any* contact could jeopardise a conviction, it is imperative that the witness officer should not see the suspect. This risk is not reduced simply by not asking the officer if he recognised the suspect, and answer D is therefore incorrect. In *R* v *Lennon* [1999] EWCA Crim 1309, a suspect was arrested for public order offences after his description was circulated by the police officers who witnessed the offence. After the suspect was placed in a van, the officers accidentally went in the van and identified the suspect. The court held that the person was a 'known' suspect and the identification evidence should have been excluded. Also of interest here is *K* v *DPP* [2003] EWHC 351 (QBD appeal).

Evidence and Procedure, para. 2.11.2.2

Answer 11.4

Answer **D** — Code D requires that a first description provided of a person suspected of a crime (regardless of the time it was given) must be recorded (para. 3.1) and that a copy of the record should, where practicable (answers A and B are therefore incorrect), be given to the defence before certain procedures such as identification parades are carried out.

This record must be made and kept in a form which enables details of that description to be accurately produced from it, in a visible and legible form (Code D, para. 3.1), which can be given to the suspect or the suspect's solicitor; answer C is therefore incorrect.

Evidence and Procedure, para. 2.11.2.1

Answer 11.5

Answer **B** — Code D of the Police and Criminal Evidence Act 1984 Codes of Practice, paras 3.12 and 3.13 state:

> Whenever:
>
> (i) a witness has identified a suspect or purported to have identified them prior to any identification procedure set out in paragraphs 3.5 to 3.10 having been held; or
>
> (ii) there is a witness available, who expresses an ability to identify the suspect, or where there is a reasonable chance of the witness being able to do so, and they have not been given an opportunity to identify the suspect in any of the procedures set out in paragraphs 3.5 to 3.10,
>
> and the suspect disputes being the person the witness claims to have seen, an identification procedure shall be held unless it is not practicable or it would serve no useful purpose in proving or disproving whether the suspect was involved in committing the offence. For example, when it is not disputed that the suspect is already well known to the witness who claims to have seen them commit the crime.

Code D, para. 3.12(ii) provides that there is no need to go through any of the identification procedures where it is not practicable or it would serve no useful purpose in proving or disproving whether the suspect was involved in committing the offence. This view is supported by the Court of Appeal decision *R* v *Chen* [2001] EWCA Crim 885. The defence in that case was one of duress but the appeal was based on the failure of the police to hold identification procedures. The Court of Appeal stated that this was not a case about identification as none of the defendants denied their presence at the scene. What they denied was their criminal participation in the activities that took place. It followed, therefore, that Code D did not apply. Other examples would be where it is not in dispute that the suspect is already well known to the witness who claims to have seen the suspect commit the crime or where there is no reasonable possibility that a witness would be able to make an identification.

In this scenario if an identification procedure had been held, the officer would have picked NANCARROW out as the driver (as she knew not only him but another occupant of the car), making an identification procedure somewhat pointless, with no useful purpose; answers A and C are therefore incorrect.

However attempts should be made to have the Dutch officer as a witness. Although several hundred miles away it is still practical (this might not be the case had he returned to Holland); answers A, C and D are therefore incorrect.

Evidence and Procedure, para. 2.11.2.3

Answer 11.6

Answer **A** — Code D, para. 3.12(ii) provides that there is no need to go through any of the identification procedures where it is not practicable or it would serve no useful purpose in proving or disproving whether the suspect was involved in committing the offence. This view is supported by the Court of Appeal decision *R* v *Chen* [2001] EWCA Crim 885. The defence in that case was one of duress but the appeal was based on the failure of the police to hold identification procedures. The Court of Appeal stated that this was not a case about identification as none of the defendants denied their presence at the scene. What they denied was their criminal participation in the activities that took place. It followed, therefore, that Code D did not apply.

What is important here though is what the accused are actually accepting; they accept that they were at the location where they were arrested, not the location where the crime was committed. This is a subtle but important distinction. As they deny being involved in the crime they deny being present at the scene it is an issue of participation and identification and an identification procedure should be held; answers B, C and D are therefore incorrect.

Evidence and Procedure, para. 2.11.2.3

Answer 11.7

Answer **C** — Nothing in Code D of the PACE Codes of Practice inhibits showing films or photographs to the public through the national or local media, or to police officers for the purposes of recognition and tracing suspects.

When a broadcast or publication is made, a copy of the relevant material released to the media for the purposes of recognising or tracing the suspect, shall be kept.

The suspect or their solicitor shall be allowed to view such material before any identification procedure is carried out, provided it is practicable; answers A, B and D are therefore incorrect.

Evidence and Procedure, para. 2.11.2.3

Answer 11.8

Answer **A** — Generally, a witness may give evidence identifying the defendant's voice (*R* v *Robb* (1991) 93 Cr App R 161), while expert testimony may be admitted in relation to tape recordings of a voice which is alleged to belong to the defendant. As this is not a tape recording but a live identification, expert testimony is not required; answer D is therefore incorrect.

In the latter case, the jury should be allowed to hear the recording(s) so that they can draw their own conclusions (*R* v *Bentum* (1989) 153 JP 538). Again this is not identification from a tape recording but live identification; answer C is therefore incorrect. The voice identification is in its entirety not just relating to the speech impediment; answer B is therefore incorrect.

In *R* v *Flynn* [2008] EWCA Crim 970 the Court of Appeal held that where the voice identification is from a recording a prerequisite for making a speaker identification was that there should be a sample of an adequate size from the disputed recording that could confidently be attributed to a single speaker. The court also recognised that expert evidence showed that lay listeners with considerable familiarity of a voice and listening to a clear recording could still make mistakes. It is therefore suggested other supporting evidence will be needed for a conviction to succeed.

Evidence and Procedure, para. 2.11.2.12

Answer 11.9

Answer **B** — Naturally, a person can consent to having his or her fingerprints taken at any time; the law deals with occasions where such consent is missing. Such cases are covered by s. 61 of the Police and Criminal Evidence Act 1984. Under s. 61(4), fingerprints of a person detained at a police station may be taken without that person's consent in the following two circumstances:

(4) The fingerprints of a person detained at a police station may be taken without the appropriate consent if—
   (a) he has been charged with a recordable offence or informed that he will be reported for such an offence; and
   (b) he has not had his fingerprints taken in the course of the investigation of the offence by the police.

As his fingerprints have already been taken, they cannot be taken again without consent or inspector's authority; answers A, C and D are therefore incorrect. Although in certain circumstances fingerprints can be taken without consent, this question is clearly aimed at where fingerprints will be taken with consent. Clearly fingerprints taken without consent will only apply where consent has been sought and not given.

Evidence and Procedure, para. 2.11.3.1

Answer 11.10

Answer **C** — Until recently, under s. 64 of the Police and Criminal Evidence Act 1984, if the person from whom fingerprints were taken was cleared of the original offence, the fingerprints must ordinarily have been destroyed as soon as was practicable. The Criminal Justice and Police Act 2001 has removed the requirement to destroy fingerprints of those persons who are not convicted, and custody officers should no longer inform detained persons of the right to destruction; answers A and B are therefore incorrect. The 2001 Act removes this obligation in relation to fingerprints where the person is cleared of the offence for which the fingerprints were taken, or where a decision is made not to prosecute. The obligation to destroy is replaced by a rule to the effect that any fingerprints or samples retained can be used only for the purposes related to the prevention and detection of crime, the investigation of any offence or the conduct of any prosecution. This means that if a fingerprint match is established at a subsequent crime scene regarding an individual who has previously been cleared of an offence, the police are able to use this information in the investigation of the crime, and answer D is therefore incorrect.

Evidence and Procedure, para. 2.11.3.3

Answer 11.11

Answer **D** — In *R (on the application of Howe)* v *South Durham Magistrates' Court* [2004] EWHC 362 (Admin) the claimant was charged with driving whilst disqualified and without insurance. At no time did he admit that he was the Christopher Howe who had been disqualified. As it was necessary for the prosecution to prove that the defendant before the court was the person disqualified from driving, the prosecution applied for a witness summons to be issued to a solicitor, who had been the solicitor acting for the Christopher Howe who was disqualified and who was also acting for the claimant in respect of the present charge. This was opposed citing that the issuing of the summons would involve a breach of legal professional privilege, also that it would violate the claimant's rights under Art. 6 of the European Convention on Human Rights by depriving him of his right to be represented by a lawyer of his choice and that it would conflict with his right not to incriminate himself.

The Administrative Court held that questions solely as to the identity of the person disqualified from driving in the original court hearing and as to the identification of the claimant as being that person did not infringe legal professional privilege; answer A is therefore incorrect. The admissible question would be whether, when the solicitor first saw the claimant in connection with the prosecution, he knew him or remembered him. The solicitor was not being called in his capacity as the claimant's solicitor, but as a person who was present in court at the relevant time. With regard to the argument that the claimant would be deprived of the solicitor of his choice, although that was important it was not an absolute right and there was no risk of injustice to the claimant if he was required to make a fresh choice of solicitor; answer B is therefore incorrect.

The court was 'mystified' by the dilemma supposedly faced by the claimant's solicitor. After all, if this witness could categorically state that their client was not the person disqualified this would have a devastating effect on the prosecution case. However if they knew the person to be disqualified, it would be embarrassing to admit they represented them knowing they were indeed guilty.

As a cautionary warning, however, the court did not view this case as any sort of licence to increase the amount of such applications by the CPS, and stated that calling a solicitor in such circumstances must only be a last resort; answer C is therefore incorrect.

Evidence and Procedure, para. 2.11.2.5

Answer 11.12

Answer **D** — DNA extracted from blood or semen stains, or even from body hairs, etc., found at the scene of the crime or on the victim is compared with samples (typically derived from mouth swabs) taken from the suspect. The process has been refined in recent years, but is essentially similar to that described by Lord Taylor CJ in *R* v *Deen*, The Times, 10 January 1994. A positive match between the two profiles does not necessarily provide comparable proof of guilt, and the courts have made it clear that DNA evidence alone will not be sufficient for a conviction; there needs to be other supporting evidence to link the suspect to the crime, and answer A is therefore incorrect. This may be any supporting evidence linking the suspect to the area or circumstances of the crime, or may come from questions put to the suspect during interview. It would include circumstantial evidence, i.e. being seen in the area. It need not be direct evidence gained by other identification procedures or otherwise, answers B and C are therefore incorrect. In *R* v *Lashley* [2000] EWCA Crim 88, in addition to the DNA evidence, evidence that the suspect had connections in the area was enough for the jury to consider the likelihood that the defendant was the assailant.

Evidence and Procedure, para. 2.11.4.1

Answer 11.13

Answer **A** — The definition of an intimate sample is:

- a sample of blood, semen, or any other tissue fluid, urine or pubic hair;
- a dental impression;
- a swab taken from any part of a person's genitals or from a person's body orifice other than the mouth.

The definition of a non-intimate sample is:

- a sample of hair, other than pubic hair, which includes hair plucked with the root;
- a sample taken from a nail or from under a nail;
- a swab taken from any part of a person's body including the mouth but not any other body orifice other than a part from which a swab taken would be an intimate sample;
- saliva;
- a skin impression which means any record, other than a fingerprint, which is a record, in any form and produced by any method, of a skin pattern and other

physical characteristics or features of the whole, or any part of, a person's foot or of any other part of their body.

So a swab from a person's penis would be an intimate sample and the Serious Organised Crime and Police Act 2005 has extended the definition beyond a 'body orifice', although it has not gone as far as declaring the penis to be a body orifice; answer B is therefore incorrect. Answer D is almost correct, apart from the caveat in the definition that states 'a swab taken from any part of a person's body including the mouth but not any other body orifice other than a part from which a swab taken would be an intimate sample'; answers C and D are therefore incorrect as a penile swab is an intimate sample.

Evidence and Procedure, para. 2.11.5.1

Answer 11.14

Answer **C** — Paragraph 6.9 of Code D of the Police and Criminal Evidence Act 1984 Codes of Practice sets out the provisions to be followed where clothing needs to be removed in circumstances likely to cause embarrassment. These are:

- no person of the opposite sex may be present (other than a registered medical practitioner or registered health care professional);
- only people whose presence is necessary for the taking of the sample should in fact be present;
- in the case of a juvenile or mentally disordered or mentally vulnerable person, an appropriate adult of the opposite sex may be present *if specifically requested by the person and the person is readily available;*
- in the case of a juvenile, clothing may only be removed in the absence of an appropriate adult if the person signifies (in the presence of the appropriate adult) that he/she prefers his/her absence and the appropriate adult agrees.
- Clearly, as consent is needed to take a sample, the use of force would be inappropriate.

In the case of a juvenile the appropriate adult need not be present if the juvenile signifies (in the presence of the appropriate adult) that he/she prefers his/her absence and the appropriate adult agrees; as the agreement of the adult is required, answer A is incorrect.

In this scenario although the juvenile did not want an appropriate adult present, and the adult agreed, this conversation would have had to take place with the adult present, which they were not; answer B is therefore incorrect. An adult does not have to be present when an intimate sample is taken, provided both the juvenile and the adult agree; answer D is therefore incorrect.

Evidence and Procedure, para. 2.11.6.7

Answer 11.15

Answer **B** — By s. 63A of the Police and Criminal Evidence Act 1984, a constable may require a person to attend at a police station to have a non-intimate sample obtained:

- where a person has been charged with a recordable offence or informed that he or she will be reported; *or*
- where the person has been convicted of a recordable offence;

and, in either case, the person has not had a sample taken in the course of the investigation into the offence, or he or she has had a sample taken but it proved either unsuitable for the same means of analysis or insufficient.

The requirement to attend a police station must be made:

- within one month of the date of charge or of conviction; *or*
- within one month of the appropriate officer being informed that the sample is not suitable or has proved insufficient for analysis.

As it is 'or', the requirement runs to the latest date in the scenario—2 May—and answers C and D are therefore incorrect.

Answer A is incorrect because it is unnecessary to obtain the consent of a person convicted of an offence, and a person can be arrested for failing to comply with the requirement.

Evidence and Procedure, para. 2.11.8.2

Answer 11.16

Answer **B** — Section 62 of PACE sets out police powers in relation to intimate samples, and the circumstances under which they may be obtained. They are subject to the consent of the person, as well as authorisation by the appropriate police officer. The Criminal Justice and Police Act 2001, s. 80(1) lowered the level of authority from superintendent to inspector; therefore answer C is incorrect. This authority remains at the same level irrespective of whether the person is in police detention or not, as outlined in Code D, para. 6.2; therefore, answers A and D are incorrect.

Evidence and Procedure, para. 2.11.6.1

Answer 11.17

Answer **D** — An officer of at least the rank of inspector (or the court) may authorise taking the fingerprints of a person who has answered bail at a court or police station, if the person answering bail has done so on behalf of a person whose fingerprints were taken on a previous occasion and there are reasonable grounds for believing that he or she is not the same person, or the person claims to be a different person from a person whose fingerprints were taken previously (s. 61(4A) and (4B) of the Police and Criminal Evidence Act 1984).

Since this power relates to a person answering bail at a police station as well as a court, answer A is incorrect. Answers A and B are also incorrect because the power may be utilised before a person has been charged with an offence. The authority to take fingerprints in these circumstances may be given orally or in writing; but if given orally, it must be confirmed in writing as soon as is practicable. Answer C is therefore incorrect.

Evidence and Procedure, para. 2.11.3.1

Answer 11.18

Answer **B** — For the purposes of taking fingerprints, appropriate consent means:

- in relation to a person who is 17 years or over, his or her own consent;
- in relation to a person who is aged between 14 and 17 years, his/her own consent *and* the consent of his or her appropriate adult;
- in relation to a person under the age of 14, the consent of his or her appropriate adult only.

WINSLETT was between the ages of 14 and 17 years, therefore consent could have been obtained from her, and from her appropriate adult; answer A is therefore incorrect. Fingerprints can be taken where a person has been warned or reprimanded under s. 65 of the Crime and Disorder Act 1998 for a recordable offence and not just convicted of a recordable offence; answers C and D are therefore incorrect.

Evidence and Procedure, para. 2.11.3.2

Answer 11.19

Answer **A** — The PACE Codes of Practice, Code D, para. 6.1 provides the following definition of intimate and non-intimate samples:

(a) an 'intimate sample' means:
- a sample of blood, semen, or any other tissue fluid, urine or pubic hair;
- a dental impression;
- a swab taken from any part of a person's genitals or from a person's body orifice other than the mouth.

(b) a 'non-intimate sample' means:
- a sample of hair, other than pubic hair, which includes hair plucked with the root;
- a sample taken from a nail or from under a nail;
- a swab taken from any part of a person's body including the mouth but not any other body orifice other than a part from which a swab taken would be an intimate sample;
- saliva;
- a skin impression which means any record, other than a fingerprint, which is a record, in any form and produced by any method, of the skin pattern and other physical characteristics or features of the whole, or any part of, a person's foot or of any other part of their body.

Answers B, C and D are *all* intimate samples; the question asked you to identify samples which were *not* classed as intimate samples, therefore if you selected any of these, the answer was incorrect. A skin impression which is not a fingerprint is a non-intimate sample.

Evidence and Procedure, para. 2.11.5.1

Answer 11.20

Answer **B** — A person who has been detained under the Terrorism Act 2000 may have his or her fingerprints taken without his or her consent in these circumstances only when authorisation has been given by an officer of at least the rank of superintendent. Answers A and C are therefore incorrect. There are no provisions for this power to be delegated to an inspector in any circumstances, therefore answer D is incorrect.

Evidence and Procedure, para. 2.11.10.1

Answer 11.21

Answer **B** — Code D, para. 6.9 of the PACE Codes of Practice outlines the provisions for taking an intimate sample, where clothing needs to be removed in circumstances likely to cause embarrassment. Paragraph 6.9 states:

> When clothing needs to be removed in circumstances likely to cause embarrassment to the person, no person of the opposite sex who is not a registered medical practitioner or registered health care professional shall be present (unless in the case of a juvenile, mentally disordered or mentally vulnerable person, that person specifically requests the presence of an appropriate adult of the opposite sex who is readily available) nor shall anyone whose presence is unnecessary.

However, in the case of a juvenile, this is subject to the overriding proviso that such a removal of clothing may take place in the absence of the appropriate adult only if the juvenile signifies, in their presence that they prefer the adult's absence and they agree.

Answer A is incorrect; the decision was made by MURPHY when his mother was not present and she should have been consulted in respect of that decision. The fact that MURPHY's mother was not readily available is immaterial—this issue is only relevant when a juvenile, mentally disordered or mentally vulnerable person specifically requests the *presence* of an appropriate adult of the opposite sex who is readily available, therefore answer C is incorrect. Paragraph 6.9 above applies to *all* juveniles under 17, therefore answer D is incorrect.

Evidence and Procedure, para. 2.11.6.7

Answer 11.22

Answer **D** — Code D requires that a first description provided of a person suspected of a crime (regardless of the time it was given) must be recorded (para. 3.1) and that a copy of the record should, where practicable, be given to the defence before certain procedures such as identification parades are carried out.

This record must be made and kept in a form which enables details of that description to be accurately produced from it, in a visible and legible form (Code D, para. 3.1), which can be given to the suspect or the suspect's solicitor. Such a record could be made electronically or be paper-based; answers A, B and C are therefore incorrect.

Evidence and Procedure, para. 2.11.2.1

12 Interviews

STUDY PREPARATION

Another area of direct practical relevance to all police officers is that of interviews of suspects. This area is heavily regulated by the Police and Criminal Evidence Act 1984 and the Codes of Practice.

Key aspects of this area are:

- cautioning;
- interview procedure at police stations and elsewhere;
- access to legal advisers;
- interviews with vulnerable people, the use of interpreters and emergency.

QUESTIONS

Question 12.1

WARBURTON is under surveillance for drug supply and is being followed by undercover officers. They follow him onto the motorway where officers from the road policing unit (RPU) stop WARBURTON's vehicle on suspicion of a speeding offence. The RPU officers then receive a radio message from the undercover officers advising them that there may be drugs in the car; following a search they find a package they believe to be controlled drugs. One of the RPU officers asks WARBURTON, 'What is this, then?'

Would the question asked by the officer be an interview as defined by Code C of the Police and Criminal Evidence Act 1984?

A Yes, as the RPU officers believed the package to be controlled drugs.

B Yes, as the other police officers had indicated there may be drugs in the car.

C No, as the officers did not suspect WARBURTON of an offence at this stage, they hadn't considered the lawfulness of the possession.

D No, the officers may have suspected but did not know the substance to be a controlled drug.

Question 12.2

Constable HAWKINS is dealing with an offence of theft, where a man is suspected to have been stealing from his mother. The man attends voluntarily at the police station and explains to the police support staff inquiry officer that he is 'there to be interviewed about a theft, but they'll never find where I've hidden the jewellery'. The man laughed out loud and winked at the inquiry officer. The inquiry officer believed the man to be joking with her.

Was what the man said to the inquiry officer a 'significant statement' as outlined in Code C, para. 11.4 of the Police and Criminal Evidence Act 1984 Codes of Practice?

A Yes, it appears capable of being used in evidence against him.

B Yes, it was said within the confines of a police station, and to a police officer or police staff.

C No, it was not said to a police officer; police staff are not mentioned in the relevant code.

D No, it is not a confession, and does not relate to a direct admission of guilt.

Question 12.3

Police officers have been called by the principal of a high school to interview a juvenile who has caused damage to school property. The principal did not witness the incident, but wishes the juvenile to be interviewed on the school premises as the youth is due to sit a GCSE in two hours. The parents of the juvenile have been contacted, but are unavailable for some time.

Can the principal be the 'appropriate adult'?

A In these circumstances, only the principal can be the appropriate adult.

B The principal can be the appropriate adult as the parents are not readily available.

C The principal can be the appropriate adult provided the parents agree.

D The principal will not be able to be the appropriate adult in these circumstances.

Question 12.4

O'REILLY has been arrested on suspicion of a burglary that occurred one month ago, and is being transported in the back of a police vehicle. On the journey O'REILLY calls out to a passer-by, 'tell Jonesy the coppers have got me'. The officers are aware that there is another suspect outstanding, and ask O'REILLY to explain who 'Jonesy' is and where he is. O'REILLY tells them. The officers then ask O'REILLY where the outstanding property is, and if 'Jonesy' is guilty of the burglary.

Is this 'interview with a person who is under arrest' lawful?

A No, such an interview can be conducted only at a police station.

B No, as they did not stop the interview after they identified the location of 'Jonesy'.

C Yes, as it was to clarify a voluntary statement made by O'REILLY.

D Yes, as the interview was to facilitate the arrest of 'Jonesy' and there was still property to be recovered.

Question 12.5

A suspect has been arrested for possession of controlled drugs, and police officers have taken him to his home address to carry out a search. During the search some cannabis is found along with items of drug paraphernalia. A large sum of money has also been found.

In relation to the questions the officers can ask of the suspect at the scene, which of the following is true?

A Questions can be asked only relating to ownership of the items found.

B No direct questions can be asked, but any comments made should be recorded contemporaneously.

C The suspect could be asked where the money had come from.

D The suspect could be asked the location of other premises where drugs could be found.

Question 12.6

Constable PAUX is about to interview a suspect on suspicion of theft. The officer has been made aware that the suspect made an unsolicited comment.

Which of the following best describes what an unsolicited comment is?

A A comment implicating them in an offence before they are suspected of any involvement and before they are cautioned.

B A comment implicating them in an offence before they are suspected of any involvement but after they are cautioned.

C Any comment made before they are cautioned, that may or may not be admissible as evidence.

D Any comment made after they are cautioned, that may or may not be admissible as evidence.

Question 12.7

CALLARD has been arrested and is about to be interviewed on audio. Initially CALLARD stated he did not want a solicitor and the interview commenced. During the interview CALLARD states that he now wants to speak to his solicitor, however, as the officer is closing the interview CALLARD asks what will happen next. The officer explains that he will be put back in his cell pending the arrival of his solicitor. CALLARD states he just wants to be bailed and again says that he does not want a solicitor.

In the circumstances outlined above, can the audio-recorded interview proceed?

A Yes, provided an officer of the rank of inspector or above has given agreement for the interview to proceed in these circumstances.

B Yes, provided an officer of the rank of inspector has given agreement and the suspect agrees in writing.

C No, as CALLARD has stated that he has changed his mind over legal advice during the interview his solicitor must be contacted.

D No, CALLARD changed his mind due to what the officer said, only the custody officer can give advice as to detention, a solicitor should be called.

Question 12.8

Constable CHAN is interviewing a young person and an appropriate adult has been called. Whilst speaking to the appropriate adult the officer suspects that they have a hearing defect and can't hear what is being said. The adult makes no mention of this and is happy to be present during the interview.

In these circumstances what action should the officer take?

A The officer should ask an interpreter to sit in at the interview.

B The officer should ask the adult if they want an interpreter and act on their verbal reply.

C The officer should ask an interpreter to sit in at the interview and make a contemporaneous written record of the interview.

D The officer need take no action as it is not the suspect who has hearing difficulties.

Question 12.9

STODDARD has been arrested and is in custody at the police station suspected of a series of rapes; this followed a description obtained from his various victims, a first description was obtained and recorded. The suspect has, in accordance with his rights, asked for his solicitor to be called. Prior to the arrival of his solicitor STODDARD is examined by the police surgeon and samples obtained. Officers also attend at STODDARD's home address and carry out a search in compliance with s. 18 of the Police and Criminal Evidence Act 1984 and various items are seized as being of evidential value. Prior to the first interview the interview co-ordinator is considering what will be disclosed to STODDARD's solicitor.

In relation to the various items obtained what *must* be disclosed to the solicitor at this stage of the investigation?

A Only the custody record.

B The custody record, and the record of first description.

C The custody record, the record of first description and the details of the items seized.

D At this stage, there is no mandatory disclosure, it is discretionary for the investigating officer.

Question 12.10

Detective Sergeant STROUD is carrying out a visually recorded interview with a suspect for murder. The suspect is a well-known gang member and fearing for his own safety, Detective Sergeant STROUD wishes to hide his identity and sit with his back to the camera. There have been no specific threats made against Detective Sergeant STROUD, however the gang members have issued a generic warning to any officer concerned in the investigation of the murder.

In relation to the correct procedure, which of the following is true?

A The officer can do this, but must record on the interview record the reasons for this.

B The officer can do this, but must record on the custody record the reasons for this.

C The officer cannot do this as the suspect is not a person detained under the Terrorism Act 2000.

D The officer cannot do this as no specific threat has been made against him.

Question 12.11

MORE is being interviewed by detectives in relation to an allegation of fraud. During the audio-recorded interview, MORE alleges that his rights under PACE Code C were breached and that he wishes to make a formal complaint.

Which of the following is correct?

A The audio recording should be stopped and an inspector summoned to deal with the complaint.

B The custody officer is responsible for deciding whether the interview should continue or not in these circumstances.

C The interviewing officer should make a note in his or her pocket notebook, and later, on the custody record, of the complaint.

D The custody officer should be summoned immediately, and the audio recording left running until he or she arrives.

Question 12.12

NORMAN is in custody for an offence. She requested legal advice and was allowed to consult on the telephone with the duty solicitor. Shortly afterwards, another solicitor, GULLIVER, summoned by NORMAN's father, attended at the police station.

In relation to GULLIVER, which of the following is correct?

A GULLIVER must be allowed private consultation with NORMAN.

B NORMAN does not need to be told about GULLIVER as she has already received legal advice.

C NORMAN must be told that GULLIVER is present and should be allowed a consultation.

D NORMAN does not need to be told about GULLIVER as she did not request advice from him.

Question 12.13

Constable DAWSON is interviewing a foreign national and has an interpreter present. The suspect has expressly wished to make a statement under caution in accordance with PACE Code C, Note 12A.

How should this statement be recorded?

A The suspect must record it and the interpreter prepare a translation of it, the suspect shall then sign both statements.

B The interpreter will record the statement in the language it is spoken and then shall sign it themselves, a translation will be made in due course.

C The interpreter will record the statement in the language it is spoken and the suspect shall sign it.

D The interpreter will record the statement in the language it is spoken and the suspect shall sign it, the interpreter shall then immediately provide a translation.

Question 12.14

A suspect fell from a roof during a burglary and was arrested but had to be taken to hospital. The officers are wondering under what, if any, circumstances they can interview the suspect as there are persons missing.

In relation to this which of the following is correct?

A They cannot interview the suspect whilst they are a patient in hospital.

B They can interview the suspect with the agreement of a responsible doctor.

C They can interview the suspect only with the agreement of the doctor in charge of the suspect's care.

D They can interview the suspect with the agreement of the doctor in charge of the suspect's care and the custody officer at the nearest designated station.

Question 12.15

KNIGHT was arrested for an indictable offence and, when his detention was first authorised, he asked to consult with a solicitor. However, there has now been a delay of over an hour in his solicitor arriving at the police station. The superintendent in charge of the station has now authorised an interview to take place with KNIGHT, without the solicitor being present, because there are urgent questions that need to be asked of him, and awaiting the solicitor's arrival will cause an unreasonable delay to the process of the investigation.

If KNIGHT were to make no comment during the interview, without his solicitor being present, would a court be able to draw adverse inferences from his silence?

A Yes, provided it can be shown that the superintendent has correctly applied the codes of practice with her decision.

B No, as KNIGHT has not been allowed to consult with a solicitor.

C Yes, unless the defence can show that there has been an intentional breach of the codes of practice by the police.

D No, if the defence can show that KNIGHT indicated at the start of the interview that he did not wish to be interviewed without his solicitor being present.

Question 12.16

Constable VENISON was interviewing GOUDY, who had been arrested the previous evening for an assault. The interview was being conducted on audio, in an interview room at the police station. During the interview, GOUDY disclosed to Constable VENISON that he was assaulted by the arresting officer the previous evening, and stated that he wished to make a formal complaint.

What action should Constable VENISON now take, in respect of the complaint made to her?

A She should stop the audio recording immediately and ask the custody officer to attend the interview, where the complaint may be repeated in his or her presence.

B She may carry on the interview, provided she informs the custody officer that a complaint has been made at the conclusion of the interview.

C She should stop the audio recording immediately and inform the custody officer that a complaint has been made.

D She may carry on the interview, provided she informs the duty inspector that a complaint has been made at the conclusion of the interview.

Question 12.17

The Police and Criminal Evidence Act 1984, Code C, para. 13.4 gives guidance in relation to written statements under caution from suspects, when the statement is made in a language other than English, and an interpreter is present.

What does this code of practice state in relation to who should write the statement under caution?

A The interpreter should write the statement in the language in which it is made, and translate it there and then.

B The interviewee should write it in his or her own language, and the interpreter should translate it there and then.

C The interpreter should write the statement in the language in which it is made, and translate it in due course.

D The interviewee should write it in his or her own language, and the interpreter should translate it in due course.

Question 12.18

O'SULLIVAN was in detention, having been arrested for burglary. Two people escaped from the police at the scene with the stolen property. When O'SULLIVAN's detention was first authorised, he declined legal advice. Constable GOODE, the investigating officer wished to interview O'SULLIVAN straight away because of the outstanding property and to establish who had been with O'SULLIVAN. However, it was discovered that O'SULLIVAN had injured his leg and the custody officer determined he had to go to hospital after detention was authorised. The custody officer agreed that Constable GOODE could accompany O'SULLIVAN to hospital and interview him there. It transpired that O'SULLIVAN was cooperative and the officer asked him some questions in the ambulance and further questions at the hospital with permission from a doctor.

Assuming that Constable GOODE followed the codes of practice relating to cautioning suspects and legal advice prior to the interviews, how much time will count towards O'SULLIVAN's overall detention time when he returns to the custody office?

A The whole time spent away from the custody office.

B The whole time spent at the hospital.

C Only the time spent during the interview at the hospital.

D Only the time spent questioning him.

Question 12.19

Detective Constables GRAINGER and SADDIQUE were interviewing PARKES for an offence of murder. The interview was being visually recorded. About an hour into the interview, the officers decided to have a short break and Detective Constable

GRAINGER left the interview room to obtain refreshments, leaving Detective Constable SADDIQUE alone in the room with PARKES.

What advice is contained in the PACE Codes of Practice, Code F, paras 4.12 and 4.13, as to whether or not the video recording equipment should be turned off in these circumstances?

A It *must* not be turned off, because PARKES and another police officer have remained in the interview room.

B It *may* be turned off, because one of the interviewing officers has left the interview room.

C It *must* be turned off, because one of the interviewing officers has left the interview room.

D It *must* be turned off and the recording media removed, because one of the interviewing officers has left the interview room.

Question 12.20

In certain circumstances, Code C, para. 6.9 of the PACE Codes of Practice allows the removal of a legal representative from an interview because of their behaviour.

Which of the following statements is correct in relation to the authorisation required to implement para. 6.9?

A A superintendent may make such an authorisation, but if one is not available, it may be done by an inspector.

B Only an inspector or above may make such an authorisation.

C Either a superintendent or an inspector or above may make an authorisation, but only if they witness the behaviour.

D Only a superintendent or above may make such an authorisation.

Question 12.21

Constable DAVIES is interviewing EDDISON (who is accompanied by his solicitor) on tape at a non-designated police station for a common assault offence. Her colleague, Constable POBOWSKI is acting as custody officer, the nearest inspector is six miles away. At the conclusion of the interview the solicitor refuses to sign the master recording label although EDDISON does sign the label.

What action should Constable DAVIES now take?

A She should note the fact the solicitor has refused to sign, no further action is required as the suspect did sign the label.

B She should call in Constable POBOWSKI who should sign the label.

C She should call in Constable POBOWSKI who should sign the seal, only after seeking authority from the inspector to do so.

D She should write 'third party refused to sign' on the label, and sign that entry.

Question 12.22

PRIOR works for a firm of solicitors as an accredited representative and attended the custody police station one day on behalf of the firm of solicitors he had recently joined. The custody officer, Sergeant BRADBURY met PRIOR in the foyer. Unfortunately for PRIOR, Sergeant BRADBURY had just been promoted from a different force area and recognised PRIOR as a person who had been recently arrested and convicted in that area for an offence of burglary, under a different name. When challenged, PRIOR admitted that this was true, and the custody officer contacted the duty inspector.

In these circumstances, could the inspector prevent PRIOR from entering the custody office?

A No, the decision must be made by a superintendent, who must inform the Law Society if entry is refused.

B Yes, and the inspector should inform other custody staff in the area, to ensure that PRIOR is not allowed entry to those either.

C Yes, and the inspector must inform a superintendent, who must inform the Law Society if entry is refused.

D Yes, and the inspector may inform a superintendent, who may inform the Law Society if entry is refused.

ANSWERS

Answer 12.1

Answer **A** — If a person is asked questions for reasons other than obtaining evidence about his/her involvement or suspected involvement in an offence, this is not an interview (and a caution need not be given). So when does suspicion of an offence come about in this scenario? The RPU officers were told that there may be drugs in the car, at this point in time do they have suspicion that an offence has been committed? Well no, because they haven't found anything; answer B is therefore incorrect.

This point is confirmed in the case of *R* v *McGuinness* [1999] Crim LR 318, where the court confirmed that it was only when a person was suspected of an offence that the caution must be administered before questioning. Consequently, in *R* v *Miller* [1998] Crim LR 209 the court held that asking a person the single question, 'Are these ecstasy tablets?' criminally implicated the person and therefore the conversation was an interview (i.e. it would not be necessary to ask such a question if there were no suspicion that the tablets were a controlled substance). In this scenario having found the package the RPU officers believed them to be controlled drugs and therefore had suspicion that an offence had been committed. This is suspicion and not actually the point to prove in relation to that offence so therefore whether the possession was lawful or not or whether the package actually contained controlled drugs are irrelevant as to whether this was an interview and a caution required; answers C and D are therefore incorrect.

Before a person can be interviewed about their involvement in an offence, that person must be cautioned. So it might be said that an interview is any questioning of a person after such time as a caution has been or should have been administered. Where a person is arrested for an offence, he/she must also be cautioned, as any questioning will amount to an interview.

Evidence and Procedure, para. 2.12.2

Answer 12.2

Answer **A** — At the beginning of an interview the interviewer, after cautioning the suspect, shall put to them any significant statement or silence which occurred in the presence and hearing of a police officer or other police staff before the start of the interview and which have not been put to the suspect in the course of a previous interview. The interviewer shall ask the suspect whether they confirm or deny that earlier statement or silence and if they want to add anything.

A significant statement is one which appears capable of being used in evidence against the suspect, in particular a direct admission of guilt.

Whether a joke or not the statement made by the suspect would be capable of being given in evidence against them even though it was not a direct admission of guilt (although arguably it is!); answer D is therefore incorrect.

The statement can be made anywhere (not just a police station) and can be said to police staff as well as police officers; answers B and C are therefore incorrect.

Evidence and Procedure, para. 2.12.9.2

Answer 12.3

Answer **D** — Interviews at educational establishments should take place only in exceptional circumstances and with the agreement of the principal or the principal's nominee (PACE Code C, para. 11.16). This is the mandatory practice; however, it is not mandatory that the principal be the appropriate adult, and therefore answer A is incorrect. If waiting for the parents (or other appropriate adult) to attend would cause unreasonable delay, the principal can be the appropriate adult, and this is not dependent on the parent's consent and therefore answer C is incorrect. The only exception to this is where the juvenile is suspected of an offence against his or her educational establishment, as the youth is in the question. In these circumstances the principal cannot be the appropriate adult and answer B is therefore incorrect (Code C, para. 11.16).

Evidence and Procedure, para. 2.12.5

Answer 12.4

Answer **B** — The general rules for the conduct of interviews are contained in PACE Code C, para. 11.1. The suspect under arrest should be interviewed about an offence only at a police station. However, there are exceptions to this rule based on the necessity for the interview, and answer A is therefore incorrect. Code C, para. 11.1 (b) covers one of those exceptions, i.e. where delay would be likely to 'lead to the alerting of other persons suspected of having committed an offence but not yet arrested for it'. However, interviewing in these circumstances should cease once the relevant risk has been averted or the necessary questions have been put (para. 11.1). Code C, para. 11.1(c) outlines that interviewing would be lawful if delay would 'hinder the recovery of property'. One month after the offence would be unlikely to hold credence with the court. This, together with the fact that questions could not be asked regarding 'Jonesy's' guilt, makes answer D incorrect. Clarification over a voluntary statement relates to prisoners being transferred between forces, i.e. no questions may be put to the suspect about the offence while he or she is in transit between the forces except in order to clarify any voluntary statement made by him or her (Code C, para. 14.1), and answer C is therefore incorrect.

Evidence and Procedure, para. 2.12.6

Answer 12.5

Answer **C** — The courts have recognised that there may be times when a person who is under arrest will be asked questions other than at the police station. One such example is where the arrested person is present while officers search his or her home address, and answer B is therefore incorrect. In *R* v *Hanchard*, 6 December 1999, unreported, the questions which were admissible included whether cannabis at the address belonged to the suspect and where a large quantity of money had come from (answer A is therefore incorrect). Questions going beyond what is needed for the immediate investigation are in breach of the PACE Code of Practice. Asking for evidence of offences unconnected with the search clearly would be such a breach, and therefore answer D is incorrect.

Evidence and Procedure, para. 2.12.6

Answer 12.6

Answer **A** — There will be occasions where suspects make unsolicited comments implicating them in an offence before they are suspected of any involvement and therefore before they are cautioned (or further cautioned if already suspected). Such statements are likely to be admissible provided the PACE Codes of Practice are complied with.

If a suspect is suspected of an offence they must be cautioned prior to questions being asked; answer B is therefore incorrect. Whether a statement is admissible or not is a matter for the court, not the officer; answers C and D are therefore incorrect.

Evidence and Procedure, para. 2.12.4.3

Answer 12.7

Answer **A** — If a request for legal advice is made during an interview, the interviewing officer must stop the interview straightaway and arrange for legal advice to be provided. If the suspect changes his or her mind again, the interview can continue provided Code C, para. 6.6 is complied with. Code C para. 6.6 states:

> In these circumstances the interview may be started or continued without delay provided that:
> (i) the detainee agrees to do so, in writing or on the interview record [answer B is therefore incorrect] made in accordance with Code E or F; and
> (ii) an officer of inspector rank or above has inquired about the detainee's reasons for their change of mind and gives authority for the interview to proceed.

Confirmation of the detainee's agreement, their change of mind, the reasons for it if given and, subject to para 2.6A, the name of the authorising officer shall be recorded in the written interview record or the interview record made in accordance with Code E or F.

It is the suspect's right to consult with a solicitor. If during the interview they want advice, and prior to it being arranged they change their mind again, that is their right and the interview can proceed without legal representation; answer C is therefore incorrect.

Although technically issues relating to detention are that of the custody officer, whilst in the interview the interviewing officer is responsible for the Police and Criminal Evidence Act 1984 rights of the suspect; again it is their choice to have or not have legal representation, and answer D is therefore incorrect.

Evidence and Procedure, para. 2.12.9.13

Answer 12.8

Answer **A** — As a confession can be very damning evidence against a defendant, it is important to provide safeguards that give all suspects the same level of protection. The PACE Codes of Practice recognise certain groups as being in need of additional protection. These groups include juveniles, people who do not speak English, those suffering from a mental impairment and those who are deaf. Such suspects must not be interviewed without the relevant person being present.

If the suspect appears to be deaf or there is any doubt about his/her hearing or speaking ability, an interpreter should be found (unless he/she agrees in writing to proceed without an interpreter; answer B is therefore incorrect) (Code C, para. 13.5). This requirement also applies in the case of the appropriate adult who appears to be deaf or there is doubt about his/her hearing or speaking ability; answer D is therefore incorrect (Code C, para. 13.6).

If the suspect is deaf or there is doubt about his/her hearing ability, a contemporaneous written record should be made as well as the audio recording, this only applies to the suspect and not an appropriate adult; answer C is therefore incorrect. This record should be the same as where there is no audio record of the interview (Code E, para. 4.7).

Evidence and Procedure, para. 2.12.9.15

Answer 12.9

Answer **A** — It is important not to confuse the duty of disclosure to a person once charged with the need to disclose evidence to a suspect before interviewing them. After a person has been charged, and before trial, the rules of disclosure are clear and almost all material must be disclosed to the defence.

However, this is not necessarily the case at the interview stage of the investigation. There is no specific provision within PACE for the disclosure of any information by the police at the police station, *with the exception of the custody record*. In respect of the provision of a copy of the 'first description' of a suspect it should be noted that Code D (para. 3.1) states that a copy of the 'first description' shall, where practicable, be given to the suspect or their solicitor before any procedures under paras 3.5 to 3.10, 3.21 or 3.23 are carried out. In other words, the disclosure requirement is that a copy of the 'first description' shall, where practicable, be given to the suspect or their solicitor *before a video identification, an identification parade, a group identification or confrontation takes place*. Therefore, an officer disclosing information to a solicitor at the interview stage (which is taking place in advance of any identification procedures), need not provide the 'first description' of a suspect at that time.

Further, there is nothing within the Criminal Justice and Public Order Act 1994 that states that information must be disclosed before an inference from silence can be made. Indeed, in *R* v *Imran* [1997] Crim LR 754 the court held that it is totally wrong to submit that a defendant should be prevented from lying by being presented with the whole of the evidence against him or her prior to the interview.

So only the custody record and the initial descriptions needs to be disclosed; answers B, C and D are therefore incorrect.

Evidence and Procedure, para. 2.12.9.7

Answer 12.10

Answer **B** — Nothing in Code F of the Police and Criminal Evidence Act 1984 codes of practice requires the identity of an officer to be recorded or disclosed if:

(a) the interview or record relates to a person detained under the Terrorism Act 2000; or

(b) otherwise where the officer reasonably believes that recording or disclosing their name might put them in danger [answer C is therefore incorrect].

Note that there is no need for a specific threat to be made against a particular officer; answer D is therefore incorrect.

In these cases, the officers will have their back to the camera and shall use their warrant or other identification number and the name of the police station to which they are attached. Such instances and the reasons for them shall be recorded in the custody record; answer A is therefore incorrect.

Evidence and Procedure, para. 2.12.9.10

Answer 12.11

Answer **D** — If the suspect makes a complaint regarding his or her treatment since arrest, the interviewing officer must inform the custody officer and follow PACE Code C, para. 12.9, which states:

> If in the course of the interview a complaint is made by the person being questioned or on his behalf concerning the provisions of this code then the interviewing officer shall:
> (i) record it in the interview record; and
> (ii) inform the custody officer, who is then responsible for dealing with it in accordance with section 9 of this code.

Note that it is recorded on the interview record, and answer C is therefore incorrect. Code C, para. 9.2 states that 'a report must be made as soon as practicable to an officer of the rank of Inspector or above who is not connected with the investigation'. However, it is not necessary to stop the audio recording; indeed, it should be kept running in accordance with Code E, Note 4E, and answer A is therefore incorrect. Code E, Note 4E also outlines that 'continuation or termination of the interview should be at the discretion of the interviewing officer' and not the custody officer, and therefore answer B is incorrect.

Evidence and Procedure, para. 2.12.9.8, App. 2.5

Answer 12.12

Answer **C** — If a solicitor arrives at the station to see a suspect, the suspect must be asked whether he or she would like to see the solicitor *regardless of what legal advice has already been received* and regardless of whether or not the advice was requested by the suspect; answers B and D are therefore incorrect (PACE Code C, para. 6.15). Note that it is the suspect's choice whether to speak to the solicitor, who has no automatic right of consultation even if summoned by a relative, and answer A is therefore incorrect. However, where a solicitor does arrive at the police station to see a suspect, that suspect has to be told of the solicitor's presence and must be allowed to consult with the solicitor should he or she wish to do so.

Evidence and Procedure, para. 2.12.9.13

Answer 12.13

Answer **C** — Statements under caution, particularly of a detained person, are less common than interviews. If a person has been interviewed and it has been audio or visually recorded or an interview has been recorded contemporaneously in writing, a statement under caution should normally be conducted only at the person's express wish (Code C, Note 12A).

When completing the statement, the person must always be invited to write down what he/she wants to say and should be allowed to do so without any prompting, except that a police officer may indicate which matters are material or question any ambiguity in the statement. In the case of a person making a statement in a language other than English, Code C, para. 13.4 states:

(a) the interpreter shall record the statement in the language it is made;

(b) the person shall be invited to sign it; [answer B is therefore incorrect]

(c) an official English translation shall be made in due course. [Answer D is therefore incorrect.]

(In these cases, para. 13.4 means that the person will not be invited to write the statement him/herself which is an exception to the guidance in Annex D; answer A is therefore incorrect.)

Evidence and Procedure, para. 2.12.10

Answer 12.14

Answer **B** — Note that a person in police detention at a hospital must not be questioned without the agreement of a responsible doctor (Code C, para. 14.2); answer A is therefore incorrect. If a person is questioned in these circumstances, he is entitled to consult a solicitor. The Code does not mention, unlike drink/drive legislation, the doctor in immediate charge of the person's care; answers C and D are therefore incorrect.

Evidence and Procedure, para. 2.12.6

Answer 12.15

Answer **B** — The case of *Murray* v *United Kingdom* (1996) 22 EHRR 29 changed the situation in respect of adverse inferences being drawn from silences, where the detainee has asked to speak to a solicitor prior to interview and has not been allowed to do so. The ruling in *Murray* also caused a change to the Codes of Practice. There will, of course, be instances where the police can legitimately deny a detainee access to a solicitor prior to interview, and the situation described in the scenario complies with Code C, para. 6.6(b)(ii), where a superintendent may authorise an interview to take place without a solicitor being present, when the detainee has requested one, when the solicitor has been contacted and awaiting his or her arrival will cause an unreasonable delay to the process of the investigation.

However, when this power is utilised, Code C states that there will be a restriction on the court drawing adverse inferences from any silence; this is regardless of whether the superintendent has correctly applied the Codes of Practice (answer A is therefore incorrect). There will be no requirement for the defence to show that there has been an intentional breach of the Codes of Practice (answer C is therefore incorrect), or that the defendant indicated at the start of the interview that he did not wish to be interviewed without his solicitor being present (answer D is therefore incorrect). The detainee is simply afforded protection by the Codes of Practice because he or she has not been allowed access to a solicitor during interview, when he or she has asked for one.

Evidence and Procedure, para. 2.12.4

Answer 12.16

Answer **B** — Under Code E, Note 4F, if a complaint is made during an interview about a matter not connected with the conduct of the interview itself, the interviewing officer has the decision whether or not to continue the interview. Therefore, there is no need to stop the interview, and answers A and C are incorrect. When the interviewing officer does carry on with the interview, he or she should inform the detainee that the matter will be brought to the custody officer's attention at the conclusion of the interview. The interviewing officer must then do this as soon as practicable at the conclusion of the interview. Answer D is incorrect, as the interviewing officer has no duty to inform an inspector (although the custody officer will have to do so, when the complaint is brought to his or her attention).

Lastly, even though there is no necessity to call the custody officer to the interview room, Code E, Note 4F states that if a custody officer is called to deal with a complaint, the audio recording should be left running until the custody officer has entered the room and spoken to the interviewee. Answer A is incorrect for this reason also.

Evidence and Procedure, para. 2.12.9.8

Answer 12.17

Answer **C** — Code C, para. 13.4 states that where a person makes a statement under caution in a language other than English, the interpreter should record the statement in the language in which it is made, the person must be invited to sign it, and an official English translation must be made in due course. There is no provision in the Codes of Practice for the interviewee to write the statement, therefore answers B and D are incorrect. Also, there is no requirement for the statement to be translated immediately, and answer A is therefore incorrect.

Evidence and Procedure, para. 2.12.10

Answer 12.18

Answer **D** — While the situation in the question is unusual, the actions of the police were perfectly legal. Under the PACE Codes of Practice, Code C, para. 14.2, if a person is in police detention at a hospital they may not be questioned without the agreement of a responsible doctor. Note 14A continues: 'if questioning takes place at a hospital under paragraph 14.2, or on the way to or from a hospital, *the period of* *questioning concerned* counts towards the total period of detention permitted' (emphasis added). Answers A and B are therefore incorrect. Answer C is incorrect, because both the interview on the way to the hospital and the interview at the hospital will count towards the overall detention time.

Note that in circumstances where a person is interviewed away from the custody office, it would be advisable as far as possible to record the interview on a portable tape recorder to demonstrate that the Codes of Practice have been complied with. Also, the situation would have been different if the detainee had requested legal advice when detention was first authorised. In this case, permission to interview without the solicitor being present would have to be granted either by a superintendent (if the matter was urgent—Code C, para. 6.6(b)) or by an inspector (if the detainee changed his/her mind—Code C, para. 6.6(d)).

Evidence and Procedure, para. 2.12.6, App. 2.4

Answer 12.19

Answer **B** — The advice concerning visually recorded interviews is contained in Code F of the PACE Codes of Practice. Code F, para. 4.12 states that:

> When a break is to be a short one, and both the suspect and a police officer are to remain in the interview room, the fact that a break is to be taken, the reasons for it and the time shall be recorded on the recording media. The recording equipment may be turned off, but there is no need to remove the recording media. When the interview is recommenced the recording shall continue on the same recording media and the time at which the interview recommences shall be recorded.

Since the officers only intended the break to be a short one, para. 4.12 applies in these circumstances. The above paragraph states that in these circumstances, the officers *may* turn off the recording equipment, as both the suspect and an officer have remained in the room. Since there is a choice, answers A and C are incorrect. There is no requirement to remove the recording media, because one of the officers and the suspect are still in the room, and there is no likelihood of it being interfered with. Answer D is therefore incorrect.

Whether or not the recording equipment is turned off is a matter for the officers to decide in the circumstances. Further advice is contained in Note 4E, which states that the officer:

> should bear in mind that it may be necessary to satisfy the court that nothing occurred during a break in an interview or between interviews which influenced the suspect's recorded evidence.

Note that in extended breaks, where the suspect leaves the interview room, the recording equipment *must* be turned off and the recording media removed (see para. 4.12).

Evidence and Procedure, para. 2.12.9.12

Answer 12.20

Answer **A** — Provision is made under the PACE Codes of Practice, Code C, para. 6.9 to remove a solicitor from an interview, if the interviewer considers a solicitor is acting in such a way that their conduct is such that the interviewer is unable to put questions to the suspect properly. Further guidance is contained in para. 6.10, which states that the interviewing officer must stop the interview and consult an officer not below superintendent rank, if one is readily available, and otherwise an officer not below inspector rank not connected with the investigation. Since either of these officers may take the decision, answers B and D are incorrect. Note 6E states:

> An officer who takes the decision to exclude a solicitor must be in a position to satisfy the court the decision was properly made. In order to do this they may need to witness what is happening.

It is not mandatory that the authorising officer witnesses the behaviour (therefore answer C is incorrect); however, it would be advisable to do so in order that an informed decision is reached. In practice, it is advised that the authorising officer listens to the audio recording of the interview to assist in the decision-making process. The solicitor could then be given a warning and the interviewing officer advised to stop the interview if it re-occurs. This way, the solicitor will have been given every opportunity to correct their behaviour.

Evidence and Procedure, para. 2.12.9.13, App. 2.4

Answer 12.21

Answer **B** — At the conclusion of an audio-recorded interview the interviewer must sign the label and ask the suspect and any third party present to sign it also.

If the suspect or third party refuses to sign it, an inspector, or if not available a custody officer, shall be called into the interview room and asked to sign it (Code E, para. 4.18).

The inspector is not available so the custody officer should sign the seal and there is no need to seek any authority prior to doing so; answer C is therefore incorrect.

The interviewer has no further part to play where a third party refuses to sign the label; answers A and D are therefore incorrect.

Evidence and Procedure, para. 2.12.9.18

Answer 12.22

Answer **D** — An accredited or probationary representative sent to provide advice by, and on behalf of, a solicitor shall be admitted to the police station for this purpose unless an officer of inspector rank or above considers such a visit will hinder the investigation and directs otherwise (PACE Code C, para. 6.12A). Answer A is incorrect.

The inspector should take into account in particular whether the identity and status of an accredited or probationary representative have been satisfactorily established and/or they are of suitable character to provide legal advice, e.g. a person with a criminal record is unlikely to be suitable unless the conviction was for a minor offence and not recent (para. 6.13).

The exclusion of an accredited or probationer solicitor has to be considered in relation to the specific investigation and whether that person is likely to interfere with the investigation, and the decision has to be made in relation to each individual case. It is *not* permissible to have blanket bans on such persons (*R* v *Chief Constable of the Northumbria Constabulary, ex parte Thompson* [2001] 1 WLR 1342). Answer B is therefore incorrect.

In relation to informing the Law Society, if an inspector considers a particular solicitor or firm of solicitors is persistently sending probationary representatives who are unsuited to provide legal advice, they should inform an officer of at least superintendent rank, who may wish to take the matter up with the Law Society. This is not mandatory in every case and would depend on the company itself. Answer C is therefore incorrect.

Lastly, if the inspector refuses access to an accredited or probationary representative, the inspector must notify the solicitor's company, to give them an opportunity to make alternative arrangements (para. 6.14).

Evidence and Procedure, para. 2.12.9.13, App. 2.4

Question Checklist

The checklist below is designed to help you keep track of your progress when answering the multiple-choice questions. If you fill this in after one attempt at each question, you will be able to check how many you have got right and which questions you need to revisit a second time. Also available online, to download visit www.blackstonespolicemanuals.com.

	First attempt Correct (✓)	Second attempt Correct (✓)
1 Sources of Law		
1.1		
1.2		
1.3		
1.4		
1.5		
1.6		
2 The Courts		
2.1		
2.2		
2.3		
2.4		
2.5		
2.6		
2.7		
2.8		
2.9		
2.10		
3 Instituting Criminal Proceedings		
3.1		

	First attempt Correct (✓)	Second attempt Correct (✓)
3.2		
3.3		
3.4		
3.5		
3.6		
3.7		
3.8		
3.9		
3.10		
3.11		
3.12		
3.13		
3.14		
4 Bail		
4.1		
4.2		
4.3		
4.4		
4.5		
4.6		
4.7		
4.8		

	First attempt Correct (✓)	Second attempt Correct (✓)
4.9		
4.10		
4.11		
4.12		
4.13		
4.14		
4.15		
4.16		
4.17		
4.18		
4.19		
4.20		
4.21		
4.22		
5 Court Procedure and Witnesses		
5.1		
5.2		
5.3		
5.4		
5.5		
5.6		
5.7		
5.8		
5.9		
5.10		
5.11		
5.12		
5.13		
5.14		
5.15		
5.16		
5.17		
5.18		
6 Youth Justice, Crime and Disorder		
6.1		
6.2		
6.3		

	First attempt Correct (✓)	Second attempt Correct (✓)
6.4		
6.5		
6.6		
6.7		
6.8		
6.9		
6.10		
6.11		
6.12		
6.13		
6.14		
6.15		
6.16		
6.17		
6.18		
6.19		
7 Evidence		
7.1		
7.2		
7.3		
7.4		
7.5		
7.6		
7.7		
7.8		
7.9		
7.10		
7.11		
7.12		
7.13		
7.14		
7.15		
7.16		
7.17		
7.18		
7.19		
7.20		
7.21		

	First attempt Correct (✓)	Second attempt Correct (✓)
8 Exclusion of Admissible Evidence		
8.1		
8.2		
8.3		
8.4		
8.5		
8.6		
8.7		
8.8		
8.9		
8.10		
8.11		
9 Disclosure of Evidence		
9.1		
9.2		
9.3		
9.4		
9.5		
9.6		
9.7		
9.8		
9.9		
9.10		
9.11		
9.12		
9.13		
9.14		
9.15		
9.16		
9.17		
10 Custody Officer's Duties		
10.1		
10.2		
10.3		
10.4		

	First attempt Correct (✓)	Second attempt Correct (✓)
10.5		
10.6		
10.7		
10.8		
10.9		
10.10		
10.11		
10.12		
10.13		
10.14		
10.15		
10.16		
10.17		
10.18		
10.19		
10.20		
10.21		
10.22		
10.23		
10.24		
10.25		
10.26		
10.27		
10.28		
10.29		
10.30		
10.31		
10.32		
10.33		
10.34		
10.35		
10.36		
10.37		
10.38		
10.39		
10.40		
10.41		
10.42		

	First attempt Correct (✓)	Second attempt Correct (✓)
11 Identification		
11.1		
11.2		
11.3		
11.4		
11.5		
11.6		
11.7		
11.8		
11.9		
11.10		
11.11		
11.12		
11.13		
11.14		
11.15		
11.16		
11.17		
11.18		
11.19		
11.20		
11.21		
11.22		

	First attempt Correct (✓)	Second attempt Correct (✓)
12 Interviews		
12.1		
12.2		
12.3		
12.4		
12.5		
12.6		
12.7		
12.8		
12.9		
12.10		
12.11		
12.12		
12.13		
12.14		
12.15		
12.16		
12.17		
12.18		
12.19		
12.20		
12.21		
12.22